AMBASSADORS

of

RECONCILIATION

Volume I

AMBASSADORS
of
RECONCILIATION

VOLUME I

NEW TESTAMENT REFLECTIONS ON
RESTORATIVE JUSTICE AND PEACEMAKING

CHED MYERS & ELAINE ENNS

ORBIS BOOKS

Maryknoll, New York 10545

Founded in 1970, Orbis Books endeavors to publish works that enlighten the mind, nourish the spirit, and challenge the conscience. The publishing arm of the Maryknoll Fathers and Brothers, Orbis seeks to explore the global dimensions of the Christian faith and mission, to invite dialogue with diverse cultures and religious traditions, and to serve the cause of reconciliation and peace. The books published reflect the views of their authors and do not represent the official position of the Maryknoll Society. To learn more about Maryknoll and Orbis Books, please visit our website at www.maryknollsociety.org.

Manufactured in the United States of America.

Myers, Ched.
    Ambassadors of reconciliation / Ched Myers and Elaine Enns.
    p. cm.
    Includes bibliographical references.
    ISBN 978-1-57075-831-7 (pbk. : v. 1)
    1. Restorative justice—Biblical teaching. 2. Bible. N.T.—Criticism, interpretation, etc.
I. Enns, Elaine. II. Title.
    BS2545.J8M94   2009
    261.8—dc22
                        2008049652

To Nelson and Joyce Johnson: mentors, colleagues, friends.
With love and respect.

Human beings suffer,
They torture one another,
They get hurt and get hard.
No poem or play or song
Can fully right a wrong
Inflicted and endured.

The innocent in gaols
Beat on their bars together.
A hunger-striker's father
Stands in the graveyard dumb.
The police widow in veils
Faints at the funeral home.

History says, don't hope
On this side of the grave.
But then, once in a lifetime
The longed-for tidal wave
Of justice can rise up,
And hope and history rhyme.

So hope for a great sea-change
On the far side of revenge.
Believe that further shore
Is reachable from here.
Believe in miracles
And cures and healing wells.

—Seamus Heaney (from "The Cure at Troy," 1990)

CONTENTS

INTRODUCTION

> To say "Christ" means to say "reconciliation" or to say "peace" . . .
> If he "is peace," then he is by nature a social, even a political event,
> which marks the overcoming and ending of barriers, however deeply
> founded and highly constructed these appear to be . . . When this
> peace is deprived of its social, national, or economic dimensions,
> when it is distorted or emasculated so much that only "peace of
> mind" enjoyed by saintly individuals is left—then Jesus Christ is
> being flatly denied.
>
> —Markus Barth, *The Broken Wall* (1959: 44)

> It is no longer a choice between violence and nonviolence in this
> world; it's nonviolence or nonexistence.
>
> —Martin Luther King, Jr., "I See the Promised Land"
> (Washington, 1986: 280)

Our world has never been more in need of courageous and creative alternatives to violence and injustice. Street crime, police abuse, and domestic
violence are epidemic, while there has never been a time in history more
militarized. More people are enslaved today than two centuries ago, and
poverty is the number one killer around the globe. Torture seems to have
again become acceptable, and even our entertainment culture is ruled by
the gun. From personal alienation and family abuse to urban uprisings
and social prejudice, and from a domestic war against immigrants to an
international war against real and imagined terrorism, we are caught in an
escalating spiral of violence.

This is why Martin Luther King, Jr., in his last speech the night before
he was assassinated forty years ago, delivered the ultimatum cited above:
our future is nonviolence or nonexistence. And it is why Markus Barth,
a perceptive biblical scholar (and son of the great theologian Karl Barth),
wrote during the darkest days of the Cold War that "to propose in the
name of Christianity, neutrality or unconcern on questions of international, racial or economic peace—this amounts to using Christ's name in

vain" (1959: 45). In the spirit of both dictums, we offer this first of two volumes exploring faith-rooted restorative justice and peacemaking.

In their comprehensive overview of the prospects and problems in the rapidly expanding field of restorative justice, Howard Zehr and Barb Toews write:

> In a mere quarter century, restorative justice has grown from a few scattered experimental projects into a social movement, and then into an identifiable field of practice and study. Moving out from its origins within the criminal justice arena, restorative justice is being applied in schools, in homes, and in the workplace. Restorative justice approaches and concepts are being used to address issues on the micro level—among individuals, within communities—but, as illustrated by South Africa's Truth and Reconciliation Commission, are also being applied to the macro level. Restorative justice programs are being operated and promoted by individuals and by community-based organizations, but also by government bodies. Some advocates are arguing that restorative justice has implications for our social and economic systems, but also for the way we live our personal lives. (2004: vii)

The body of literature concerning active nonviolence has also proliferated in the last twenty-five years, as have academic peace studies programs.[1] This project, however, grew not out of an academic context, but from a long-running conversation between Elaine Enns, a restorative justice trainer and mediator, and Ched Myers, a nonviolence organizer and educator.

It will be helpful for us to stipulate at the outset what we mean by "restorative justice and peacemaking." This practice represents a range of nonviolent responses to injustice, violation, and/or violence with the aim of

1. reducing or halting the presenting violence in order that
2. victims and offenders (as well as their communities and other stakeholders) can collectively identify harms, needs, and responsibilities so that
3. they can determine how to make things as right as possible, which can include covenants of accountability, restitution, reparations, and (ideally) reconciliation.

We will nuance and analyze the concepts embedded in this working definition in volume II, but let us make clear two key assumptions. First, we think this definition applies both to interpersonal and political contexts.

Second, we are referring to a spectrum of diverse but interrelated strategies of peacemaking, which explains why this project addresses issues of "restorative justice" *and* "nonviolent action." We are all too aware that lamentably, these two trajectories tend to diverge in most contemporary theory and practice, and we hold them together intentionally, for reasons that will be examined in volume II, chapter 2.

In thinking how we might make a small but useful contribution to this dynamic but fractured field, we discerned three gaps that we hope to help fill. Our first concern, and the focus of volume I, is the need for continuing theological and biblical reflection to be done within our circles. Although many recent restorative justice and peacemaking initiatives have emerged from Christian communities, popular theological reflection has lagged, while the important work emerging in some academic circles has not been widely "translated."[2] In particular, there have been too few serious explorations of how contemporary practices might illuminate the Bible, and vice versa, which this volume hopes to do. As an activist theologian known for his "political" readings of scripture, Ched took the lead in writing these chapters.[3]

A second concern is that our movements are not always sufficiently analytical in our diagnoses of, and responses to, the epidemic of violence that plagues our world. In volume II, part 1, we offer three conceptual models we have found useful in our work. These models inform our approach both to the biblical and to the biographic material. A third concern is that while there has been an explosion of theoretical literature concerning various aspects of restorative justice and peacemaking in the last decade, many of these are, in our opinion, overly abstract. This may perhaps reflect an anxiety to justify our field before the bar of conventional legal, moral, or political theory. While apologetics is important, it does not sufficiently reflect the exciting, creative, and sometimes risky real-life experimentation that is occurring on the ground. This is why we decided to take a more narrative approach in volume II, part 2, profiling nine contemporary North American colleagues whose work represents a wide spectrum of personal and political responses to violence and injustice. Elaine, a mediator and restorative justice trainer for two decades, took the lead in conducting and writing up these interviews.

As should already be evident, we write primarily from and for the Christian community—understood in the widest ecumenical sense—in the English-speaking First World. This is our own convictional, vocational, and geopolitical context. We live in Southern California and are members of the Mennonite Church, though our work is broadly cross-denominational. We have a double goal for this project:

1. For those unfamiliar with faith-rooted restorative justice and peacemaking, we seek to provide a primer that summarizes key concepts and practices, and that points to further resources. We believe these ways of thinking and doing can transform both the church's internal life and its public witness.

2. For experienced faith-rooted practitioners, we hope to advance a vigorous conversation about how to broaden and deepen our theological and analytical understandings and concrete engagements.

We would hope, however, that values-based practitioners from other religious or ethical traditions might find our study of use as well.

It is not enough for Christian practitioners to appeal to a handful of scriptural "sound-bites" or favorite proof texts to support their restorative justice and peacemaking work. Our task must include a rereading of the entire Bible, to determine how our convictions are borne out in the tradition. The present volume seeks to contribute to this by offering careful expositions of four texts from the New Testament:

- Chapter 1 looks at a passage from Paul's second epistle to the Christians at Corinth, probing the meaning of his call to become "ambassadors of reconciliation," whence the title of this project.

- Chapter 2 examines Mark's account of Jesus' early ministry through the lens of public nonviolent action, revealing why peacemaking must first be peace disturbing.

- Chapter 3 shows how Jesus' so-called "church order" teaching in Matthew 18 firmly grounds its process for adjudicating interpersonal violation in an analysis of social power and historic context.

- Chapter 4 addresses the divine vision of cosmic reconciliation and the peacemaking power of Christ's cross in the epistle to the Ephesians, along with its theological, ecclesial, and political implications.

These passages represent core samples of how the New Testament "shows" and "tells" restorative justice and peacemaking.

The chapters in volume I proceed according to the widely accepted first-century chronology of New Testament material: Paul (2 Corinthians probably dates from the mid-50s c.e.); Mark (late 60s c.e.?); Matthew (mid-80s c.e.?); and Ephesians (90s c.e.?). Some of these passages are relatively familiar (and in some circles well-worn) within contemporary faith-rooted restorative justice and peacemaking movements. We have, however, offered a more detailed and contextual examination of how they might guide and challenge our work. Other texts are not as widely used among us; we have sought to show their relevance. We encourage similar work in the Hebrew Bible and other parts of the New Testament, because we believe the whole biblical tradition supports a vision of restorative justice and peacemaking.

In these expositions we have endeavored to balance exegetical integrity, social context, and theological depth with a desire to be accessible to a wide audience. Technical language or issues have been placed in footnotes so as not to impede the reader. Our approach, which emphasizes both the socio-historical context and the political character of the New Testament witnesses, will be new to many readers. We have, for this reason, proceeded with attention to textual detail, so we aren't perceived as making unfounded generalizations. We have also provided numerous secondary references, both to introduce readers to the significant and exciting recent scholarship that supports our readings and to provide suggestions for further study. These expositions should be read with the biblical text in hand.

The two volumes of our project are meant to be studied together, as complementary stages of the "hermeneutic circle."[4] The New Testament texts exposited below suggest how the earliest church understood the call to become "ambassadors of reconciliation," while the models and practitioners introduced in volume II illustrate what this vocation might look like concretely today. We hope that these witnesses, scriptural and contemporary, will animate our Christian imaginations to experiment more passionately with restorative justice and peacemaking.

This project was completed during 2008, which marks the fortieth anniversary of Martin Luther King's murder in Memphis, April 4, 1968. Some elder colleagues in the African American church challenged us to commit this year to reflecting on the meaning of these last "forty years in the American wilderness" since our greatest prophet was gunned down by his own government.[5] This project is part of our response. To that end, we have woven in references to the life and work of Dr. King throughout this first volume, because he remains the most germane and compelling modern American representative of faith-rooted restorative justice and peacemaking. As the great Trappist monk and social commentator Thomas Merton put it just before King was killed, the civil rights movement "has been one of the most positive and successful expressions of Christian social action that has been seen anywhere in the twentieth century. It is certainly the greatest example of Christian faith in action in the social history of the United States" (1968: 130f.).

We have intentionally used King, his social movement, and his "dream" as an "analogical aid" to help recover the sharp edge of our New Testament texts. The latter are, after all, removed in time and space from us, and have long been dulled in our churches by spiritualizing, decontextualized or overly academic readings. For many New Testament scholars, these analogies will seem too unqualified, while lay readers may find them jolting. But this simply underlines the huge gulfs between the seminary, the sanctuary, and the street, which this volume seeks to bridge. We see in King's life and witness not just an inspiring and instructive example, however. It is also a warning, for our society is, four decades on, scarcely closer to his dream of a "beloved community." Instead, as we write this, we are still at war abroad, and still deeply divided by race, class, and gender at home, just as we were in 1968.

On April 19, 1995, a U.S. government office complex in downtown Oklahoma City was bombed, claiming 168 lives and leaving over 800 persons injured. It was one of the deadliest acts of terrorism on U.S. soil. The perpetrator was a young, economically struggling advocate of white supremacy and a military veteran of the first Gulf War. This terrible moment—like the Middle Passage, the Salem witch trials, Wounded Knee, My Lai, and so many others—offered Americans a mirror into which to look in order to see the violence in the heart of our national story. Standing in front of the poignant Memorial Park in Oklahoma City today is a statue of Jesus weeping. It alludes to the moment in Luke's Gospel where Jesus approaches Jerusalem and tearfully laments: "Would that you knew the things that make for peace!" (Luke 19:42). We offer these volumes to all persons of faith who are trying, through experimentation and critical reflection, to discover the things that make for peace in our weary world.

1

"AMBASSADORS OF RECONCILIATION"

Witnessing to the Restorative Justice of God
(2 Corinthians 5:16-6:13)

Cheap grace is the deadly enemy of our Church. We are fighting today for costly grace . . . Cheap grace is grace without discipleship, grace without the cross, grace without Jesus Christ . . .
—Dietrich Bonhoeffer, *The Cost of Discipleship* (1963: 45f.)

Just as the Apostle Paul left his little village of Tarsus and carried the gospel of Jesus Christ to practically every hamlet and city of the Greco-Roman world, so too am I compelled to carry the gospel of freedom beyond my particular hometown. Like Paul, I must constantly respond to the Macedonian call for aid. Moreover, I am cognizant of the interrelatedness of all communities and states. I cannot sit idly by in Atlanta and not be concerned about what happens in Birmingham. Injustice anywhere is a threat to justice everywhere. We are caught in an inescapable network of mutuality, tied in a single garment of destiny.
—Martin Luther King, Jr., "Letter from Birmingham City Jail"
(Washington, 1986: 290)

Martin Luther King's work as a minister and public theologian was defined by the historic struggle to overcome institutional racial segregation in U.S. society. His concern for equality and social justice shaped his preaching and public oratory, focused his organizing with the Southern Christian Leadership Council (SCLC), and led him repeatedly to acts of civil disobedience. After the passage of the Civil Rights Act of 1964 and the Voting Rights Act of 1965, the SCLC turned its energies toward what King called "the second phase" of the civil rights movement: challenging the scourge of economic disparity in the United States. This led King to stand with a sanitation workers' strike in Memphis, Tennessee, where he was assassinated on April 4, 1968.[1]

A deep sense of solidarity with racially and economically marginalized fellow citizens—what King called the "inescapable network of mutuality"—was both his motivation and his goal in civil rights campaigning. It was grounded in his vision of the "beloved community." This idea can, according to Smith and Zepp (1974b), "be traced through all of his speeches and writings, from the earliest to the last":

> In 1957, writing in the newsletter of the newly formed Southern Christian Leadership Conference, he described the purpose and goal of that organization as follows: "The ultimate aim of SCLC is to foster and create the 'beloved community' in America where brotherhood is a reality . . . King's was a vision of a completely integrated society, a community of love and justice . . . In his mind, such a community would be the ideal corporate expression of the Christian faith." (1974a: 361)

The "beloved community" was King's way of talking about the reality Jesus called the Kingdom of God.[2]

This vision took King into an Alabama jail in 1963—American apartheid's heart of darkness—from where he penned his famous epistle. In the letter, King expresses his conviction that his mission was simply following in the footsteps of the apostle Paul.[3] Yet few North American Christians today see that connection, much less appreciate that Paul was *also* fundamentally concerned with issues of race and class justice. To explore this, we turn to an examination of 2 Corinthians.

1A. Paul in Corinth:
Struggling for the Beloved Community

At the heart of one of Paul's best-known theological formulations describing Christian conversion is a summons to a "ministry of reconciliation" (2 Cor 5:18). This passage represents perhaps the earliest New Testament articulation of the vocation of restorative justice and peacemaking. Just as we need to know something about Dr. King's social location within the real world of "Jim Crow" in mid-twentieth-century America in order to appreciate his work, we must understand Paul's theology of reconciliation in the context of his commitment to ethnic peace and economic equity in the teeth of a hostile first-century Roman imperial society.

Like King, Paul was an educated member of a racial-ethnic Jewish minority which was systematically segregated within the dominant Roman society. Both experienced religious discrimination as well: King as a member of the marginalized Black Church, Paul as a member of a Christian sect that was unauthorized by the Roman imperial pantheon and which uneasily orbited on the fringes of the Judean diaspora. The hard catechism of experience taught both these disciples the deep connections between national, economic, and religious oppression—and liberation.

The way Paul has been portrayed by most modern theologians (liberal and conservative alike) gives the impression that a singular focus on conversion and spiritual formation made him reticent to challenge contemporary Greco-Roman social norms, to which he allegedly urged his churches to conform. But over the last fifteen years biblical scholars such as Elsa Tamez (1993), Neil Elliott (1994, 2008), and Richard Horsley (1997, 2000) have contended that Paul's writings should be freed from the powerful interpretive biases of dogmatic or pietistic Protestantism and read instead in their own socio-historical context. They have shown that Paul's theology and ethics subverted imperial religion and politics, while nurturing alternative communities he called *ekklēsiai*. In the Epistle to the Galatians, Paul appears to stake his entire ministry on the conviction that these *ekklēsiai* should recognize "neither Jew nor Greek, neither slave nor free, neither male nor female" (Gal 3:28). Yet the same letter hints that Paul's missionary project threatened to founder on these very disparities of race, class, and gender, which other Jewish Christian leaders were apparently unwilling to challenge (Gal 1:6-2:14).

On one hand, Paul was fiercely critical of the decadence and injustice of the Roman Empire. Recently, Neil Elliott has offered a paradigm-shattering reading of Paul's manifesto to the Romans. That epistle is not, he argues, so much a tract about universal sin and redemption as about God's specific judgment on the hubris of the empire and its rulers:

> In his monumental commentary on Romans, Robert Jewett declares, "The argument of Romans revolves around the question of which rule is truly righteous"—Christ's or Caesar's—"and which gospel has the power to make the world truly peaceful." This important insight has long been blunted, if not completely obscured, by the tendency of Christian interpretation to read Romans 1-3 in terms of a universal human "plight" that requires divine salvation . . . But when Paul juxtaposes divine justice (*dikaiōsynē . . . theou*) and human injustice

(*adikian anthrōpōn*, 1:17-18), he is not describing plight and solution. He is contrasting two contemporary dominions, two regimes, that stand fundamentally opposed to each other . . . (2008: 73)

Elliott contends that in his indictment of "human beings who through their injustice suppress the truth" (Rom 1:18), "Paul intends his hearers to recognize definite allusions to none other than the Caesars themselves" (ibid.: 79).

Elliott catalogues the brutality, predatory sexual abuse, and arrogance of the three emperors most contemporary to Paul (assuming a date of Romans between 55 and 58 C.E.):

- **Gaius** Julius Caesar (the infamous "Caligula," who ruled 37-41 C.E.);
- Tiberius **Claudius** Nero (ruled 41-54, who placed Palestine under direct Roman rule); and
- **Nero** Claudius Caesar (54-68, responsible for the first widespread persecution of Christians).

Elliott points out that severe denunciations of the horrific personal and political character of these rulers can also be found in other writers of the period. The Roman historian Suetonius (writing in the early second century) called Gaius "the Monster," while the Jewish philosopher Philo (writing just before Paul) referred to Gaius as "a master avid for slaughter and thirsting for human blood" (ibid.: 80f.). These authors, like Paul, attribute the demise of Gaius and Claudius (both apparently by political assassination) to "the justice of God." Nero, however, would prove to be the worst: under his rule Paul was executed, and Rome burned.

Elliott concludes that the apostle's famous rant against "human ungodliness and wickedness" in Romans 1:18-32 refers to divine judgment on the world system headed by these corrupt characters:

His hearers, living in the very city where the savagery of one emperor after another was notorious, would easily have heard his phrases as allusions to the imperial house . . . The specific sequence Paul describes—refusal to honor God; descent into idolatry; sexual debauchery and degradation; unrestrained ruthlessness—seems an almost clinical recital of the conduct of these men. Instead of imputing to Paul a heated, irrational exaggeration as he describes general human sinfulness . . . we can read every phrase in this passage as an accurate catalog of misdeeds of one or another recent member of the Julio-Claudian dynasty. (Ibid.: 82)

Paul's (earlier) correspondence with the Corinthian Christians anticipates Romans' sweeping indictment of empire: "Among the mature we impart wisdom, although it is not a wisdom of this age or of the rulers of this age, who are doomed to pass away . . . for if they had understood it, they would not have crucified the Lord of glory" (1 Cor 2:6, 8).

If Elliott's thesis about the Epistle to the Romans is correct, it is all the more astonishing that, despite his unequivocal antipathy toward the empire, Paul refused to exclude Roman citizens from the circle of YHWH's grace. This theology of radical inclusion was deeply disconcerting to both Jewish theological ethnocentrism and to Hellenistic ideologies of superiority. In Greco-Roman antiquity, the cultural, economic, and political conflict between Jew and Gentile was considered to be the "prototype of all human hostility" (D. Smith, 1973: 35). These two communities were institutionally and historically alienated (Dix, 1953)—not unlike the modern legacy of racial apartheid, or the protracted struggle between Israelis and Arabs in the Middle East, or Protestant Loyalists and Catholic Republicans in Northern Ireland. But Paul's beliefs about the "called out" community of the *ekklēsia* prohibited him from abiding by such social divisions. It instead motivated him to build a "beloved community," just as King's faith did 1,900 years later across a similar divide, despite his denunciation of white supremacist culture (see below, 4A).

Though the early church's leadership had tactical and strategic differences on "race-mixing," Paul implies in Gal 2:10 that there was apostolic consensus that the *ekklēsiai* should express a "preferential option for the poor," as liberation theologians put it (see, e.g., Rieger, 1998). Indeed, economic chasms were as deep as ethnic ones in the Mediterranean world of Paul's time, with huge gaps between the Roman elite and the working and slave classes. Passages such as 1 Corinthians 1:26ff. suggest that "Paul's assemblies were mostly composed of urban poor folks who lived near the line between subsistence and crisis . . . After all, Paul himself was poor, an itinerant worker who supported himself by physical labor. He may have chosen a life of downward mobility, but most of the people in his assemblies did not."[4]

The Corinthian epistles provide the best insights into how Paul tried to resist Roman norms of class stratification and ethnic segregation. Corinth was a leading Greek city that had been sacked by the Romans in 146 B.C.E., then rebuilt a century later as a Roman colony and repopulated with immigrants, entrepreneurs, military veterans, and freed slaves. By Paul's time it was characterized by a culture of "new wealth." This prosperity was largely due to Corinth's strategic location astride two major marine trade routes.[5] The city Paul encountered was thus ambitious, competitive, and marked by huge disparities between its *nouveau riche* and its large laboring and slave classes. This is why one of the main themes of Paul's second letter to the Christians at Corinth, written sometime in the mid-50s c.e., is his struggle to counter the prevailing Roman culture of patronage, materialism, and elitism.[6]

For example, Paul continually had to defend his apostleship against critics who accused him of being a race and class "traitor"—not unlike what Dr. King encountered from white church leaders in the American South. Another charge by Paul's ideological opponents was that he shouldn't be trusted because his public rhetorical style didn't conform to what elite society expected of a "philosopher" (2 Cor 11:6). An analogy today might be ostracism by academia for refusing to parade formal credentials or play the "publishing game" because of a conviction that the gospel prioritizes practice over professional intellectualism.

Apparently some Corinthian believers (as with many North American Christians today) were also more impressed with displays of charismatic oral performance by those who preached a sort of "prosperity theology" than with fidelity to the Way of Christ (10:1-10). Against such prestige-oriented Christianity, Paul pits his own commitment to costly discipleship (4:8-11). He contrasts himself with "hucksters of the Word of God" (2:17) and those who "pride themselves on position" (5:12), defending his apostolic credentials in terms of suffering rather than self-advancement; of service rather than status; and, most importantly, of grace rather than merit. For similar reasons, Dr. King turned down prestigious pulpits, honorary doctorates, official postings, and sweet retirement deals, choosing rather to stay immersed in the struggle for racial and economic justice.

Paul was keenly aware that the cornerstone of social stratification in Roman antiquity was the patronage system. This is described by Bruce Malina and Richard Rohrbaugh as:

> socially fixed relations of generalized reciprocity between social unequals in which a lower-status person in need (called a client) has his needs met by having recourse for favors to a higher-status, well-situated person (called a patron) . . . The client relates to the patron as to a superior and more powerful kinsman, while the patron looks after his clients as he does his dependents. (1992: 74)

Ben Witherington correlates the rise of patronage to two factors (1995: 22ff.). As the more hierarchical structures of the Roman Empire imposed themselves on traditional participatory institutions around the Mediterranean world, patronage increasingly defined all social relations: family, craft guilds, tribal structures, etc. The other factor was the increasing erosion of the social safety net under the pressure of economic "structural adjustments" throughout the *Pax Romana*—such as displacing locally sustainable farms with agriculture for export (for how this impacted Palestine, see below, 2A). Resulting landlessness and the atrophy of village mutual aid made personal patronage a practical necessity.

Conventions of patronage functioned in economic, social, and political spheres, and affected Corinthian Christians at many levels (for a detailed examination, see Chow, 1997). Thus elite critics also disparaged Paul's refusal to support his apostolic ministry either by professional religious begging (as in the Cynic tradition) or as an "in-house philosopher" sponsored by a wealthy patron (as in the Sophist tradition). Paul steadfastly, and in the eyes of some Corinthians, unreasonably, avoided becoming a client of the rich, insisting on supporting himself through a trade. This lowered Paul's prestige in the eyes of members of the aristocracy, since working with one's hands was considered "debasing" (2 Cor 11:7).[7] To make matters worse, Paul *did* accept support for his Corinthian ministry from poorer communities in Macedonia, shaming the relatively more-well-off Corinthians (11:8f.; see 8:1f.).[8]

Paul's commitment to "downward mobility" and "patronage from below" were concrete ways he believed he could subvert the social fabric of the status quo and make space for the gospel. He did this because he recognized the patronage ethos as the glue that held all the oppressive relationships of the empire in place. Following the Christ who had been executed by that empire, Paul instead embraced the status of a "slave" (the lowest social class), in order that he might serve *all* people, unbeholden to those of high political or economic standing (1 Cor 9:19). As Allen Callahan puts it, in Corinth Paul was "waging resistance to Roman hegemony after the fashion of those without power, privilege, or prestige in the world, slaves, former slaves, and their descendants" (2000: 223).

Paul hoped, of course, that his converts would *also* reflect these "upside-down" social relationships in their lives together. So when he heard that the Christians at Corinth were mimicking (consciously or unconsciously) the class divisions of Roman society in their *ekklēsia*, he was deeply frustrated. We see this reflected in two conflicts addressed in 1 Corinthians, which was written a few years before. One was the issue of eating meat sacrificed to idols (1 Cor 8-10). Most meat available at the Corinthian markets came from animals that had been used in pagan temple sacrifices, and only the more affluent could afford to eat it. Paul stood with the poorer majority of the church, which was scandalized over this practice. Worse, some of these same privileged Christians were interpreting Paul's "gospel of freedom" as license to participate *in* Roman temple feasts (1 Cor 8; 10:7-31). Paul strongly objected to this because not only were these public gatherings often debauched, but also because he knew they functioned to legitimize patronage, to promote the imperial cult, and to consolidate exclusionary economic-political solidarity among upper classes.

An even deeper concern was that wealthier Corinthian Christians were apparently seeking to reproduce the ethos of a Roman *symposium* when the church would gather for the Lord's Supper. This meant ranking guests in terms of social status, with those of higher class eating with the host in the dining room while lower-class participants ate in the porticoes and received leftover food (1 Cor 11:17-34; see Witherington, 1995: 191ff.). This infuriated Paul, who denounces such practices as a "profanation" of the body of Christ. He even speculates whether such abominations might lead to illness and death, and rhetorically kicks the offenders out of the Christian feast (1 Cor 11:34a).

On the positive side, one important aspect of Paul's ethos that illustrates how he tried to promote social solidarity across class and ethnic boundaries was the "collection" project. Mentioned in every one of his epistles, it called for economic sharing between rich and poor and between Gentile and Jewish Christians. Its rationale is given most complete articulation in 2 Corinthians 8-9, where Paul tries to persuade the Corinthians to follow through on promises they made to participate. Here we see Paul's theology of grace grounded in a concrete strategy of wealth redistribution, backed by a remarkable principle stated in a carefully crafted doublet:[9]

> I do not mean that others should be relieved and you afflicted; rather, it is a matter of equality. So your present surplus should help their need so that their abundance might help your lack—in order that there may be equality. (2 Cor 8:13f.)

The term "equality" (Gk. *isotēs*), so important to our modern notions of justice, is actually rare in the New Testament, appearing only here and in Colossians 4:1. Yet in the following verse Paul underlines this principle by invoking the central "instruction" of the Exodus *manna* story: "The one who had much did not have too much, and the one who had little did not have too little" (2 Cor 8:15 = Exod 16:8; see Myers, 2001a: 10ff.). Paul's argument makes it clear that he saw international economic mutual aid not as a practice of "charity," but of fundamental justice.

Finally, Paul's inclusive stance toward non-Jewish Christians was constantly being challenged by Jewish Christians, who argued that Gentile converts should adopt practices and conventions of the Mosaic Law (such as keeping *kosher*). Paul believed that such obligations represented a fatal barrier to the task of building a truly multicultural church, which he thought should be based on Jesus' *ethos* rather than his *culture*. Given the fact that Jews were a hard-pressed minority culture within the Roman empire, this was a remarkable strategy of inclusion. As an educated Jew trained in Torah, Paul was empathetic with his people's struggle to retain their identity and group cohesion, particularly given the fragmentation resulting from the Mediterranean diaspora. Indeed, Paul had once worked as part of an "internal security" operation to root out heterodox Jews throughout Judea and Samaria, which according to both Acts 8:1-3; 9:1f. and Galatians 1:13f., 23 had involved both the imprisonment and even execution of Jewish Christians!

But he had been profoundly changed by his experience on that fabled Damascus road (Acts 9:3ff.; Gal 1:15f.). He appears to have made the connection that if it was wrong to persecute his own kinsfolk for their unorthodox commitments to "the Way," then it was just as wrong to try to make Gentile Christians conform to the same brand of "orthodox" Judaism. For this Paul was branded an ethnic traitor who was "diluting" or "compromising" the integrity of Israel (a charge he tries to counter in Rom 9-11). It is worth keeping in mind, by way of analogy, that Dr. King's advocacy for racial integration was criticized not only by his white adversaries; it was also attacked by leaders in his own community, both from the left by advocates of Black Nationalism, and from the right by Black conservatives, including many ministers.[10] Internal conflict is inevitable whenever a minority community tries to forge liberation both for itself *and* for the oppressor majority, as was the case with both the apostle Paul and the prophet King.

In sum, Paul was serious about the church's "adamant opposition to Roman imperial society" (Horsley, 1997: 242). Yet he refused to see this as a strictly ethnic strategy of resistance among Jews; he expected Gentile Christians, too, to defect from their own entitlements and loyalties. He believed that his small Christian house gatherings, sprinkled around the eastern empire, were to model an alternative society liberated from patronage, hierarchy, economic disparity, and racial hostility. Dr. King, two millennia later, called this the vision of "a beloved community." It is such a community that Paul believed Christ had called into being, a "new creation" in which "everything old has passed away and everything has become new" (2 Cor 5:17), a text to which we now turn.

1B. Reconciliation as Divine Invitation and Challenge (5:16-6:2)

Our passage begins with two categorical declarations, the first in a string of rhetorical doublets:

Therefore, from now on we regard no one from a human point of view. Even though we once knew Christ from a human point of view, we know him no longer in that way.

Therefore, if anyone is in Christ, there is a new creation: everything old has passed away. See, everything has become new! (2 Cor 5:16-17)[11]

The apostle urges disciples to view the world no longer "from a human point of view"—literally, "according to the flesh." The "flesh" (Gk. *sarx*) does *not* refer to our bodies or our sexual passions, the widespread misunderstanding of Christian pietism.[12] Rather, it is one of Paul's favorite metaphors for the deeply rooted, socially conditioned *worldview* we inherit from our upbringing. It is the sum total of personal and political constructs and conventions that define what it means to be a member of a given culture—in other words, the way most folk think and act. A key example of the perspective of the "flesh" that we raise throughout this project is the dominant assumption that the "moral" response to violation is punishment. To challenge this cultural conviction quickly engenders passionate and often irrational resistance that is both broad (i.e., the majority opinion) and deep (welling up from the core of individual psyches). This is the power of the "flesh" in Paul's sense.

Paul believed that this social formation, however majoritarian, is fundamentally deforming to the biblical understanding of what it means to be human. The flesh dictates what and how we "know," constrains our imagination, and locks us into habitual enslavements of all kinds.[13] Philosopher Daniel Quinn (1992) remetaphorizes this socialization as "Mother Culture"; New Testament scholar Walter Wink refers to it as the "domination system" (1992a: 13ff.). The deep biblical metaphor would be "bondage under Pharaoh." But this is always apprehended through the Exodus lens of YHWH's promise of liberation. Thus, the apostle's next assertion is that those who are in communion with Christ have adopted a radically new perspective (5:17).

Paul's vocabulary of the "new creation," which eclipses the "old things that have passed away," places the whole passage in a decidedly apocalyptic—which is to say world-transformative—framework.[14] Conversion is not only an inner change of heart, or a private change of mind, but a *revaluation of everything*. This is at once both profoundly personal and political.[15] But Paul does not want this apocalyptic language misunderstood as implying a divinely ordained destruction of the world, as so many modern fundamentalists have done.[16] *This* revolution is for the purpose of restoring the world through the great work of "reconciliation," a word Paul now deploys emphatically and repeatedly. Verses 5:18-19 read:

A   All this is from God, who reconciled us to Godself
        through Christ,
  B   and has given us the ministry of reconciliation;
A' that is, in Christ, God was reconciling the world to
        Godself (not counting their trespasses against them)
  B' and entrusting the message of reconciliation to us.

Each theological assertion (A) is linked immediately to a practical one (B), reiterated in a parallel doublet.[17] Let us look at each in turn, because here we are at the core of Paul's theological vision.

The theological assertion articulates the extraordinary idea of God's conciliatory initiative. God is portrayed not as the recipient of Jesus' "sacrifice" but as the One acting through Jesus' execution. Reconciliation is not something accomplished *by* Christ *for* God, nor inflicted *on* Christ *by* God, but forged *by* God *in* Christ. This wreaks havoc on the medieval (but still widespread) doctrine that Christ's death functions to placate an angry or offended deity (see Bartlett, 2001). Rather, the cross represents a fundamentally restorative initiative by the divine victim toward the human offender: "While we were yet enemies we were reconciled to God by the death of God's Son," as Paul puts it in Romans 5:10f. In the narrower sense, God is one with Jesus-the-victim of imperial crucifixion; but in the more cosmic sense, God is victimized by *every* expression of human injustice and violence.[18] Yet this God absorbs the violent injustice of the offender, and offers the gift of forgiveness. The powerful notion of the "moral authority of victim initiative" is central to restorative justice, and will recur throughout both volumes of this project.

It is significant that the semantic field of the verb "to reconcile" (Gk. *katallassō*, used only by Paul in the New Testament) is *economic* here, not expiatory. In Aristotle, it connotes an exchange of money to establish equivalence of value (we still speak of "reconciling" a bank statement). Frances Young and David Ford examine this rhetoric in the wider context of 2 Corinthians as a whole, which uses a wide variety of "economic analogies."[19] They point out that Paul metaphorizes God as a kind of "central storehouse" in an alternative economy, providing unlimited abundance. Christians, in turn, are to practice mutual aid. As we noted in the previous section, the apostle's project of international ecclesial sharing is articulated in 2 Corinthians 8-9 as a work of "grace" (Gk. *charis*). This economic discourse resonates with the Hebrew Bible's tradition of Sabbath and Jubilee.[20] The unilateral seventh- and forty-ninth-year "release" from debt-bondage (Deut 15; Lev 25) is alluded to in God's decision "not to count our trespasses against us" (the explanatory addition in 2 Cor 5:19). Christ heralds the renewal of this divine economy of grace: the old "debt system" is passing away.

The practical part of the doublet (B) makes it clear, however, that in order to participate in this divine Jubilee disciples must embrace the "ministry of reconciliation" (5:18). This mandate is couched in the language of gift rather than obligation: this vocation is "given" (5:18b), the message "entrusted" to us (5:19b). Yet with the gift comes responsibility, which is taken up in the next verses:

> So we are ambassadors for Christ, since God is making an appeal through us. We entreat you on behalf of Christ, be reconciled to God! For our sake God made him to be sin who knew no sin, so that in him we might become the justice of God. (2 Cor 5:20f.)

This "appeal" (Gk. *parakaleō*) can be understood both as an invitation and a challenge, and it comes through the agency of disciples acting as "ambassadors."

In the Greek-speaking Roman Empire, "ambassador" (Gk. *presbeutēs*; Lat. *legatus*) had thoroughly political connotations.[21] The *legatus* represented imperial interests, especially in foreign (and often occupied) lands: facilitating intelligence gathering, negotiating trade deals, wielding threats, or offering compromises, etc. But this was not Paul's meaning. While Caesar's envoys throughout the Mediterranean world strove to defeat enemies and to bend nations and peoples to the will of the *Pax Romana*, the emissaries of Christ were to appeal to those same nations and peoples to be reconciled to God and one another (2 Cor 5:20b).

The indicative mood now gives way to imperative, a transition typical of Paul's rhetorical style.[22] Divine *realities* are waiting to be *realized* in our lives, so Paul as the emissary of Christ pleads, "Be reconciled to God!"[23] But this "balancing of the books" is demanding because, as we shall see, it is predicated on making peace with those from whom one is alienated, including one's ethnic or political enemies (below, 4B). Thus Paul emphasizes the need for "ambassadors" to facilitate this challenging social vision.

The divine imperative is followed by a conditional subjunctive: "For our sake God made him to be sin who knew no sin, so that in him we might become the justice of God" (5:21). Christ "took on the debt system" in order to liberate us from its totalitarianism (see Rom 8:3f.). Jesus' empowered "political body" somehow "grounded" the pathology of the body politic like a lightening rod (below, 4B). This commitment to absorb the violence of the offender is a difficult notion, but nevertheless the core of redemptive nonviolence, as demonstrated in a number of our testimonies in volume II.[24] When we embody such commitment, we "become the justice of God," a key Pauline phrase, appearing some ten times in his letters (see Grieb, 2002: 19ff.). As Elliott recognizes, it is a polemical phrase, asserting that divine fairness is utterly opposed to Roman *iustitia* (justice; 2008: 59ff.). Nor should it be equated with *our* functional notions of retributive justice. The deeply engrained retributive logic of the domination system—the way we think "according to the flesh"—stipulates that debtors must be imprisoned and offenders punished. In stark contrast, God models in Christ the practice of victim-initiated reconciliation.[25] As Christopher Marshall (2001) has shown, this restorative logic lies at the heart of the New Testament theology of redemption—even though our churches persist in hanging on to a cosmology of ultimate divine retribution (below, 4C).

For Paul, the proper response to God's expression of grace is to work for liberation in the world: "As we work together with Christ, we urge you also not to accept the grace of God in vain" (2 Cor 6:1). Paul invites disciples to "cooperate" with God's restorative initiative in Christ.[26] If, however, we do not practice this divine Jubilee toward others, we have "accepted grace in vain" (2 Cor 6:1b).[27] While Paul often laments that *his* work might be futile (e.g., 1 Cor 15:14; Gal 2:2; Phil 2:16), only here does he dare suggest that *our* lack of follow-through might in fact jeopardize God's work. It is surely one of the most chilling theological assertions in the New Testament, a radical indictment of what Dietrich Bonhoeffer famously called "cheap grace" (1963: 45ff.).

To complete his appeal, Paul cites Isaiah 49:8, a hymn to the liberation of Israel from captivity: "For God says, 'At the acceptable time I have listened to you, and on the day of salvation I have helped you'" (2 Cor 6:2a). Paul existentializes the old prophetic vision with one more emphatic doublet:

Behold, *now* is the acceptable time!
Behold, *now* is the day of salvation! (2 Cor 6:2)[28]

The apostle's rhetorical strategy here recalls Luke's portrait of Jesus' inaugural sermon at Nazareth. After reading another Isaianic oracle envisioning the "acceptable year," Jesus announces to the synagogue: "*Today* this scripture has been fulfilled in your hearing" (Luke 4:19, 21; see Prior, 1995).

Paul sweeps away our classic religious excuses for non-engagement—namely, that such idealistic practices are for other people, or some other place, or some other time. No, argues the apostle, restorative justice is *our* vocation, *here* and *now*. But what does it require?

1C. The Cost of Nonviolent Discipleship (6:3-13)

It is no accident that Paul follows his exhortations with a litany of the hardships he has endured as a result of his "ambassadorship":[29]

> We are putting no obstacle in anyone's way, so that no fault may be found with our ministry, but as servants of God we have commended ourselves in every way: through great endurance, in afflictions, hardships, calamities, beatings, imprisonments, riots, labors, sleepless nights, hunger; by purity, knowledge, patience, kindness, holiness of spirit, genuine love, truthful speech, and the power of God; with the weapons of righteousness for the right hand and for the left; in honor and dishonor, in ill and good repute. (2 Cor 6:3-8a)

There is a cost to a discipleship of restorative justice in a world of protracted violence and persistent oppression. Paul is, after all, a *legatus* who operates without the official sanction of the Jewish authorities, much less a consular letter of appointment from the emperor![30]

But for Paul the only legitimation of his apostleship is his own sufferings in solidarity with Christ (6:4; see 5:12), which he catalogues in three groups of three:

- The first group summarizes the hardship, "inevitable distress," and restrictions that disciples must typically endure (6:4b).[31]
- The second group is Paul's record of political persecution: beatings, imprisonments, and riots (6:5a)—all in the plural (see Wansink, 1996; below, 4D).
- The third group focuses on the physical wear and tear of his work: tiring labor, sleeplessness, and hunger (6:5b).

In response to these injustices and stresses, however, Paul strove to maintain a demeanor of nonviolent composure, so that his witness might "place no obstacle before anyone" (6:3). He believed that only the nonviolent weaponry of God's "justice, love, truth" had the power ultimately to transform the world (6:7).[32] We hear this conviction echoed by Dr. King when he accepted the Nobel Peace Prize in 1964: "I believe that unarmed truth and unconditional love will have the final word in reality. This is why right temporarily defeated is stronger than evil triumphant."[33]

Seven antitheses complete Paul's apostolic self-portrait:

> We are treated as impostors, and yet are true; as unknown, and yet are well known; as dying, and see—we are alive; as punished, yet not killed; as sorrowful, yet always rejoicing; as poor, yet making many rich; as having nothing, and yet possessing everything. (2 Cor 6:8b-10)

These offer a sobering reminder of Paul's ambassadorial reality. Unlike the fame and fortune enjoyed by Caesar's envoys, Paul acknowledged that he was unknown and poor—though not in the alternative reality of God. While imperial legates enforced "law and order" in the provinces, Paul was criminalized—yet persisted defiantly, "alive amidst death" (6:9). Whereas officials of the *Pax Romana* rejoiced in conquest and possession, Paul knew the grief and dispossession of the empire's victims—yet celebrated the alternative economy of God, whose grace was freely distributed, "making many rich" (6:10).

Paul reminds the Corinthians that despite his own economic and political marginalization, his work among them has always been expansive and motivated by compassion:

> We have spoken frankly to you Corinthians; our heart is wide open to you. There is no restriction in our affections, but only in yours. In return—I speak as to children—open wide your hearts also. (2 Cor 6:11-13)

Unlike tight-lipped, hard-hearted imperial diplomats, the apostle speaks warmly but honestly with his communities; indeed, this whole epistle is an attempt to talk openly about difficult matters with the Corinthian community.

For a second time Paul alludes to the "restrictions" placed on him by the authorities, and to the consternation this causes among his compatriots (6:12).[34] Yet despite his own proscribed freedom, Paul insists he is not trying to constrain his churches; in fact, it is *their* lack of solidarity with God's restorative mission that inhibits them. Paul concludes his extended appeal to the Corinthian assembly by asking them to draw on child-like instincts to "throw their hearts wide open" (6:13), in order to resume their trusting relationship with him and their fidelity to the gospel.[35] This exhortation might well be addressed to those of us who are white, middle-class Christians today, since we are notoriously "restricted" in our solidarity and seem to have such a difficult time opening our emotions, our trust, and our pocketbooks to those who are doing risky or controversial justice and peace work—especially to those from different racial and/or class backgrounds.

It is no wonder that later New Testament traditions referred to Paul, with no hint of irony, as an "ambassador in chains" (Eph 6:20; below, 4E). The apostle inhabited the empire's jails because he represented God's *restorative* justice, which challenged the retributive politics of Caesar's world. Paul understood his suffering to be meaningful because it expressed solidarity with his Lord—"bearing in my body the dying of Jesus" he calls it in 2 Cor 4:10. In this way he was "co-operating" with the God who suffers with *all* victims of personal and political violence, yet who seeks to win back the offenders as well.

Paul's thesis in 2 Cor 5:16-6:13 is that reconciliation is the dream of God, who through Christ has modeled restorative justice as the only means of achieving it. But this theological indicative means to press upon the Corinthian Christians an imperative: they must renounce whatever dominant culture privileges and prejudices they have internalized by virtue of their socialization into imperial society, in order to become a "beloved community" across class and race lines. Paul writes as an envoy with an urgent message to those in the assembly who have become alienated from his decidedly nonimperial ethos: "Be reconciled now!" (5:20). At the same time, he invites and challenges these Corinthians, as did Dr. King with the religious leaders in Birmingham, to become *themselves* ambassadors of reconciliation (below, 4D). But he follows this with a reality check: such work requires a discipleship of nonviolence that can prove costly in the real world of empire and its discontents.

Paul's challenge and invitation to become "ambassadors of reconciliation" were beautifully embodied in our own history by the "Journey of Reconciliation," one of the important actions that laid the foundation for the emergence of King's civil rights movement. In April 1947, the day before Jackie Robinson broke the color barrier in major league baseball, eight white and eight black travelers took a two-week bus and train trip from Washington, D.C., to Louisville, Kentucky. Sponsored by the Fellowship of Reconciliation and the Congress of Racial Equality, the ride's co-leaders were Bayard Rustin, a gay black man, and George Houser, a white Methodist minister.

With a strategy of whites sitting in the back seats, blacks in front and both side-by-side, they aimed to force the Southern states to implement an earlier Supreme Court decision barring segregation on interstate public transportation. Along the way the group spoke at NAACP gatherings and churches, and endured numerous arrests for violating local segregation laws. In Chapel Hill, North Carolina, they were attacked by an angry mob of white cab drivers, and the white minister who took them in was forced by threats to evacuate his family. Four of the riders were arrested, convicted, and served thirty days on a chain gang, one of whom was Rustin (his journalistic account of conditions in the jail led to the termination of chain gangs). The journey was a direct inspiration for the later Civil Rights Freedom Rides of the 1960s (Bauer, 2006).

Paul's appeal in 2 Corinthians represents the earliest literary articulation of the Christian vision of restorative justice and peacemaking. In the following chapters, we will examine how the apostolic church embraced Paul's invitation and challenge to discipleship.

2

"A HOUSE DIVIDED
CANNOT STAND"

Jesus as a Practitioner of Nonviolent Direct Action
(Mark 1-3)

It was precisely and specifically by the shores of the Sea of Galilee
that the radicality of Israel's God confronted the normalcy of Rome's
civilization under Herod Antipas in the 20s of the first century C.E.
  —John Dominic Crossan, *God and Empire* (2007: 122f.)

Nonviolent direct action seeks to create such a crisis and establish
such creative tension that a community that has constantly refused
to negotiate is forced to confront the issues. It seeks so to dramatize
the issue that it can no longer be ignored . . . We have not made
a single gain in civil rights without determined legal and nonviolent pressure. History is the long and tragic story of the fact that
privileged groups seldom give up their privileges voluntarily . . . We
know through painful experience that freedom is never voluntarily
given by the oppressor; it must be demanded by the oppressed.
  —Martin Luther King, Jr., "Letter from Birmingham City Jail"
                                    (Washington, 1986: 291f.)

Ten days before Martin Luther King, Jr., was killed, the great American rabbi Abraham Heschel asserted that the very future of our country
might well depend on how the legacy of this extraordinary man would be
handled.[1] If "the untranquil King and his peace-disturbing vision, words
and deeds hold the key to the future of America," wrote Vincent Harding later, "then we owe ourselves, our children and our nation a far more

serious exploration and comprehension of the man and the widespread movement with which he was identified" (2008: 65).

Unfortunately, the way King is officially honored on our national holiday has little to do with the leader of the most significant religious and political movement in U.S. history, which dramatically and permanently changed the landscape of American race relations. Rather, Dr. King is portrayed as a lovable, harmless icon of peace and tolerance. King's legacy has been widely domesticated, captive to street names and prayer breakfasts. And his revolutionary message typically is reduced to a vague and sentimental sound bite, in which his "dream" can mean anything to anyone (see Harding's perceptive analysis, ibid.: 56ff.).

King's *historic* voice, however, was prophetic in every sense of the word. His oratory was often polarizing and upsetting to the status quo; even more so, his campaigns of civil disobedience. This subversive voice is perhaps best heard in his famous "Beyond Vietnam: A Time to Break the Silence" speech, delivered on April 4, 1967, at Riverside Church in New York City.[2] In this talk, King—who was by then a famous civil rights leader and Nobel Peace Prize recipient—publicly articulated his opposition to the Vietnam War for the first time. Government authorities— notably FBI chief J. Edgar Hoover—were furious that King had joined his considerable moral authority to the antiwar movement. King called on listeners to face the "giant triplets" of racism, materialism, and militarism that were (and are) strangling the "soul of America." It is not surprising that exactly one year later this prophet was gunned down in Memphis (see Douglass 2000). The Vietnam War was, of course, an earlier example of the United States trying to secure "regime change" in a foreign country, as is the current case in Afghanistan and Iraq. Thus, the *real* King is highly inconvenient for a nation that has canonized him and then ignored his clarion call to examine the "deeper malady within the American spirit."

The same can be said about Jesus of Nazareth. The portrait we get in the Gospels—of an anointed man who ministered among the poor, relentlessly challenged the rich and powerful, and was executed as a political dissident—is a far cry from the stained-glass-window Christ we encounter in many churches. This seems to be a pattern in human culture: we are far more comfortable with dead prophets than living ones. We honor them publicly only after they are safely disposed of, after which they are put on display in museums and shrines. Jesus understood this tendency well: "Woe to you!" he exclaimed, "For you build the tombs of the prophets whom your ancestors killed" (Luke 11:47).

James Lawson, a retired Methodist minister now in his eighties, has been a major figure in faith-rooted activism in the United States.[3] One of King's closest colleagues, he has continued to work tirelessly in the tradition

of nonviolent activism for social justice. Speaking at a King holiday com-
memoration in Los Angeles a few years ago, Lawson said: "If you want to
understand King, you must look at Jesus." Lawson was acknowledging that
King was a committed Christian disciple who understood the call of the
gospel as a vocation of advocacy for the oppressed, of love for adversaries,
and of nonviolent resistance to injustice. Despite his secularization as a
putative national hero, King's leadership role in the civil rights movement
simply cannot be understood apart from his faith. He organized in church
basements, prayed as he picketed, sang gospel hymns in jail, preached to
presidents, and challenged church leaders to join him (most poignantly in
his 1963 "Letter from Birmingham City Jail," see below, 4D).

But Lawson was saying more than this. He was alluding to the undeni-
able, if uncomfortable, parallels between the Jesus story and the ministry
of Dr. King. Like King, Jesus was a member of an ethnic community
that suffered great discrimination at the hands of a world power. Both of
them:

- spent time listening to the pain of the dispossessed and broken
  among their own people, and advocating on their behalf;
- worked to build popular movements of spiritual and social
  identity and renewal, which included practices of nonviolent
  noncooperation with and resistance to injustice;
- proclaimed a vision of God's "beloved community" in ways that
  got them into trouble with both local, national, and imperial
  authorities;
- were widely perceived as operating in the biblical prophetic
  tradition by both allies and adversaries;
- animated dramatic public protests resulting in arrest and jail;
- were deemed such a threat to national security that their inner
  circles were infiltrated by government informers; and
- in the end, were killed through an official conspiracy because of
  their work and witness.

These parallels have been oddly absent, however, from the longstanding
but often abstract theological debates as to whether or not Jesus was a
"pacifist," or whether he was politically engaged.[4]

King not only looked *to* Jesus; he looked *at* Jesus. Too many Christians
apprehend Jesus in a highly spiritualized way, ignoring the fact that he lived
and died in times that were as contentious and conflicted as our own. The
Nazarene's world was not the fantasy-scape we so often imagine the Bible
to inhabit. It was tough terrain, not so unlike that of the United States at
the time of Dr. King's death: a world of racial discrimination and class

conflict, of imperial wars abroad and political repression at home. It was a world presided over by a political leadership that (directly or indirectly) engineered the demise of the prophet, then issued stern but pious calls for law and order in the wake of his "tragic death." The converse of Lawson's assertion, therefore, also applies: If we want to understand Jesus, we would do well to look at King. Indeed, the more we study the civil rights movement, the more the Gospels come alive. Remembering the challenges that Dr. King faced trying to build a social movement for racial justice in the teeth of the hostile system of American apartheid can help us re-imagine how difficult it must have been for Jesus to proclaim the Kingdom of God in a world dominated by imperial Rome two thousand years ago.

In order to move the theological conversation about Jesus and violence beyond the favorite proof texts of both pacifists (e.g., Matt 26:52) and nonpacifists (e.g., Luke 22:36), we propose to explore the Jesus story as a narrative of King-style active nonviolence. In volume II (2B) we discuss nonviolent direct action (NVDA) as the peacemaking strategy of "last resort." NVDA is how groups who have been violated and their allies work to build their social power and to pressure their oppressors to come to the table when the latter are unwilling to submit to arbitration, mediation, or negotiation. Struggles for wholeness, peace, justice, and freedom face real adversaries. Gene Sharp defines NVDA generically as an approach that endeavors to deny the adversary "the human assistance and cooperation which are necessary if he is to exercise control."

> The term nonviolent action refers to those methods of protest, noncooperation and intervention in which the actionists, without employing physical violence, refuse to do certain things which they are expected, or required, to do; or do certain things which they are not expected, or forbidden, to do. (1970: 28, 31)

As King writes in his jail letter: "The purpose of the direct action is to create a situation so crisis-packed that it will inevitably open the door to negotiation" (Washington, 1986: 292).

Often, however, violation is depersonalized, the result of social structures of inequity or exclusion, or political policies of oppression (we analyze this in vol. II, 1B). Just as often, those structures or policies seem inscrutable, invisible, or unchangeable to communities who are paralyzed by "the way things are." In this case, the first task of NVDA is conscientization. Victims need to break through their resignation, and perpetrators their denial, and develop "eyes to see" both the actual causes of dehumanization and the possible alternatives. In order for interpersonal or social conflict to be transformed, therefore, it must first be articulated. Conditions of injustice embedded in a given social order (whether a church, neighborhood, or nation) need to be unmasked through experience-based social analysis and action. Thus, ironically, for conflict to be *resolved* it must often first be *provoked*.

This is why great figures such as Jesus, Gandhi, and King, though eulogized in retrospect as great "peacemakers," were in fact accused in their own time of being "disturbers of the peace." King drew his strategic inspiration from Gandhi, who in turn was inspired in part by Jesus. Gandhi used the term *satyagraha* to describe his campaigns: the "force of truth" that was personal and political, militant but not military in its engagement with structures of oppression (see Gandhi 2001; Bondurant 1971). Ched has shown how the account of Jesus' ministry in Mark's gospel can be read through the hermeneutic lens of *satyagraha* (1988). Here we will summarize and expand a portion of that approach in a reading of Jesus' inaugural ministry in Mark 1-3, where "by the shores of the Sea of Galilee . . . the radicality of Israel's God confronted the normalcy of Rome's civilization under Herod Antipas" (Crossan).

2A. "Let's Catch Some Big Fish!": Jesus' Call to Discipleship in a World of Injustice (1:14-20)

The careful reader of the early chapters of Mark will note that already by 3:6 the local authorities are plotting to execute Jesus, after what appears to be only a few weeks of public engagement! This is long before Jesus has marched on the capital city, confronted moneychangers in the Temple, and challenged the whole political order (Mark 11:1-23; 13:2)! What is it, then, about his teaching, exorcism, and healing work that threatened those in power? To discern this, we must review the components of Jesus' first "campaign" in and around Capernaum. Mark portrays Jesus as a prophet who proclaims liberation, especially for marginalized people; advocates on behalf of the sick and distressed; acts to disrupt the status quo; and creates a community of resistance and renewal. Each of these were also elements of Gandhi's and M. L. King's work two millennia later.

Crossan reminds us that Jewish subjugation under the Roman Empire was the *matrix*, not merely the *background*, of the Jesus story. A matrix, he explains, "is interactive and reciprocal—it changes you and you change it. Southern racism was the matrix, for example, not just background, for the Rev. Martin Luther King, Jr." (2007: 99). Mark's Gospel was written in a temporal and spatial matrix of intense economic and political conflict: the Judean revolt against Roman occupation between 66-70 c.e.[5]

Judean discontent with the imperial domination of Palestine had, after seven decades of sporadic nationalist uprisings, finally culminated in a full-fledged armed insurgency.

The iron rule of Herod the Great (40-4 B.C.E.) had solidified the grip of Hellenistic culture and Roman hegemony over Jewish Palestine, while impoverishing the masses through rapacious taxes and tributes that subsidized grand royal building schemes, including the rehabilitation of the Second Temple in Jerusalem. Debt burdens forced many off their traditional lands; economic policies disrupted village life; and poverty increased, while the elite lived in luxury. After Herod's death in 4 B.C.E., a series of Herodian dynasties continued policies of client loyalty to Caesar and exploitation of the peasant majority through the time of Jesus. During Mark's time four decades later, Palestine was under direct Roman colonial rule. Thus the matrix of his Gospel was deeply shaped by all aspects of the "spiral of violence": structural oppression, reactive violence, and counter-reactive military suppression (see vol. II, 1B). Only by studiously ignoring this socio-historical context has the church been able to depoliticize the Gospel. We contend that from the outset of Mark's narrative, Jesus is portrayed not as transcending or ignoring this matrix, but vigorously engaging it. To make this case, we will look at the politics of characterization, setting, and plot in the early episodes of the Gospel.[6]

1. Characterization: Jesus and John the Baptist. At one point mid-way through the Gospel, Mark suddenly inserts a cameo about Herod (that is, Antipas, tetrarch of Galilea and Perea from 4 B.C.E. to 39 C.E.). The king is anxious that Jesus of Nazareth might somehow be the spirit of John the Baptist coming back to haunt him (Mark 6:14-16). Mark uses this to introduce his sordid "flashback" account of how Herod had executed the Baptist as a political dissident (6:17-29). According to Mark's narrative, Herod is not entirely wrong in his perception, since Jesus did in fact adopt John's message (1:14f.). The disturbing implication for the king is that John's proclamation of repentance in light of the "Kingdom of God" persisted despite his murder—suggesting that there was a more serious popular *movement* to be reckoned with.

It is surely significant that of all the mentors Jesus might have chosen to "initiate" him, he makes his way to John to be baptized (1:4-11). John is portrayed as a feral figure, subsisting on a diet of insects and honey—which is to say, what he could forage from the land (1:6). He invites his people into the wild, sacred waters of the Jordan—far from the ritual baths of the city. Moreover, his costume—camel-hair skins—invokes the memory of the great prophet Elijah (2 Kgs 1:8), who in his day also challenged kings (and queens!; 1 Kgs 18-19). But Elijah's story lacked "closure," because he disappeared into heaven—*at the Jordan* (2 Kgs 2:6-14)! Moreover, Malachi promised that God would send Elijah back to Israel "before the great and terrible day of the Lord" in order to turn the people around (Mal 4:5f.). So Mark presents John-as-Elijah at the Jordan, exhorting the people to "turn around"—a call to an entire nation to alter their historic direction radically, not just for an individual change of hearts.

While we don't know much about John the Baptist outside of the New Testament witnesses, the Jewish historian Josephus, a contemporary of Mark, confirms that Herod Antipas executed John for stirring up a popular insurrection. Thus, Mark reports that Jesus' public ministry begins "after John is arrested by Herod" (1:14). (The flashback story of 6:14-30 explains that John was arrested because of his public criticisms of Herod's marital and political alliances.) The fact, then, that Mark's Jesus publicly identifies with *this* politically notorious figure, whose days are numbered because of his vocation of speaking truth to power, not only makes the Nazarene complicit in John's rebel movement but also connotes a sort of "passing of the torch" in a prophetic revival.[7]

Another analogy to Dr. King can shed light on the importance of Jesus' "alignment" with John. Mark wrote roughly forty years after the deaths of both prophets. While that world seems remote to us, the world of Memphis in April of 1968 does not. We, too, write forty years after King was killed, in what we now know was a government conspiracy to silence his prophetic voice (see below, notes to introduction, n. 5). This assassination occurred exactly one year after his public and militant excoriation of U.S. foreign policy in the Riverside speech. Our experience is that to align ourselves publicly with *this* Dr. King—not the domesticated saint, but the radical critic of racism, poverty, and militarism—in another moment of foreign intervention is indeed controversial.[8] This helps us understand the meaning of Jesus' identification with John the Baptist.

2. *Setting: Wilderness, Nazareth, Capernaum.* Mark tells us that people came from the center of society—Judea and Jerusalem—to meet John the Baptist in the Jordan wilderness (Mark 1:5). This setting functions to remind us of the origins of Israel's faith: the God of Exodus stands outside civilization, undomesticated and free. YHWH can only be encountered at the margins. This location, both real and symbolic, is intensified immediately after Jesus' baptism: the Spirit "drives" Jesus deeper into the wilderness. This may be understood as a sort of "vision quest," in which Jesus retraces the footsteps of his ancestors back to their mythic place of origin in order to discover where they were "tempted" and went wrong (1:12f.; see Myers, 1993). So from the outset of Mark's story, a spatial tension is set up between the existing world order, which is controlled by the

Jerusalem and Roman elite, and the "radical renewal of Israelite identity" brewing in the wilderness.

Equally significant is the fact that Jesus is introduced as hailing "from Nazareth in Galilee" (1:9). Despite the fact that this village was obscure (and otherwise unattested in ancient literature), Mark emphasizes it throughout his story (1:24; 10:47; 14:67; 16:6). What was, however, noteworthy about Nazareth was that it lay a mere three miles southwest of Sepphoris. Sepphoris (also known as Zippori or Diocaesarea) had been built a century before Jesus on a Greek city plan, and was later fortified by Herod as the capital of Lower Galilee, complete with a theater and a royal palace. After Herod's death in 4 B.C.E., a major Judean insurrection broke out, and one of the most important skirmishes was the sacking of the royal armory at Sepphoris, led by one "Judas, son of Ezekias" (see Josephus, *Antiquities,* 17:271; *Wars,* 2:56). In retaliation, Varus, the Roman legate of Syria, razed the city.

Richard Horsley and Neil Silberman relate how Herod Antipas moved shortly thereafter "to impose Roman-style order" on the region:

> Among his first acts was the establishment of a modern administrative center from which security forces, market inspectors, and tax collectors could be easily dispatched. The former regional capital of Sepphoris lay in ruins as a result of the recent uprising, and Antipas ordered that it be reconstructed as a modern Roman city with a palace, treasury, archives, and forum. When it was completed, he brought in a new population of loyal functionaries and workers—to replace the former inhabitants who had been killed by Varus's legions or sold off into slavery. He named the new city Autocratoris—literally . . . "belonging to the Emperor." (1997: 24)

If Jesus of Nazareth labored as a carpenter or construction worker in Nazareth, it is highly likely that he got work as a young man rebuilding Sepphoris, one hour's walk away.[9] Its destruction and reconstruction as an imperial city would have had a profound impact on his consciousness (on this see, Crossan, 2007: 108ff.).

A third setting of social significance in Mark is the Sea of Galilee and the harbor village of Capernaum, introduced respectively in 1:16 and 1:21. The Sea of Galilee, a large freshwater lake about seven miles wide and thirteen miles long, was rich in fish. Its shore was dotted with villages connected with the local fishing industry, the most prosperous segment of Galilee's economy.[10] The known harbors of the first century strongly correlate with locations named in the gospel tradition, including Bethsaida, located near the inflow of the Jordan River (cf. Mark 8:22-26), Gadara (cf. Mark 5:1), and Migdal.[11]

In 14 c.e., Caesar Augustus died and Tiberius became emperor. To curry the new emperor's favor, Herod Antipas began building a new capital city called Tiberias on the shores of the Sea of Galilee.[12] There he built a royal palace, where it is likely he beheaded John the Baptist. The primary function of this city was to regulate the fishing industry around the Sea of Galilee, putting it firmly under the control of Roman interests. The construction work at Tiberius may have drawn Jesus to the Sea from Nazareth after 19 c.e., and as an itinerant laborer he would have moved up the coast from harbor to harbor. This explains how Jesus appears in Capernaum, a major harbor and an important center of the fishing trade, and the narrative center of gravity in Mark 1-3.

K. C. Hanson (1997) gives a compelling portrait of the political economy of the fishing industry around the Sea of Galilee during this period, which provides further detail of the matrix of oppression narrated in Mark. All fishing was regulated by the state for the benefit of the urban elite—either Greeks or Romans who had settled in Palestine following military conquest or Jews connected with the Herodian family. They profited from the fishing industry in three ways. First, they controlled the sale of fishing leases, without which locals could not fish. These rights, and often capitalization as well, were normally awarded not to individuals but to local kinship-based "cooperatives" (Gk. koinōnoi)—such as the brothers Simon and Andrew or the Zebedee family, whom we meet in Mark 1:16-20 (see Luke 5:7-10). Second, they taxed the fish product, its processing, and levied tolls on product transport. Local administrators handled royal leases, contracts, and taxes—such as "Levi son of Alphaeus," whom we meet in Mark 2:14. Third, they steadily restructured the industry for export, so that the majority of fish were salt preserved or made into a fish sauce and shipped to distant markets throughout the empire.

Herod Antipas saw the new city of Tiberias as a way to

> make the small inland lake of Galilee into a real "sea," his own private "little Mediterranean" pond. The Roman client-king developed his own microcosmic version of Caesar's claim to own all the oceans and waterways of the realm and everything in them. (Spencer, 2005: 145)

But these "structural adjustments" of the local economy, made possible by the infrastructural improvements (roads, harbors, and processing factories) carried out by the Herodians, functioned to marginalize and impoverish formerly self-sufficient native fishing families. Leases, taxes, and tolls were exorbitant, while the fish on which local people depended as a dietary staple were extracted for export. Thus, fishermen were at the bottom of an increasingly elaborate economic hierarchy. Elites looked down on them, even as they depended on their labor: "The most shameful occupations are those which cater to our sensual pleasures," wrote the Roman poet Cicero pejoratively, "fish-sellers, butchers, cooks, poultry-raisers and fishermen" (Hanson: 99). "The fisher," attests an ancient Egyptian papyrus, "is more miserable than any other profession."[13] With such rigid state control of their livelihood and the oppressive economics of export, it is hardly surprising that in Mark's story fishermen are the first converts to Jesus' message about an alternative social vision!

3. Plot: Jesus' Rhetoric about His Kingdom Mission. The content of Jesus' inaugural proclamation in Mark provides a third lens into the matrix of his world. Mark begins with a summary of his Galilean message: "The time is fulfilled, and the Kingdom of God is at hand; repent, and believe in the gospel" (Mark 1:15). This invocation suggests that Jesus took sides in the long-running debate within the biblical tradition between those who saw the Israelite monarchy as blessed by God and those who saw it as a sign of apostasy. In reasserting the exclusive sovereignty of God in the face of an obviously corrupt Herodian dynasty that was busy selling out Palestine to the Romans, Jesus sought a renewal of the "confederate" roots of free Israel.

The Sinai covenant envisioned a decentralized style of self-governance: because YHWH was king over Israel, royalist politics were *precluded*. Thus after the Canaanite city-states are vanquished (see Josh 12), the victorious military leader Gideon rejects attempts to make him king: "I will not rule over you . . . YHWH will rule over you" (Judg 8:22f.). Instead, local "judges" administer the tribal confederacy. Hebrew Bible scholar Norman Gottwald (1985: 135ff.) believes this intertribal, egalitarian social organization represented a revolutionary alternative to the dominating rule of the Bronze Age Cannaanite city-states who were aligned with imperial Egypt.[14]

First Samuel 8 narrates the decline of this system because of internal corruption and external military threats. Disillusioned with their experiment in self-determination, the people go to the elder Samuel to demand that he appoint "a king to govern us, like other nations" (1 Sam 8:5). "They have not rejected you," says God to Samuel, "they have rejected me from being king over them" (8:7). God then instructs Samuel to warn the people about "the ways of the king," which include forced conscription, militarism, state expropriation of labor and resources, an economy geared to the elite, and taxation (8:11-17). The grim litany concludes, "And you will be his slaves." The moral of the story: In choosing a centralized monarchy, a people freed from slavery recreated Pharoah's society of domination. This is, we have seen, precisely the world of Palestine under Roman occupation during the time of Jesus.

But Jesus does not propose this renewal of God's radical sovereignty as a utopian dream that can be realized only in another place (i.e., heaven) and time (i.e., the afterlife). Mark leaves no room for otherworldly religion: "The time is *now*; the Kingdom is *here*." Horsley believes we should take this announcement "literally, not metaphorically, and exclusively, such that the imperial rule of Caesar was on the way out" (2001: 28). This rupture constitutes what Mark for the second time (see 1:1) calls the "gospel" (Gk. *euangelion*). This choice of terms was itself polemical and political. According to the *Theological Dictionary of the New Testament*, the emperor

> gives *euangelion* its significance and power . . . Because the emperor is more than a common man, his ordinances are glad messages and his commands are sacred writings . . . He proclaims *euangelia* through his appearance. (2:724)

Theissen believes that Mark's use of *euangelion* "would have had a special ring to it" in Palestine toward the end of the Roman-Jewish war:

> It was here in the eastern part of the empire, in its terrible crisis, that Vespasian had been proclaimed emperor—the man who succeeded in putting an end to civil war and rebellion and restoring peace. Josephus calls the news of his proclamation as emperor "good news: . . . Every city kept festival for the *euangelia* and offered sacrifices on his behalf." (1991: 270)

But Mark's "good news" is challenging, not parroting, imperial propaganda. It implies that Caesar's hegemony is being eclipsed by a powerful prophet who has been anointed by the rebel John the Baptist in Jordan's holy waters, and who heralds the restoration of God's true sovereignty.

From a plot perspective, Mark's segue from Jesus' militant annunciation of the Kingdom to a conversation with peasant fishermen along the shores of Galilee's sea is rather jolting (1:17a). Conventional apocalyptic hope would not expect a mundane fishing cooperative to be the place or people among whom the new world dawns. But in terms of a campaign of NVDA in a world of oppression, this scene makes perfect sense. If

Tiberius was ground zero in Herod's project of Romanizing the regional economy, then Capernaum up the coast, a village profoundly impacted by such policies, was the logical place to commence building a movement of resistance. Restless peasant fishermen had little to lose and everything to gain by overturning the status quo. This is not unlike Gandhi's attempts to mobilize the "untouchable" classes in India in campaigns such as his famous Salt March (Bondurant, 1958: 100ff.), or M. L. King's outreach to young, disaffected Blacks after the urban uprisings of the mid-1960s (Branch, 2006: 284ff.).

"And Jesus said to them, 'Follow me and I will make you fish for people'" (Mark 1:17b). This famous phrase is beloved to evangelicals, who have traditionally interpreted it to connote the vocation of "saving souls." But we miss the point if we remove this text from its social matrix, and if we ignore the roots of this metaphor in the Hebrew Bible, where it appears in no less than four prophetic oracles. Jeremiah envisions YHWH "sending for many fishermen" in order to catch the wayward people of Israel, specifically "those who have polluted the land with idols" (Jer 16:16-18). The prophet Amos targets the elite classes of Israel, whom he calls "cows of Bashan," warning that YHWH will haul them away like sardines to judgment: "The time is surely coming upon you [who oppress the poor and crush the needy] when they shall take you away with hooks, even the last of you with fishhooks" (Amos 4:1f.).

The most clearly anti-imperial version is found in Ezekiel's rant against Pharaoh, denouncing the empire's delusion that it "owns" the Nile. God vows to yank the "dragon" of Egypt right out of the river, "hook, line, and sinker," along with all the fish that it claims exclusive rights to (Ezek 29:3f.). A fourth text from Habakkuk, on the other hand, could well capture the lament of those hard-pressed fishermen about how the enemy "emptied" their marine resources:

> You have made people like the fish of the sea, like crawling things that have no ruler. The enemy brings all of them up with a hook; he drags them out with his net, he gathers them in his seine; so he rejoices and exults. Therefore he sacrifices to his net and makes offerings to his seine; for by them his portion is lavish, and his food is rich. Is he then to keep on emptying his net, and destroying nations without mercy? (Hab 1:14-17)

Jesus—who knew the prophetic literature *and* sought to embody it anew in his context—was using an idiom that "exposed and provoked" the conflict in order to address it. It mixed both the prophetic sense of warning to the oppressor classes and the lament of those oppressed by the privatizers of the Sea of Galilee's commonwealth. He was summoning these marginalized workers to join him in, to use modern parlance, "catching some Big Fish" and restoring God's justice for the poor. So the revered image of "fishing for people" should be understood more in the sense of Dr. King's struggle "for the soul of America" than Billy Graham's altar calls.

Little wonder, then, that Mark records the response of these exploited fishermen to Jesus' "good news" as immediate (a scenario he repeats twice, 1:18, 20). In antiquity, leaving the workplace would have entailed both loss of economic security and a rupture in the social fabric of the extended family as well. In that sense, to join this movement demanded not just an assent of the heart but an uncompromising break with "business as usual." But the verb "they left their nets" (Gk. *aphiēmi*) is used elsewhere in Mark to connote release from debt, as well as forgiveness of sin and liberation from bondage. It is, in other words, a "Jubilee" verb. In fact, an epilogue to the later call-of-the-rich-man story defines "leaving" home, family, and work specifically in terms of the discipleship community's practice of social and economic redistribution (Mark 10:28f.). Jesus is calling these disaffected workers out of an exploitive system and back to a network of "fictive kinship" that practices mutual aid and cooperation.[15]

In sum, Mark's prologue (1:1-15) and first discipleship call story (1:16-20) describe a world in political, social, economic, and religious crisis. The tension of local disenfranchisement by imperial forces of "globalization" was intensified by the dramatic appearance of prophets who called their people to "repentance"—which is to say, to change radically the direction in which their history is headed. Mark's Jesus aligned himself with the radical Elijah-figure prophet John the Baptist, and when the latter was silenced by Antipas, Jesus took up his cause and began building a movement of discipleship. Mark's ensuing narrative sketches out the contours of this movement.

2B. Healing Political Bodies, Challenging the Body Politic (1:21-2:12)

The "rhythm" of Jesus' first campaign in Mark can be outlined as follows:

- 1:16-20: *sea*: call of fishermen, Jubilee response
- 1:21-28: *synagogue on Sabbath*: struggle over authority to teach

- 1:29-34: *home*: strategic healing and exorcism
- 1:35-39: withdrawal to wilderness
- 1:40-45: healing of leper, confrontation with purity code
- 2:1-12: *home*: healing of paralytic, confrontation with debt code
- 2:13-17: *sea/home*: call of tax collector, Jubilee table fellowship
- 2:18-22: dispute over fasting
- 2:23-28: dispute over Sabbath rights to glean
- 3:1-6: *synagogue on Sabbath*: struggle over authority to heal
- 3:7-12: withdrawal to *sea*: healing and exorcism
- 3:13-19: mountain: naming of discipleship community
- 3:20-34 *home*: family and authorities try to silence Jesus

In this sequence it is not difficult to identify patterns of movement and recurring themes.

In Jesus' very first public action (1:21-29), conflict erupts in a Capernaum synagogue. The setting represents the heart of the local social order: the holy space of synagogue and the holy time of Sabbath. The story is structurally framed by the reaction of the crowd to Jesus' teaching, which introduces tension between Jesus and the scribes:

> 1:22: And the crowd was <u>astonished</u> at Jesus' <u>teaching</u>, for he taught them as one who had <u>authority</u>, unlike the scribes.

> 1:27: And they were all <u>amazed</u>, so that they questioned among themselves saying, "What is this? A new <u>teaching</u>! With <u>authority</u> he commands even the unclean spirits and they obey him!"

This frame, with its repeated vocabulary, articulates the episode's central issue: who exercises authority in this communal space? In the middle of the narrative, an unclean spirit appears protesting Jesus' presence: "Why do you meddle with us?" (1:23f.; see Judg 11:12; 1 Kgs 17:18). The demon's defiance quickly however turns to fear: "Have you come to destroy us?" Who is the "we" on whose behalf the demon speaks?

Mark's framing device suggests that the demon represents the voice of the scribal class whose "space" Jesus is invading. The synagogue on the Sabbath is their turf, where they teach and interpret Torah. This unclean spirit, then, seems to personify scribal anxiety over Jesus' threat to their hegemony. The first order of business, then, for Mark's Jesus, is to exorcise the spirit of internalized submission among the people, whose hearts and minds are ruled by those who interpret the world to them.

Mark 1:21-28

²¹ They went to Capernaum; and when the <u>Sabbath</u> came, he entered the <u>synagogue</u> and taught.

Setting: Jesus enters scene, center of sacred/civic space and time

²² They were <u>astounded</u> at his <u>teaching</u>, for he taught them as one having <u>authority</u>, and <u>not as the scribes</u>.

Plot: Teaching as practice of social power; implied conflict between scribes and Jesus

²³ Just then there was in their synagogue a man with an unclean spirit, ²⁴ and he cried out: "<u>What have you to do with us</u>, Jesus of Nazareth? Have you <u>come to destroy us</u>? <u>I know who</u> you are, the Holy One of God."

Character: I/we: voice represents the "spirit of social orthodoxy"

²⁵ But Jesus rebuked him, saying, "<u>Be silent</u>, and come out of him!" ²⁶ And the unclean spirit, throwing him into convulsions and crying with a loud voice, came out of him.

Plot: Jesus exorcises the voice of internalized submission.

²⁷ They were all <u>amazed</u>, and they kept on asking one another, "What is this? A new <u>teaching</u>—with <u>authority</u>! He commands even the unclean spirits, and they obey him." ²⁸ At once his fame began to spread throughout the surrounding region of Galilee. ²⁹ And immediately he left the synagogue . . .

Setting: Jesus exits scene, having gained reputation as a liberator.

This exorcism seems to create the space for Jesus to commence his compassionate ministry to the masses (1:29-34).

This episode is characteristic of every one of Jesus' healings in Mark. He intervenes on behalf of the "political body" of a sick or possessed person in a way that personally liberates, even as it raises larger questions of justice in the "body politic."¹⁶ As a social animator, Jesus addresses specific presenting conditions *and* seeks root causes of why people are silenced or marginalized. This is why his healings and exorcisms are interpreted either as liberation or lawless defiance in the narrative, depending upon one's commitment to, or status within, the prevailing social order. This first skirmish of Jesus' public ministry symbolically articulates the fundamental diagnosis of a situation of oppression: the monopoly that those in power hold over popular spiritual and political imagination must be broken in order to animate a movement of change.

Concise and demystifying social analysis and inspiring proclamation of new possibilities can tap into latent dissatisfaction among oppressed people and fire their hopes for a better world. We see this in Dr. King, whose preaching "with authority" mobilized African Americans who had never accepted Jim Crow, but had been resigned to its apparent invincibility. It was through such proclamation that King the peacemaker became a local, then regional, then national "troublemaker."

Those who build movements of opposition and renewal must think not only strategically but tactically as well. The little vignette that follows the dramatic inaugural exorcism in Mark is easy to pass over (1:29f.). But it suggests that Jesus paid close attention to timing in his public work. The phrase in 1:28, translated in the RSV "his fame spread . . . " (Gk. *hē akoē autou*), is literally "that which was being heard about him"—that is, reports and rumors. As Mark indicates at several points in the narrative (e.g., 1:45; 8:27), popular hearsay is rarely reliable and easily manipulated by the authorities (15:6ff.), so it must be "managed" as much as possible.[17]

In this case, Jesus decides to withdraw from public space, accompanying Peter to his extended family home. Throughout Mark's story, the "house" (Gk. *oikos*) is a safer domain for the discipleship movement, whereas the synagogue or the Temple is always a site of conflict. At home the fishermen gather, and draw Jesus' attention to Peter's ill mother-in-law. There is a high correlation between sickness and poverty in Mark's world (dramatically articulated in the story of the woman with the flow of blood, 5:25ff.). Though culturally inappropriate for a nonrelative, Jesus touches Peter's mother-in-law, raising her to "serve" (a metaphor in Mark for discipleship; 1:31). Word of this spreads like wildfire, and "the whole village" gathers at the humble threshold of the fisherman's shack (1:32f.). But Mark tells us that Jesus waits to heal in public until "that evening, at sundown" (1:34), so as to avoid violating the Sabbath. The question of healing on the Sabbath will be broached soon enough (3:1ff.; see below, 2D); for now, Jesus is choosing his battles. Such tactical decisions are key to any NVDA campaign; Jesus was neither random in his engagements nor oblivious to their political ramifications.

We encounter another dimension of Jesus' rhythm in the next episode: he withdraws further from public for a time of prayer and reflection (1:35). Disengagement for purposes of centering and contemplation are crucial for nonviolent leaders, essential if one is to resist pressures to compromise, self-aggrandize, or give up (see Douglass, 2006b). Gandhi steadfastly practiced and promoted prayer and fasting as integral to *satyagraha* (1983: 275f.). Dr. King drew deeply on the mystical theology of Howard Thurman.[18] Disciplines of meditation and prayer are embraced by all great faith-rooted apostles of nonviolent action, from César Chávez and Oscar Romero to Dorothy Day and Desmond Tutu. At the same time, Mark's Jesus is forever being pressed back into action, as he is in 1:36f. He understands the fundamentally public nature of his prophetic mission: "For that is why I came out" (1:38f.).

The next episodes further indicate how Jesus moves through social space. Two healings suggest that Jesus is proximate to marginalized people as an intentional strategy of solidarity. Jesus' willingness to have social contact with a leper is subversive enough, given the presumption of contagious impurity. But 1:40 indicates that the leper is *challenging* Jesus to "declare him clean" (1:40-45). Given the fact that diagnosing and curing skin diseases were both the exclusive domain of priests (Lev 13-14), Jesus' intervention would be problematic, analogous to "practicing without a license" in the context of a healthcare system monopolized by doctors, hospitals, and medical-legal codes.[19] The leper's solicitation of Jesus implies there was a crisis in the organic health system of first-century Jewish Palestine. He was either disillusioned with the care he received from the local priest, or was questioning his second-class status. Either suffices to explain Jesus' reaction of gut-wrenching compassion (or in some manuscript traditions, anger, Gk. *orgistheis*, 1:41). Jesus touches the leper *and* presumes the priestly prerogative of declaring him clean. This sets up another crisis: while Mark reports that "the leprosy left him" (1:42), public perception would have presumed that Jesus had contracted the contagion.

The epilogue to the story is telling. Jesus ennobles the leper by dispatching him to "make a witness against" the priestly system by "paying for services not rendered" (1:44). The man is not up to this protest, however, and instead spectacularizes the intervention by publicizing it. As a result, Jesus has to go underground as a transgressor of multiple social boundaries (1:45). As this vignette suggests—as well as countless other biblical tales, such as Moses' constant frustration with his people along the way of the Exodus—organizing people can be difficult, unpredictable and often unruly. Not everyone wishes to change, and many are content to settle for small improvements in their personal lot, instead of joining the struggle for greater good.

After an indeterminate period, Jesus returns to Capernaum. Word gets out, and pressing crowds of broken folk gather again (2:1). Assuming that this episode is again at Peter's family home, we have another instance of drama "at the threshold" (2:2, Gk. *pros tēn thyran*, as in 1:33). This time the scenario intensifies, as the earthen roof is dug up and a physically disabled man lowered through (2:3f.). The fact that local authorities are hovering around the scene suggests that Jesus' unorthodox behavior is now on their radar (2:6). After implied conflict in the first three healing stories, we here encounter an open skirmish for the first time.

The healing again deals with the "political body" in terms of the body politic. Instead of simply curing the paralytic's body, Jesus challenges the system by unilaterally releasing him from sin/debt (2:5). The scribes object vehemently, claiming that only God can forgive (2:7). But this is a defense of their *own* social power, since as interpreters of Torah *they* determined the protocols by which people were released from sin/debt. Jesus defies their warning, asserting for the first time directly the counter-authority of the "Human One" (2:8-11).[20] The episode concludes similarly to the opening sequence with the amazement of the crowd (2:12=1:27). But here the reaction, like the conflict, is intensified, implying a moment of worshipful awe.[21]

A "social map" of Second Temple Judean culture is important to help modern readers understand why the paired healings in 1:40-2:12 engender opposition. Two mutually reinforcing codes regulated social behavior: purity and debt. The purity code established what was clean and unclean in order to maintain ethnic group and class boundaries, and was adjudicated by priests. One's status was determined by birth (e.g., tribal affiliation), body (male/female, disabled, or sick/"healthy"), and behavior (cultic obligations of purification). The debt code, on the other hand, was under the jurisdiction of the scribal class. The Law regulated individual and social responsibilities, criminal behavior, and economic rules, determining sins of commission (e.g., stealing an ox, or adultery) and omission (e.g., not paying tithes or observing the Sabbath).

It is important to remember that there was no differentiation between sacred and secular in this culture. These two stories address what we would call the "healthcare" (purity) and the "criminal justice" (debt) systems respectively. Jesus questions three key aspects:

- the power to *diagnose* illness or *interpret* legal codes;
- the power to *change* someone's status in the system (treatment/adjudication);
- the *cost* of disposition to the subject.

Thus, when Jesus breaks the rules or engages in debates with priests or scribes who are senior administrators of (and spokespersons for) the status quo, he is involved in social criticism. "Disturbing the peace" by articulating oppressive conditions is obviously threatening to those whose status and identity is bound to the dominant social codes and structures.

Dr. King's work, too, centered around advocacy on behalf of those for whom the American social system was not working, from the Montgomery bus boycott in 1955-56 to the Memphis sanitation workers' strike in 1968. King's visits to the rural South and urban North, to Watts and Appalachia, were no mere photo opportunities. He genuinely solicited the views of economically and racially marginalized people. His plan for a Poor People's March on Washington represented the pinnacle of his vision of social inclusion (Chase, 1998). Perhaps more than any single aspect of his ministry, King's tenacious politics of solidarity was what made him dangerous in the eyes of the authorities. And it is what put him on the path of inevitable conflict with the Powers, as it did Jesus.

2C. Unmasking Economic Injustice, Embodying Economic Alternatives (2:13-3:6)

After this skirmish, Jesus again withdraws to the sea (2:13), a safe space for reflection (see 4:1) and the point of origins of his campaign (1:16). His next encounter is with "Levi son of Alphaeus sitting at the tax office" (2:14). K. C. Hanson asserts (1997) that one of the main tasks of tax collectors was to sell and regulate fishing leases, making this brief discipleship invitation story an interesting counterpoint to the call of the fishermen in 1:16-20. Elaborating on Hanson, F. Scott Spencer comments:

> Levi's tax office or customs house by the Sea of Galilee in Capernaum constituted a daily, tangible reminder of the . . . system. [He was] one of Herod's minions, and perhaps, by virtue of his location, the very one who leased the fishing rights for Peter and associates and levied the first tariffs on their catches . . . The original audiences would doubtless have assumed a propensity toward cheating and profiteering, with the help of police enforcement . . . (cf. Luke 3:12-14). Moreover, Levi's name . . . —evocative of the priestly tribe of Israel supported by the people's tithes and offerings—may have elicited a sardonic smirk: here someone who symbolizes legitimate, voluntary "taxation" in Israel's theocratic kingdom is working for "King" Herod (in Rome's hip pocket) to impose extra, onerous tax burdens on God's people. (2005: 147)

What a remarkable strategy: Jesus challenges not only the oppressed to join his movement, but street-level oppressors as well!

This "odd coupling" in the discipleship community is predicated, however, on a change in social and economic practice. The next scene is Levi's house—doubtless a contrast to the fisherman's abode of 1:29 and 2:1! Here Mark paints a portrait of "debtors and debt collectors" sharing extraordinary table fellowship (2:15). Clearly, some sort of "Jubilee" rearranging of social power and roles has occurred in the respective responses of the fishermen and their economic overlords to the call of Jesus!

Table fellowship was a primary indicator of identity and status in Mediterranean antiquity. Thus, the local authorities again show up, objecting to this inappropriate blurring of social boundaries (2:16). Jesus' retort captures brilliantly the fundamental perceptual difference between those who uphold the status quo and those who see its problems and contradictions (2:17).[22] Using a healthcare metaphor, he points out that those who see no "wounds" in the body politic will not welcome attempts to "heal" it; only those who feel the pain of a given social situation will be motivated to change it. Or, as a contemporary bumper sticker puts it, "If you think the system is working, ask someone who isn't!"

On the heels of this come two more food controversies. The conflict around *who* disciples eat with is followed by debates about *when* to eat (2:18-22) and *where* it is appropriate to eat (2:23-28). In a traditional agricultural society, the table is the primary site of consumption, the field of production. These settings represent what today we call the *economic* sphere. Hence, this sequence can be read as Jesus' protest concerning the politics of food in Palestine. Each episode illustrates a different aspect of "Sabbath economics" (see Myers, 2001a), as Jesus unmasks ways in which access to sustenance and agricultural wealth was being inequitably distributed in Israel.

The Pharisees are here introduced to the story (2:16, 18, 23). They were leaders of a renewal movement whose strategy was to promote and facilitate popular ability to meet purity and debt obligations and Torah piety. A powerful political force during the Herodian period, the Pharisees were serious rivals of the Jesus movement, and their vision of practical, Torah-centered Judaism essentially prevailed after the fall of the Temple. They figure prominently in these food controversies because of their key role in regulating production, distribution, and consumption of agricultural products in Jewish Palestine.[23] Their control over planting and harvesting, marketing and eating was resented by many subsistence peasants who could not afford to conform to Pharisaic rules of holiness.

The fasting debate represents another escalation of tensions, with the authorities going on the offensive. In a fascinating glimpse of "movement politics" in the first century, the Pharisees attempt to drive a wedge between the followers of Jesus and those of John the Baptist (2:18). Jesus' response invokes a banquet metaphor, implying that the poor need shared abundance, not the religious abstinence or ritual piety of the privileged (2:19). He then introduces apocalyptic images for the first time in Mark, warning that the "old" cannot hold the "new" (2:21f.), an allusion to the critical nature of that historical moment.

The next episode completes the sequence, returning to the central issue of Sabbath (2:23-28). This time the space is not a synagogue (1:21) but a grain field, to which the disciples are helping themselves. For a second time, the Pharisees object to their practice of eating (2:24; see 2:16), issuing a warning to Jesus about working on the Sabbath. The authorities may also, however, be accusing them of stealing, since this seems to be the subject of Jesus' response. Jesus' sarcastic quip ("Have you never read . . . ?") prepares us for an ingenuous bit of midrash. He draws their attention to a story in which the insurgent guerilla fighter David and his followers commandeer the sacred shewbread from a local sanctuary (2:25f.; see 1 Sam 21:1-6; Lev 24:5-9). The implication is that the actions of Jesus' disciples pale in comparison to the Israelite hero's violation of cultic vessels. Moreover, Jesus adds a telling rationale to the account: they expropriated bread "because they were hungry" (2:25b). This represents an oblique allusion to the Torah principle of "gleaner's rights": the edges of every field belong to the needy poor and sojourner.[24] Against the Pharisees' "reductive" ethic, focused on keeping the Sabbath holy via prohibition, Jesus pits an expansive ethic, re-authorizing the work of gleaning on the Sabbath as the divinely ordained right of hungry people.

Mark's three food stories narrate a campaign of conscientization and direct action aimed at recovering the ethos of Sabbath economics. This is made explicit in Jesus' summary assertion (2:27), which can be paraphrased as follows: "The economy was made for humans, not humans for the economy" (or in contemporary parlance, "Food for people, not for profit"). The sequence concludes with a second invocation of the Human One (2:28; see 2:10), and the unequivocal claim that he is sovereign *even over economics*. Though this would come as news to most Christians in capitalist cultures, it is *good* news for the poor.

The second synagogue episode is structured as a kind of trial scene: in the public glare, the authorities stand poised, ready for the suspect to "cross the line" (3:1f.). However, Jesus turns from defendant to prosecutor (3:4), pressing a Deuteronomic ultimatum (see Deut 30:15ff.). Faced with a wall of silent resistance, Jesus proceeds to break the law, in the classic tradition of civil disobedience, in order to raise deeper issues about the moral health of the community (3:5). The authorities, for their part, begin to deliberate about how to get rid of Jesus (we suspect that the same sort of conversations took place in Washington, D.C., after King's Riverside speech).

There are two powerful "inversions" here from Mark's first synagogue conflict, befitting the culmination of the campaign:

- in 1:22, 27 the crowd marvels at Jesus' "authority" (Gk. *exousia*); in 3:4 Jesus lays before his audience the question of what "is authorized" on the Sabbath (Gk. *exestin*);
- in 1:24, the demon (symbolizing the scribal class) worries that Jesus has come to "destroy" them (Gk. *apolesai hēmas*); in 3:6, the authorities plot how to "destroy" Jesus (Gk. *auton apolesōsin*).

There are, at the same time, logical difficulties with this story:

- rabbinic teaching would actually have allowed for rescuing a life on the Sabbath;
- the man's hand injury was not life threatening, and thus could have been addressed after the Sabbath was over;
- if Jesus' healing is affected only through speech (3:5), then this would not constitute a clear violation of the Sabbath.

Either Jesus is pushing a specious argument or the authorities are over-reacting—or both. But these contradictions/exaggerations signal that we should instead apprehend this story as a sort of political cartoon. Let us examine it closely as the concluding expression of how a political body symbolizes the body politic.

In an important forthcoming book on this passage, linguist Kurt Queller shows how these incoherencies make sense when read through the lens of Sabbath-economics traditions in the Hebrew Bible.[25] He contends that a sophisticated web of scriptural allusions "point toward a reading of the narrative not just as a literal report, but rather as a midrashic elaboration of *haggadic* (narrative) themes drawn from Exodus and of *halakic* (legal/ethical) themes drawn from Deuteronomy."

Queller's identification of how Mark's showdown echoes the Septuagint (Greek) version of Exodus is summarized in the following table:

3:1: Jesus "goes in again" (Gk. *eisēlthe palin*) to the synagogue	= Moses "goes in" (Gk. *eisēlthe*) repeatedly before Pharaoh to demand that the Israelite slaves be released (Exod 5:1; 6:11; 7:10; 8:1; 9:1; 10:1, 3).
3:3: Jesus commands the man to arise "into the midst" (Gk. *eis to meson*)	= YHWH causes the people to go "into the midst" (Gk. *eis meson*) of the sea, and on to freedom. YHWH also causes the pursuing Egyptians to go "into the midst" (Gk. *eis meson*) of the sea, to their destruction (Exod 14:16, 22, 23).

3:5a: The authorities are silent because of their "hardness of heart"	= Pharaoh's heart is hard (e.g., 7:22; 14:4).
3:5b: Jesus commands: "Stretch out your hand" (Gk. *ekteinon tēn cheira sou*)	= YHWH commands Moses: "Stretch out your hand" (Gk. *ekteinon tēn cheira sou*) over the sea (Exod 14:16, 21; cf. 10:12).
3:5c: The hand is "restored" (Gk. *apekatestathē*)	= The Reed Sea is "restored" (Gk. *apekatestē*), drowning the Egyptian army and saving the Israelites (Exod 14:27).

All this gestural resonance functions to invoke Israel's primal liberation story, and signals to the reader that this synagogue episode is no mere skirmish but goes to the heart of Jewish identity.

Queller then points out two important echoes of the Deuteronomic Sabbath tradition as well. Jesus' question in 3:4 ("Is it lawful on the Sabbath to do good or to do harm, to save life or to kill?") reiterates the great Mosaic exhortation to the people on the cusp of the Promised Land: "I have set before you life and death, blessing and curse; therefore choose life, that you and your descendants may live" (Deut 30:19).[26] Conversely, Jesus' anger (Gk. *orgē*, 3:5) at the silence of his adversaries echoes YHWH's anger (Gk. *orgē kyriou*) if the covenant is broken (Deut 29:20). Queller argues persuasively that there is an "antithetical mirroring" between the authorities' silence and the exhortation of Deut 30:14 ("The word is very near to you: it is in your mouth and in your heart for you to do"):

> The "word" to be done is already "in [their] mouth"—but they refuse to say anything in response; it is "in [their] heart"—but their heart is hardened against it. It is "in [their] hands, to do it"—but as Jesus turns again to address the man, our attention is directed back to an inert hand which ostensibly, in its current "withered" state, cannot be expected to *do* anything.

The withered hand thus symbolizes "the visible embodiment of the community's unwillingness, despite the 'nearness' of the word, to do it."

How does this conflict illuminate the Sabbath question? Queller notes that Deuteronomy generally focuses more on a positive ethos than on prohibitions, and points specifically to the Sabbath-year debt-release program (Deut 15). Indeed, there we find more strong resonances with Mark 3:1-6, particularly the repeated demand that the "hearts" and "hands" of lenders must remain "open" to the poor, and a warning not to "counsel in your heart" to freeze credit in the period just before debt cancellation (Deut

15:7-11). Queller suggests that debt release is the specific Sabbath practice of "doing good" alluded to in Mark's symbol of the hand.[27]

Queller concludes: "The shadowy figure with the withered hand at the center of Mark's story appears to be emblematic for a curse resulting from covenant infidelity." His reading explains the otherwise strangely disproportionate reaction of the authorities. Their plot to kill Jesus is a "response—at once calculated and bewildered—of a powerful elite when confronted with a challenge to the moral basis of its authority, which is being staged provocatively (albeit symbolically) within a domain heretofore considered sacrosanct." They are attempting to turn the divine "curse" invoked by Jesus because of their breach of the Sabbath covenant back on him—scapegoating the whistleblower, we might say today.

Indeed, the structural indebtedness addressed in Deuteronomy 15 was in antiquity, and remains today, a "life and death" issue for the poor.[28] To "close one's hand" by freezing credit is literally to "kill" them, while to make loans available to the economically marginalized is literally "to save life." This cause and effect may routinely be obfuscated in elaborate financial systems then and now, but the Bible insists on unmasking it. Thus, hard on the heels of a confrontation in a field in which Jesus invokes the gleaning principle at the heart of Torah's vision of Sabbath economics, he restores the "withered" hand of selfishness to its proper "stretched out" position of generosity. This summary symbolic action hopes to stop the spread of "Pharaoh's disease" among the leaders of his people, whose hearts have been hardened by injustice. It is the zenith of his *satyagraha* campaign around the economically struggling fishing village of Capernaum.

The crisis between Jesus and the authorities has escalated significantly between the two synagogue episodes in Mark 1-3. The narrative in between establishes a pattern for Jesus' ministry that prevails through the rest of the story. He and his disciples shuttle between a polarized cast of *characters*: on one hand, the skeptical elites; on the other, the needy and importunate "crowds." Mentioned some thirty-eight times in Mark, the crowds represent those for whom illness, disability and indebtedness were an inseparable part of the cycle of poverty. The *settings* of Mark's story paint an accurate portrait of the economic and political situation in the decades prior to the Roman-Jewish war, in which significant portions of the Palestinian population had become dispossessed. And the *plot* shows Jesus waging a nonviolent struggle against "hard-hearted" elites who void the covenant with their silent, privileged complicity in the murderous disparity of wealth.

In the first part of his campaign, Jesus challenges interpretations of Torah that rationalize the status quo (1:21-28), transgresses social boundaries to bring personal and political wholeness to the impure (1:29-45), and unilaterally releases sin/debt (2:1-12). In the second sequence, he brings debt collectors and debtors together in Jubilee fellowship (2:13-17), insists that the poor's involuntary "fasting" must be relieved (2:18-22), legitimates the right of hungry people to glean (2:23-28), and climaxes the campaign with an act of civil disobedience that indicts his prosecutors for failing to *practice* Sabbath economics (3:1-6). We can now understand why at this point, though only a fifth of the way through Mark's story, the elites want Jesus neutralized.

Like Jesus at Levi's house, the modern civil rights movement discovered the subversive power of a "strategic meal." On February 1, 1960, four Black college students walked into a Woolworth store in Greensboro, North Carolina, sat down at the "whites-only" lunch counter, and waited to be served. Their protest went on for days, gaining national attention, and within six weeks sit-in demonstrations had spread to ten Southern states. Ultimately, more than 75,000 students, both Black and white, participated throughout the country, giving a huge push to the movement (Bishop, 1994: 223ff.). Indeed, King became convinced soon after that the struggle for racial justice would also need to become a campaign for economic democracy. It was this conviction that took him to his Calvary in Memphis as he stood with striking low-wage workers.

Mark's two Sabbath civil disobedience actions—the grainfield gleaning and the synagogue showdown—bring to mind Gandhi's famous 1930 Salt March, which protested the British monopoly (it was illegal for anyone except the British government to manufacture or sell salt in India). The march began in Ahmadabad with seventy-six followers, and covered 241 miles to the coastal city of Dandi, by which time the numbers had grown into the thousands (a scenario repeated thirty-five years later in King's Selma to Montgomery march). Standing at the Arabian Sea, Gandhi bent down and scooped up a handful of salt—the "pinch heard 'round the world"—dramatizing his advocacy for the right of Indians to procure their own salt. He was soon after imprisoned for this *satyagraha*, which highlighted the economic dimensions of imperial oppression.[29]

Similarly, Jesus' attempts to "speak truth to power" will indeed have costly consequences in the story. This becomes inevitable after his second "campaign of direct action" in Jerusalem in the second half of Mark (11:1-13:2; see Myers, 1988: 290ff.). Midway between these two campaigns, like a fulcrum on which the narrative balances, stands a conversation between Jesus and his disciples in which he invites them to embrace the "way of the cross" (8:27-9:1; ibid.: 241ff.). This allusion to Rome's execution of political dissidents shows that Jesus, like Gandhi and King after him, understood the cost of serious nonviolent struggle for justice. To prepare himself for the greater showdowns to come, then, Jesus follows this first campaign with another withdrawal, in order to reflect on his mission and consolidate his community (3:7ff.).

2D. Truth and Consequences:
Building a Community of Resistance (3:7-35)

Jesus' first NVDA campaign is spatially defined in its beginning (1:16), middle (2:13), and end (3:7) by Jesus' location at the Sea of Galilee. This seems to be a safe place, where disciples are called and instructed. Mark tells us that seekers converge there from the far southern (Idumea) and northern (Sidon) limits of Palestine, and from both center (Jerusalem) and margins ("beyond the Jordan"; 3:8). There is also the incessant press of the "crowds": the unemployed, displaced, sick, and unclean who were doubtless following rumors that Jesus could help them (3:9f.).

At the sea, Jesus continues to practice exorcism, which Mark understands to be as integral to the messianic vocation as preaching (3:11, 14f.). Modern theological liberals tend to ignore or psychologize Gospel exorcism stories, while conservatives ignore their public and political character. In antiquity, exorcism was common, and today still has a place in traditional cultures. But Jesus was not just another shaman demonstrating his power to vanquish evil spirits. Horsley contends that Mark narrates exorcism stories not to glorify the miracle worker but to invoke the Hebrew Bible tradition of holy war.[30] Whatever else it is, exorcism in Mark is a struggle over the authority to "name." The disciples may be confused about who Jesus is (see 4:41; 8:27-30), but the demonic forces are not. They seek to bring this truly free Human One back under their control by "outing" him as God's chosen (1:24). They seem to know that such a title will generate unrealistic expectations among his supporters, and violent opposition among his adversaries—as indeed will be the case in Mark's story.[31]

This is why Jesus forbids unclean spirits to "make him known" (3:12). This brings to mind the Exodus tradition, where YHWH will not be named (Exod 3:2-15). Indeed, Jesus refuses to embrace any of the honorific "titles" given to him, whether by opponents (14:61; 15:2f.) or friends (8:28f.). Instead, he adopts the apocalyptic moniker "the Human One" (2:10, 28; see 8:31; 14:62). Demons (and humans; see 8:29; 15:39) may have the right *name* for Jesus, but if they do not follow his Way, they are silenced. On the other hand, it is possible to be a disciple even if one has Jesus' name *wrong*, as in the case of blind Bartimaeus (10:47ff.). This indicates again the priority of practice over profession in Mark's Gospel.

Jesus the exorcist turns the table on demons, unmasking *them* as "presenting symptoms" of the domination system. Mark's later account of the Gerasene demoniac explicitly symbolizes the political struggle for sovereignty: the unclean spirits are named "Legion"—the imperial forces occupying Palestine (see Myers, 1988: 190ff.; Horsley, 2001: 141ff.). It is precisely Jesus' militant engagement with these "spirits" of oppressive authority that will bring scribal investigators from Jerusalem to discredit his exorcist work—by calling him "names" (3:22ff.)! Jesus' exorcisms, then, are about who has the power to *frame reality* (today, for example, we might associate this with the media). Naming the truth of a situation is fundamental to any nonviolent campaign of liberation. Certainly Dr. King understood this when, in his Riverside address, he courageously "outed" racism, militarism, and materialism as the key pathologies holding America hostage (see notes to chapter 2 below, n. 2).

In a further nod to the Deuteronomic tone of the previous synagogue showdown, Jesus next ascends a mountain (3:13).[32] But unlike the old Sinai story, in which the people were not allowed to follow Moses up (see Exod 19:16-25), Jesus summons his leadership group to meet with him there. In another demonstration of the power of naming, the disciples are commissioned to take up the mission of liberation (3:14-19a).[33] This alludes both to the organizing of the Twelve Tribes (see Gen 49; Num 1) and to Joshua's appointment of leaders on the eve of his dramatic crossing into the Promised Land (see Josh 3-4). The Twelve do not, however, symbolize the *replacement* of Israel, as Christian supercessionists imagine. Rather, the number invokes the memory of Israel's decentralized, self-governing tribal confederacy in covenant with YHWH. This antiroyalist tradition has already been broached in Jesus' proclamation of the sovereignty of God at the outset of the story (Mark 1:15; above, 2A). This "summit" meeting with twelve leaders further indicates that Jesus was promoting a social strategy of renewal, drawing on two of the most revered traditions of Israel: God's covenant with Moses on Sinai, and the free tribal confederacy in the wilderness. It is not surprising, then, that the very next episode brings officials from Jerusalem to investigate this movement—and a homily from Jesus about "revolution" (3:19ff.)!

Jesus again returns "home" (back at Peter's family house?), which for a third time is surrounded by the crowd (3:20, as in 1:32f. and 2:1f.). But two sinister counteroffensives now commence. The first is Jesus' own family (literally, "those from him," Gk. *hoi par' autou*), who, "convinced he is out of his mind," have come to rein him in (3:21). The second are scribes from the capital, out on a "witch hunt" (3:22ff.). The composition of 3:21-35 is a "sandwich," a favorite Marcan technique of beginning one story, interrupting it with another, and then returning to finish the first, thus establishing a relationship between the two episodes:

A 3:20f.: family comes to "get" him
   B 3:22-30: scribes come to "get" Jesus
A' 3:31-34: family summons him again

Mark recognizes that the two pillars of socialization, the clan and the state, both conspire to domesticate people under the status quo. Let us look at both parts in turn.

Kinship obligations overdetermined personality, identity, and vocational prospects in the ancient Mediterranean world. We can assume that Jesus' family is trying to muzzle him in for his own protection, but also for the sake of their reputation in the community, since his nonconforming behavior is shaming them. But the scene is rife with tension. In 3:31 they are identified as his "mother and brothers," introducing the important aspect of an absent father.[34] If Jesus was the oldest son, Mark's scenario reverses the traditional role—he is supposed to be taking care of his mother. The implied estrangement is underscored through spatial inversion: the disciples and the crowd are "inside" the home, while the family is "outside" (Gk. *exō*, 3:31; see 4:11). Communication is also indirect: the family's summons is relayed through the crowd (3:32). The conflict climaxes with Jesus' almost dismissive retort: "Who are my mother and my brothers?" (3:33).

But Jesus isn't being petulant; he is stressing the conviction—crucial for his movement—that in order to weave an alternative social fabric, even the most basic conventions and constraints of kinship must be reexamined. Scott Bartchy (2003) has done important research on sibling rhetoric in the New Testament, and makes a strong case that the nurturing of nonpatriarchal "fictive kinship" was central to the organizing strategy not only of Jesus but of Paul as well.[35] The premonarchic Hebrew tribal confederation was consociated on the basis of a myth that each clan was a "sibling" of Jacob. Similarly, Jesus embraces disciples as kin, radically redefining "family" in terms of *practice* (3:35), reiterating the subtext of the preceding synagogue showdown.

In the middle of the sandwich comes the official investigation, which parrots the family's accusations, if not their concern:

Family: "He is beside himself" (3:21).
Scribes: "He is possessed" (3:22).

Both equate personal sanity and political sanctity with maintenance of the status quo; to dissent is either lunatic or traitorous. Smarting from Jesus' challenge to their authority (1:25; 2:10), the scribes try to undermine Jesus' popular standing by charging that he serves the "prince of demons." This is the predictable political strategy: neutralize the opposition by identifying it with the mythic arch-demon.[36] In our political context this would be tantamount to calling Jesus a "communist" or, more recently, a "terrorist."

Who is "sane" in this polarized atmosphere depends entirely on whose point of view we adopt. Mark chooses this acrimonious debate to introduce Jesus' discourse of parables (3:23), the venerable prophetic rhetoric of speaking truth to power. These metaphorical stories freighted thinly-veiled political meanings, as in Nathan's unmasking of King David's murderous duplicity.[37] In a strategy he will employ later with other Jerusalem leaders (see 11:27ff.), Jesus begins with a pointed question: "How can Satan cast out Satan?" (3:24). He is, in effect, returning the scribal "compliment." He follows with a triplet about internal contradictions in the Judean body politic:

> A divided kingdom <u>cannot stand</u>.
> A divided house <u>cannot stand</u>.
> Satan divided in revolt against himself
> <u>cannot stand</u> but is coming to an end. (3:25f.)

Though theocratic in name, the Judean state is doomed because it is in fact ruled by the Principalities and Powers.

The last phrase of the parable makes Jesus' subversive intentions clear, likening his mission to a thief who "must bind the strong man in order to ransack the goods in his house" (3:27). The image is, perhaps, inspired by Isaiah: "The captives of the strong one will be liberated; the prey of the tyrant will be rescued" (Isa 49:24f.). It will emerge as one of the Gospel's master metaphors. Jesus (a.k.a. the "stronger one" heralded by John the Baptist in 1:8) intends to overthrow the "strong man" (a.k.a. the elite establishment, represented by the demon in 1:24). Later Jesus will go into the Jerusalem Temple, "cast out" the *real* "thieves," who steal from the people, and put a halt to the trading of "goods" in that "house" (11:15-17).[38] Shortly after, Jesus insists it cannot stand (13:2), and exhorts his disciples to keep vigil over the house as it awaits its true Owner (13:34-37). However unsettling this metaphor of criminal breaking and entering may seem to our modern, middle-class churches, the tradition of the Lord's advent "like a thief in the night" is common in the New Testament (see Matt 24:43; 1 Thess 5:2, 4; 2 Pet 3:10; Rev 3:3; 16:15). As if to acknowledge that these are hard words, Jesus ends the exchange by issuing a blanket pardon for those who fail to understand his vision (3:28, the first of many solemn "Amen" sayings in Mark). But he can do nothing for those who insist on demonizing acts of liberation accomplished in the power of the Spirit (3:29f.).

Here, in the "epilogue" to Jesus' first campaign, the ideological struggle is broken wide open. His suggestion that insurrection (Gk. *anestē*, 3:26) is inevitable in a corrupt social order essentially legitimates the right of the people to rebel. In the first three chapters of Mark, Jesus has subjected every aspect of collective life—religion, economics, politics and family—to scrutiny by "the will of God." His practice of militant nonviolence escalates later in the Jerusalem narrative, from his subversive "street theater" as he enters the capital (11:1-10) to his "blockade" of the Temple (11:11-25). There he interrogates every level of authority (11:27-12:17) and repudiates the politics (12:35-40) and economics (12:41-13:2) of the Temple state. But he also rebukes those who imagine that war can overthrow the domination system (13:5-13). Disciples are instead exhorted to resist the propaganda of armed messianic struggle (13:3-8, 14-23), to face the consequences of their nonviolent witness (13:9-13) and to embrace an apocalyptic politics that looks for the complete demise of the Powers (13:24-33). In the Passion narrative, Jesus models the *via crucis* in his arrest, trial, and execution as a dissident (14:1ff.). This last section of Mark's Gospel articulates his deep conviction that the nonviolent cross is the only weapon powerful enough to prevail over the Powers and transform the world (see Douglass, 2006a; below, 4C).

Jesus the *satyagrahi* is a far cry from the heavenly Christ we usually encounter in our churches. The same is true of "saint" Martin Luther King, Jr. As noted at the outset of this chapter, both have been widely domesticated in popular culture. But as historic figures, they were prophetic in the true sense: speaking truth to power *and* foreseeing the historic consequences of injustice. At the end of their lives, Jesus and King were hemmed in by all the factions of their respective political terrains, navigating death threats, dissent from within their own movements, and supported by only a small group of loyal (if often feckless) companions. Despite this, both chose nonviolent love without ever compromising their insistence on justice.[39] As great peacemakers who were first peace disturbers, they remain problematic for a nation and church that have canonized and then ignored them. Jesus and King gave their lives for God's beloved community, and invite us to do the same, in a world still held hostage by emperors and terrorists, militarists and corporate kingpins, ambivalent religious leaders and insular academics, paralyzed citizens and distracted "crowds."

On June 16, 1858, the young politician Abraham Lincoln gave a now-famous speech about the coming national crisis of slavery, in which he quoted Jesus' sobering parable about the fatal structural flaws of a "house" founded on oppression. "If we could first know where we are, and whither we are tending, we could better judge what to do, and how to do it," lamented Lincoln. "'A house divided against itself cannot stand.' I believe this government cannot endure permanently half slave and half free." One hundred and five years later, Dr. King stood before Lincoln's monument in Washington, D.C., and warned that "America has defaulted on her promissory note": [40]

> We have come to this hallowed spot to remind America of the fierce urgency of now . . . Now is the time to make real the promises of democracy; now is the time to rise from the dark and desolate valley of segregation to the sunlit path of racial justice . . . now is the time to make justice a reality for all God's children. (Washington, 1986: 217f.)

That August day in 1963, in turn, calls to mind a similar scene two millennia earlier: Jesus standing before a hostile synagogue leadership, reminding them of their vocation as Sabbath people (3:1-6). This incident invokes a scene yet another millennium further removed: Moses standing on the mountain overlooking the Promised Land, challenging Israel to "choose life" (Deut 30). Each represents a defining moment in the life of a people, the moment of truth and consequences. Such moments reside at the heart of redemptive history—and of nonviolent discipleship in a world of injustice.

3

REVERSING "LAMECH'S CURSE"

Jesus as a Teacher of
Restorative Justice (Matthew 18)

In our society, forgiveness is often seen as weakness. People who forgive those who have hurt them or their family are made to look as if they really don't care about their loved ones. But forgiveness is tremendous strength. It is the action of someone who refuses to be consumed by hatred and revenge.

—Helen Prejean, C.S.J. (1995)

We must develop and maintain the capacity to forgive . . . There is some good in the worst of us and some evil in the best of us. When we discover this, we are less prone to hate our enemies.

—Martin Luther King, Jr. (C. King, 1996)

The Gospels portray Jesus of Nazareth as the embodiment of what we call "full-spectrum peacemaking" (vol. II, 2b). Not only does he engage in nonviolent direct action; he also practices and teaches interpersonal restorative justice. The same prophet who "disturbs the peace" of the political status quo in order to advocate for true *shalom* with justice also demands that his followers embrace a deeply personal nonviolence. To this end, he instructs them in a communal ethos of conflict transformation and community-based reconciliation. This process offers an alternative to retributive institutions of criminal prosecution—then and now.

Our core sample for this trajectory of restorative justice and peacemaking comes from Matthew's Gospel. One of the best-known sayings of Jesus occurs at the heart of this passage: "For where two or three are gathered in my name, I am there among them" (Matt 18:20). Whenever we teach Matthew 18 to church folks, we begin with a simple quiz, asking: "To what does this venerable promise refer?" The answers, typically, are that Jesus will be present when just a handful of Christians gather for worship, prayer, and/or fellowship. But in fact, this assurance refers to the specific and difficult church practice of confronting and healing incidents of violation.

The pious misunderstanding of Jesus' pledge of accompaniment unwittingly reveals the greatest weakness among our contemporary churches: we are notoriously incompetent at facing conflict and abuse! Indeed, many church members would sooner start a new denomination than engage in the demanding work of resolving hurtful clashes or correcting oppressive behavior, as the history of our denominations attests. But the great challenge of working to transform violation is precisely why this remarkable promise attaches to *this* Christian practice. Whenever the *ekklēsia* gathers to "make things right" between offenders and victims, the mystical Christ will assuredly be "in our midst."

3A. Matthew's Minority Ethic

In order to appreciate Jesus' teaching in Matthew 18, it is important to review briefly the sociohistoric context of the First Gospel.[1] "Matthew" was first attested as its author by Irenaeus at the end of second century c.e. Because we know nothing of this figure, some scholars see the name as a cipher for the Greek word "disciple" (*mathētēs*). Indeed, this narrative means to be a manifesto of early Christian life and faith. This is suggested by the long-recognized literary structure of Matthew's story of Jesus. It is composed around five lengthy teaching discourses, each of which concludes with the phrase, "When Jesus finished these words":

1. the Sermon on the Mount (5:1-7:28);
2. the "missionary discourse" (10:1-11:1);
3. parables (13:1-53);
4. instruction on social power and "church order" (18:1-19:1);
5. the "woes" (chap. 23), the "little apocalypse" (chap. 24), and the three concluding parables (chap. 25). Final refrain: "When Jesus had finished saying *all* these things . . ." (26:1).

These five "books" portray Jesus as a new Moses who is renewing Torah. Our focus will be on the fourth of these discourses.

Ancient patristic tradition, as well as modern scholarship, locates the provenance of Matthew in Antioch. The capital of Roman Syria, Antioch was the third largest city in the Roman Empire (after Rome and Alexandria). The city was favorably located at the axis of both land and water trade routes and surrounded by the rich agricultural region of the Orontes River valley (though it was plagued by earthquakes and flooding). It was densely populated (estimated at ca. 150,000), with a steep social hierarchy and deep divisions between an aristocracy residing in fortress-like villas and a slave and laboring majority living marginally in squalid wood tenements (W. Carter, 2000: 14ff.).

There is evidence of some eighteen different ethnic groups living in Antioch, including a significant Jewish community. The fortunes of Jews in Roman Antioch had been up and down since the city's founding, but they deteriorated during the Judean insurrection against Rome in 66-70 C.E. (ibid.: 30f.). A debtors revolt broke out in Antioch toward the end of the war, for which Jewish agitators were blamed and executed by the imperial authorities. In the wake of Rome's destruction of Jerusalem in 70 C.E., Antioch's Jewish community swelled with refugees.

The military was omnipresent because Antioch was the seat of Roman power in the east, a base for two or possibly three imperial legions. The public landscape was rife with Roman architecture and monuments that propagated imperial ideology.

> After his victory over Jerusalem in 70 C.E., Titus set up bronze figures outside the city gate leading to Daphne, which were understood to be cherubim from the Jerusalem temple. On the gate facing toward Jerusalem, he displayed a bronze figure of the moon and four bulls, a symbol of *Aeternitas*, of Rome and the Flavians forever. These figures located near the Jewish quarters in the southern part of the city and in Daphne were humiliating for Jews and a clear warning to all of the cost of not submitting to Roman control. (Ibid.: 38)

Adding insult to injury, coins were minted between 70 and 80 C.E. that celebrated the Roman defeat of the Jewish revolt. The series depicted a bound female, head down, the caption reading: *Iudea capta*. Antiochean Jews were thus reminded of their subjugation in daily commerce. In an equally galling affront, Emperor Vespasian expropriated what had formerly been the Jerusalem Temple tax and levied it on all Jews to fund the rebuilding of the pagan Temple of Jupiter in Rome!

Within this context of Roman domination, vigorous internecine debates marked Antioch's hard-pressed Jewish community, especially concerning how to reconstruct their social and religious identity in the wake of the Temple's demise as their symbolic and political center. There were many voices around the Jewish diaspora advancing diverse visions for how Judaism might survive under these challenging new circumstances, as attested in the rich trove of noncanonical literature during this period.

Matthew was one such voice, probably writing within one or two decades of the fall of Jerusalem (see Matt 22:7). His gospel offered fellow Jews a narrative of the life, teaching, death, and resurrection of a Galilean prophet who embodied an alternative "Kingdom" to the *Pax Romana*, and who promoted a way of renewed obedience to Torah. This vision was embraced by some, but vehemently rejected by the majority of synagogue leaders. Matthew scholar Andrew Overman summarizes:

> The years following the destruction of the Jerusalem temple and the first Jewish revolt were significant for both Matthean and formative Judaism. It was during this period that these two groups most actively ordered and defined their life and beliefs. At the time of the writing of Matthew's Gospel these two groups . . . were obviously in competition and, it would appear, formative Judaism was gaining the upper hand.[2]

We can see footprints of this struggle throughout Matthew. He frequently differentiates the discipleship community from "*their* synagogues," the leadership of which Jesus is intensely critical. His antipathy toward those he calls "blind guides" is most clearly evident in the scorching jeremiad of Matthew 23, in which the term "hypocrites" appears as a refrain no less than seven times![3]

On the other hand, Matthew is *also* the most Jewish of our Gospels, asserting at several points that Jesus' mission was not to "abolish" but to "fulfill" Torah (e.g., Matt 5:17-20). Matthew was no more critical of his own minority group's leadership than were the Hebrew prophets before him (or for that matter, Martin Luther King after him). His Gospel reflects one side of the vigorous Christian/Jewish dialogue that raged for the better part of a century—before the eventual Hellenization of the church (and then the advent of Christian imperialism) changed that conversation forever. Matthew could not have imagined that he would later be interpreted as a "Christian" who categorically rejected (or scapegoated!) his own people and tradition. Yet that is precisely how his Gospel has been too often read since Constantine, both in the wrongheaded theological legacy of Christian supercessionism and in the murderous political legacy of anti-Semitism.[4]

It is important, therefore, to proceed carefully with reading Matthew today. We must reject both lethal tendencies of anti-Judaic Christendom, which have drawn heavily (and selectively) on Matthean passages that negatively caricature the Pharisees or the "Jews" as a whole, with horrendous historical consequences. On the other hand, we cannot ignore Matthew's critique of his contemporaries, properly understood in context. The

First Gospel represented the perspective of an increasingly marginalized "messianic" minority that was competing for hearts and minds within an already-traumatized Jewish community, which itself was a beleaguered minority struggling to survive in the Roman imperial center of Antioch.[5] In this sense, Matthew's context was analogous to that of Martin Luther King, Jr., whose activist gospel was embraced by only a minority in the Black community, which was hard-pressed by the Cold War retrenchment of the 1950s.[6]

This "double marginalization" helps us properly interpret Matthew's views on justice and conciliation. For example, it explains why the Gospel exhibits a keen distrust of both Roman and rabbinic courts, which we encounter first in the Sermon on the Mount. An escalating series of six "antitheses" contrasts conventional wisdom with Jesus' vision of a "beloved community": "You have heard it said . . . but I say to you."[7] He exhorts disciples to practice a justice that "exceeds that of the scribes and Pharisees" (5:20) regarding legal/criminal matters such as:

- murder, insult, and accusation (5:21ff.);
- adultery (5:27ff.);
- divorce (5:31ff.);
- false testimony (5:33ff.);
- retributive justice (5:38ff.); and
- treatment of enemies (5:43ff.).

This list of "case studies" addresses both offenders (the first three) and victims (the second three), and so is worth examining as we approach Matthew 18.

From the outset of this teaching, Jesus signals his skepticism about the prevailing Judean and Roman justice systems of his time. Suggesting that the roots of lethal violence lie in unresolved conflict (5:21f.), he exhorts believers to take the moral initiative to reconcile with those they have harmed (5:23f.).[8] An intensified warning to offenders follows:

> Come to terms quickly with your accuser while you are on the way to court, or your accuser may hand you over to the judge, and the judge to the guard, and you will be thrown into prison. Truly I tell you, you will never get out until you have paid the last penny. (Matt 5:25f.)

The language here invokes a legal setting, alluding to debtor's prison and/ or punitive fines.[9] Matthew uses the term "prison" (Gk. *phylakē*) ten times in his Gospel, suggesting that it was part of his community's experience.[10] His bias is clear: he does not trust the courts to adjudicate justice, much less to heal the wounds of violation. Nor was he alone in the early Christian movement; the apostle Paul shared his antipathy toward civil courts.[11]

We should not dismiss this principled stance by the early church as irrelevant to our modern society's "rational" justice system. Racial-ethnic minorities in the United States today are similarly skeptical about the prospects of being treated even-handedly in criminal proceedings—which is entirely justified, given both the historical record and the persistent and endemic racism in prosecution and sentencing.[12] The first Christians also had such suspicions, and it was in their interest to pursue alternatives to the rabbinic and imperial courts that routinely marginalized or criminalized them (see below, 3D).

The second and third antitheses continue the focus on offenders by singling out the male exercise of domination through adultery and divorce (Matt 5:27-32). Jesus understood how vulnerable females in his society were to male abandonment (based on his mother's experience?), and saw that gender oppression was fundamental in a context of patriarchy. The strange and grim exhortation to "self-amputation" (5:29f.) represents a strident warning against behavior that objectifies or exploits.[13]

The fourth antithesis switches to victim responsibility, beginning with an exhortation to insure that one's testimony be truthful (5:33-37). The ancient Jewish legal process was reliant on the word of the accuser and of witnesses, which is why there was such strong censure of false testimony (see Deut 19:15-21; also Ps 27:12; Prov 24:28). Because the forensic process proposed by Jesus in Matthew 18:15-20 also relies so heavily on the "truth" of the victim, it is crucial that it be spoken without the artificial *bona fide* of oath taking, a widely used convention in Hellenistic society (W. Carter: 149f.).

If the integrity of the witness is compromised, the justice process breaks down. But Jesus' fifth antithesis does not follow the retributive logic of Deuteronomy that perjurers must therefore be punished for the same crime for which they falsely accused: "Eye for eye, tooth for tooth" (Deut 19:21; see also Exod 21:24). Instead, he calls for a nonviolent response, understanding that a perjurer is no longer a victim but a violator who must be exposed (Matt 5:38-42). Walter Wink's work on this passage has shown that Jesus' instructions to turn the other cheek or to give up one's coat are acts of creative, nonviolent resistance, not capitulation (1992b). This "third way" between passivity and violent struggle is the strategy of those who, in the absence of a reliable legal or mediated process, must defend their dignity and advocate for justice.[14]

Jesus culminates his instructions on restorative initiative in the sixth antithesis: inviting disciples to love their enemies. He cites the command found in Leviticus 19, a portion of Torah devoted to social ethics:

You shall not hate in your heart anyone of your kin. You shall reprove your neighbor . . . You shall not take vengeance or bear a grudge against any of your people, but you shall love your neighbor as yourself. (Lev 19:17f.)

This articulates an ethos of civility and solidarity reserved for other members of one's body politic. It was understood to be a central statute and is cited twice more in Matthew's Gospel (19:19; 22:39) and five other times in the New Testament (Mark 12:31; Luke 10:27; Rom 13:9f.; Gal 5:14; Jas 2:8), not to mention in various rabbinic writings from the period.

But Jesus unmasks the darker side of this conventional wisdom, namely, that love for one's own must sometimes translate into hatred of an enemy. In the New Testament, hatred (Gk. *miseō*) usually describes how God's people are treated by their adversaries. Luke's Magnificat, for example, cites Israel's traditional petition "to be saved from our enemies, from the hand of all that hate us" (Luke 1:71 = Ps 18:17). Those "enemies" eventually did "surround" the Jews, as Luke 19:43 puts it in an allusion to the Roman siege of Jerusalem in 70 c.e. In the generation following that national disaster, Matthew had plenty of reason to hate an imperial enemy who hated his people.

After the attacks of September 11, 2001, President George W. Bush canted repeatedly that Americans must wage and win a righteous war against "all those who hate us." We hear this exact directive reiterated in a thousand different ways from the moment we are old enough to form a thought. It is a pillar of Mother Culture, and has formed our hearts and minds through the relentless catechism of family socialization, playground protocol, the popular media, and politics as usual. The logic of supporting one's own people and nation and "giving no comfort to the enemy" is meant to be obvious and unassailable. The only thing about this age-old ethos that changes over time is the name of the enemy.

Jesus uses the sharp edge of irony to demonstrate the smallness of this conventional moral vision: "Loving those who love us back is hardly virtuous; even our enemies can do *that*." Matthew goes so far as to name the "enemy" specifically here: tax collectors (i.e., Jews who collaborated with the Roman occupier) and Gentiles (i.e., the imperial rulers themselves; 5:46f.). Gospel realism recognizes that we *will* have enemies in the world, but how we treat them defines whether we are children of the One who showers and shines on the world an undifferentiated grace (5:45). Jesus' teaching implies something much more demanding than mere pacifism, which requires only that we refuse to kill our enemies. It invites us to love them.

Love does not mean capitulation or appeasement, as the preceding passage concerning the art of nonviolently resisting an enemy's abuses makes clear. Justice remains the goal of a restorative response, which is what Matthew 18 lays out carefully. The adversary must be held accountable, but never dehumanized, never hated, and certainly never killed. Paul understood this clearly: "If your enemy hungers, feed him; if he thirsts, give him drink" (Rom 12:20). For the apostle this ethic is predicated on the character of God: "While we were *enemies* we were reconciled to God by the death of God's Son" (Rom 5:10). So too for Matthew, who concludes his antitheses with the exhortation to "be mature as your heavenly Father is mature" (5:48).

This last verse has long been used in our churches as the loophole we so desperately seek. Its purported "counsel to perfectionism" exonerates us from having to embrace the Sermon on the Mount, since as Calvinists like to remind us, we are not and never will be perfect. Indeed, we take perverse delight in making the "normative" case by spinning endless scenarios that illustrate the irredeemable depravity of criminals and enemies who no rational, moral person could *or should* love. The anthropological differentiation between friend and enemy is fundamental to Mother Culture, the agonist plot that pits the good guys against the bad guys in the narrative we call history. But the Greek word *teleios* is best translated "be mature," as it is properly rendered in the RSV of, for example, 1 Corinthians 2:6, 14:20, and Philippians 3:15. It connotes the intended *purpose* of an ethic: the end for which we were created is love, and this must ultimately include our enemies. We are to be like God in *this* specific way—by practicing restorative justice. This is the reliable foundation on which our remodeled "house" must stand (see Matt 7:24-27).

We see Matthew's minority ethic taking shape in this opening section of the Jesus' Sermon on the Mount, the first of his five "discourses." The fourth discourse, to which we now turn, continues this reasoning, outlining a practical vision of the church as a community of *relational* integrity. This teaching contributes valuable insights for modern practices of victim-offender dialogue.

3B. Challenging Social Stratification (18:1-10)

Matthew 18 is an almost unbroken discourse, which concludes with the formulaic refrain: "Now when Jesus had finished these sayings" (19:1). The start of the teaching is usually identified with the disciples' question in 18:1. However, the immediately preceding episode (17:24-27) has so many points of connection with the ensuing discourse that it could well be considered a constitutive part:

- It begins with a public dispute (17:24), but ends in a house (17:25), the space where special discipleship teaching (such as Matthew 18) often occurs in the Gospel.[15]
- At issue is the Temple tax, and more generally the authority of "kings of the earth" to extract wealth from their conquered subjects (17:24).[16] The next episode commences with a question regarding the "Kingdom of Heaven" (18:1), which, as Carter points out (2000: 93), is Matthew's alternative to the Roman Empire.
- The political economy of tax-farming implied in 17:24-27 is also described in the concluding parable of Matthew 18:23ff. (below, 3E), thus "framing" Jesus' teaching on restorative justice with two scenarios of real-world injustice.
- Peter is characterized in 17:25f. as the clueless voice of (the reader's?) resistance to Jesus, as he will be again in 18:21.
- Jesus' explanation (17:25) begins with the parabolic "What do you think?," as does 18:12.
- Jesus asserts that children of God's Kingdom are "free" (17:26; Gk. *eleutheros*, i.e., exempt from the tax); but he also wants to avoid "scandalizing" (17:27)—a major theme in Matthew 18:6-9.

In the end, Jesus resorts to a bit of political satire to address the dilemma.[17] In an enigmatic and surely symbolic action, a coin is "fished out" for payment (17:27). As an enacted parable, it leaves the reader/listener with questions (as does the parable in 18:23ff., which is also political satire; below, E). How *will* Antiochean disciples creatively steer their way through the dangerous imperial landscape, given that the consequences of not paying Caesar's tax are severe? As magical narrative, this "fish story" awakens all of us to imaginative thinking about how to navigate the difficult conundrums of life in empire. It thus serves as a suitable "prolegomenon" to Matthew 18, which offers instruction for how Christians can truly be "free" of domination.

Matthew 18 can be outlined as follows:

A 1-5: Object lesson #1: Challenging assumptions about social power
  B 6-10: Exhortation to potential offenders
    C 12-14: Central parable—the least and the lost as the center of community concern
  D 15-22: Exhortation to victims
E 23-35: Object lesson #2: A warning parable about the logic of retribution

The concentric structure serves two pedagogic purposes: repetition and drawing attention to the middle.[18] The teaching opens and closes with object lessons that challenge the disciples' deepest assumptions about power and retribution. The next layer consists of exhortations to offenders and victims respectively. In the middle of the discourse, like a fulcrum, is a parable that captures the heart of the vocation of restorative justice.

The disciples' initial question reflects both inward anxiety and outward conditioning concerning social position (18:1). People in ancient Palestine assumed that prestige was a limited good, distributed according to one's station in the social hierarchy. Our modern cultural cosmology is not different in kind, only in scope: because of the possibility of social mobility, we are far more competitive. We aspire upward in a hundred ways, large and small: better degrees, bigger pulpits, more influence, higher pay, etc. But the flip side of this upward social fixation is our tendency to scapegoat downwards. We believe that those above us somehow deserve their privilege, because they are supposedly brighter, harder working, more entrepreneurial. Conversely, those below us are equally deserving of their social disadvantages, because they are allegedly lazy, dependent, incapable. Such social conditioning lies at the heart of the culture of domination, undergirding the political and economic architecture of stratification. And it is the first target of Jesus' teaching.

The verbal exchange in this episode is also concentric, using repetition to drive home the point:

> **A** "Who is greatest (Gk. *meizōn)* in the Kingdom of Heaven?"
> > **B** ". . . unless you turn/convert and become like children
> > > **C** you will *never* enter the Kingdom of Heaven."
> > **D** Whoever humbles themselves like this child
> **E** is greatest (Gk. *meizōn)* in the Kingdom of Heaven.

Jesus emphasizes the object lesson by making a child the focus, literally calling her from the invisible margins of the scene to its center (18:2; Gk. *en mesō).* This scene is relentlessly sentimentalized in our churches, conjuring romanticized pictures of cute, happy children. That was not Jesus' point, however:

> Ethnocentric and anachronistic projections of innocent, trusting, imaginative, and delightful children playing at the knee of a gentle Jesus notwithstanding, childhood in antiquity was a time of terror. Children were the weakest, most vulnerable members of society. Infant mortality rates sometimes reached 30 percent. Another 30 percent of live births were dead by age six, and 60 percent were

gone by age sixteen. Recent estimates are that in excess of 70 percent would have lost one or both parents before reaching puberty . . . Children were always the first to suffer from famine, war, disease and dislocation . . . Children had little status within the community or family. A minor child was on a par with a slave . . . (Malina and Rohrbaugh, 1992: 117f.)

Today, children are still the most vulnerable in the social construction of poverty, both at home and abroad.

Jesus challenges the norm of upward social aspiration by imputing supreme value at the bottom of the hierarchy, urging disciples to "turn about-face" (Gk. *strephō*) and practice solidarity downward. The verb "to humble" (Gk. *tapeinoō)* is drawn from a semantic field that, in almost every other place in the New Testament, connotes the divine intention to "level" the social terrain by bringing down the exalted and lifting up the lowly.[19] In ancient society, as today, status was jealously guarded. But Jesus invites us to change social location: Whoever "receives" (Gk. *dechomai*) vulnerable persons receives Jesus, who is already with *them*.[20] This notion of Christ's mystical presence among the marginalized poor is later reiterated in 25:31-46, Matthew's famous parable of the sheep and the goats: "Inasmuch as you did this to the least of these . . . you did it to me" (25:40). Here, as there, Jesus is emphatic that our status in the Kingdom depends on our practice of this kind of solidarity.

This standard is underlined in the ensuing doublet: [21]

18:5 Whosoever receives one such child in my name receives me.
18:6 But whosoever causes one of these little ones (Gk. *mikrōn*) who believe in me to sin, it would be better for him to . . . be drowned in the depth of the sea.

This redirects the disciples' preoccupation with the "greatest" to a focus on the "littlest." But because our failure to embrace this "turning" will inevitably result in oppressive behavior, the promise of verse five is linked immediately in verse six with a warning to "potential offenders"—which is to say, all of us.

Here, we again encounter the Greek verb *skandalizō* (as we have in Matt 5:29f. and 17:27), which is repeated in each of the next four verses. Usually translated "to cause to stumble or fall away," it means "to impede" or "to make indignant."[22] Sin was always relational in antiquity, and the welfare of the "least" is here revealed as Jesus' moral barometer.[23] The metaphor of a "millstone . . . cast into the sea" has an interesting echo later in the New Testament:

- . . . it would be better for him if a millstone (Gk. *mylos onikos*) was hung around his neck, and he was drowned in the depth of the sea (Gk. *thalassa*). (Matt 18:6)
- Then a mighty angel took up a stone like a great millstone (Gk. *mylinon*) and threw it into the sea (Gk. *thalassan*), saying, "So shall Babylon the great city be thrown down . . ." (Rev 18:21)[24]

This grim image conjures the old story of the demise of Pharaoh's army in the sea (Exod 14), which will also be the fate of "Babylon" (a.k.a. Rome). The message is strident: the church should take great care not to reproduce the pathologies of an oppressive society! This leads Jesus to utter a series of "woes" in the rhetorical tradition of Isaiah or Jeremiah (Matt 18:7). The point of this prophetic refrain is to emphasize moral agency in a context of sober realism:

Woe to the world because of those who scandalize.
Scandal predictably comes,
but woe to the person by whom scandal comes!

Dehumanizing acts, habits, or social structures may be inevitable in fallen human history, but this does *not* exonerate disciples who are complicit with them.

To underscore this, Jesus repeats one of the most disturbing metaphors in the gospel tradition: the invitation to self-amputation (18:8f.; see 5:29f.). Body parts often functioned in ancient rhetoric as organic symbols for community (see, e.g., 1 Cor 12:12-27). In this case, however, hand, foot, and eye connote a person's moral intention or agency. The "fires of Gehenna" (18:9b), in turn, alludes to the public dump in Jerusalem, which was always smoldering, like trash heaps today in the Third World where the poor try to scavenge a living.[25] This gruesome image is equally avoided by modern liberals and fundamentalists (one should never give credence to a two-handed biblical "literalist"). But it becomes both comprehensible and poignant to our ears if we employ the analogy of battling substance abuse. A recovering addict knows in her flesh the searing truth that kicking a habit is very much like cutting off a part of oneself. Recovery is a life-or-death discipline, and Jesus' metaphor captures that urgency.[26]

The teaching concludes with another stern warning about the fate of "one *mikrōn*" (18:10). This refrain links the first, second, and third sections of the teaching:

18:6: But whosoever causes one of these little ones (Gk. *hena tōn mikrōn toutōn*) . . .

18:10: Watch that you do not despise one of these little ones (Gk. *henos tōn mikrōn toutōn*) . . . their angels always behold the face of my <u>Parent in Heaven.</u>

18:14: It is not the will of <u>my Parent in Heaven</u> that one of these little ones (Gk. *hen tōn mikrōn toutōn mikrōn*) . . .

We are commanded *never* to "look down on or treat as if of no value" (Gk. *kataphroneō*) vulnerable members of the community. Now comes the culminating revelation, a phrase unique in the New Testament: "In heaven their angels always behold the face of my Parent who is in Heaven" (18:10b). The notion that those who are of no account in society's eyes are omnipresent in the visage of God is a dramatic way of imaging Jesus' insistence that in the Kingdom, the "last are first" (Matt 19:30; 20:16). The notion that the "least" have an inherently privileged relationship to the divine (see 18:5) reiterates the old Exodus conviction that YHWH hears the "cry of the poor" (Exod 2:24; 3:7). In Jesus' vision, social worth has been "revalued" from the bottom up.

We can conclude from these first two sections of Matthew 18 that Jesus is serious about the imperative of social solidarity. Second-class citizenry, apartheid, or exclusion of any kind is simply unacceptable. Such may be "inevitable" in a world of empire, but there is no justification for the church's complicity in such "despising" behaviors or social structures. This is what Dr. King tried to get the ministers of Birmingham to understand in his letter: "We will have to repent in this generation not merely for the vitriolic words and actions of the bad people, but for the appalling silence of the good people" (Washington, 1986: 296).

The prerequisite for our practice of restorative justice, then, is a critical understanding of how and why social power is unevenly distributed, and a commitment to level that terrain in its own practices and self-organization (we address this in vol. II, 3A). Without a deeper rehabilitation of human dignity and social equity, restorative efforts will only be cosmetic.

3C. The Least and the Lost as Center of Concern and the Biblical Roots of Restorative Justice (18:12-14)

The third and briefest part of Jesus' discourse lies at the structural center of Matthew 18.[27] "How does it seem to you?" begins Jesus, a typical preamble to parabolic discourse.[28] This is a well-known parable, and heavily sentimentalized. We immediately form a mental image of the ubiquitous picture hanging on Sunday School walls, in which a Charlton Heston-like Jesus holds a little lamb. This is a sure way to miss the subversive power of

Jesus' storytelling. Parables are widely read and preached as quaint, poetic, or theologically figurative—but rarely as relevant to Christian disciple-ship. We spiritualize them as "earthly stories with heavenly meanings," so that tales about landless peasants and rich landowners, lords and slaves, or lepers or lawyers are lifted out of their social and historical context and reshaped into pious or moralistic fables bereft of any political or economic edge—or consequence. This interpretive strategy functions to thoroughly domesticate the parable, as we inevitably read the story in terms of our own unconscious political assumptions. Stories meant to challenge our preconceptions are thus used to legitimate them. So do we disarm the gospel's most powerful rhetorical weapons, whose purpose is to liberate us from *our* domestication under the status quo.

Parables are by design irresistibly allegorical. As Bernard Brandon Scott (1989: 7ff.) points out, the Hebrew word for parable, *mashal*, comes from the root *m-sh-l*, meaning "to be like." But the church too often jumps from trying to understand Jesus' allegory to ourselves allegorizing the allegory. The genius of these stories was that they narrated recogniz-able scenarios in plain language that illiterate peasants could understand. Jesus is talking to poor folk about poor folk, in the true style of a popu-lar educator. Here he references the social worlds of indebted fishermen (Matt 17:25-27) and lonely shepherds (Matt 18:12-14). Elsewhere it is farming (Mark 4:1ff.), day labor (Matt 20:1ff.), the village feast (Luke 14:1ff.), or exclusion from the houses of the rich (Luke 16:19ff.). These vignettes would have drawn the agrarian listener into their familiarity, only to throw a surprise twist, in order to challenge conventional assump-tions about what was proprietary and what was possible: a miraculous harvest (Mark 4:8), an enemy as a friend (Luke 10:33), or unexpected vindication (Luke 18:2ff.). Instead of seeing parables as romanticized folk wisdom, then, we should read them as "*earthy* stories with *heavy* mean-ings," as William Herzog puts it (1995: 3).

Our image of the biblical shepherd has become the victim of too many Christmas plays. In antiquity, shepherds were socially outcast, particularly among Jews because of the occupation's unclean animal contact. In this sense they represent the perfect archetype of those who are "despised." At the same time, in the prophetic literature the shepherd was also a symbol of political leadership—bad and good (e.g., Ezek 34). As we have seen (above, 2D), parables in the Hebrew Bible were also a lethal way of speak-ing prophetic truth to power. We see this supremely in Nathan's unmask-ing of King David (2 Sam 12). The court prophet spins a story about the "many" vs. the "one" sheep, symbolizing the disparity in wealth and power between the haves and the have-nots (2 Sam 12:1-4). There can be little doubt that Matt 18:12 is at least indirectly alluding to David's "scandalizing" acts of adultery and murder; it was, after all, the most infamous instance of political criminality and personal violation in Jesus' national tradition.

But what is the allegorical drift of Jesus' parable? Who is the "stray" here? Up to this point in Matthew 18, the vulnerable party has been defined as anyone victimized by social disparaging or marginalization. But the allusion to the Nathan/David story introduces the "twist": it is the "lost" one (i.e., David) who deserves the full attention of the good "shepherd."[29] This parable, as the structural center of the whole teaching, thus signals a subtle but crucial transition in Jesus' restorative logic. Not only are those who are "scandalized" the moral center of the community; the *offender*, too, as an errant member, must be "found" and restored.[30] Both victim and offender are wounded and vulnerable. The moral of the story is: "It is not the will of my Father that *one* of these little ones should be lost!"[31] This represents the bottom line of restorative justice: there is no victim whose pain does not deserve attention, and no offender who is beyond redemption. Giving "priority to a minority" means the Christian community is governed not by majority rule but by the task of restoring those whose relationships have been shattered by violation.

Before we look at how to realize this vision in practice, however, let us look briefly at how this ethos was grounded in the older tradition of the Hebrew Bible, out of which Jesus spoke and Matthew wrote. There are two trajectories in Torah that are germane to the vision of relational justice being developed in Matthew 18, and both are introduced in Exodus 21. The principle of restitution understands the offender to be a *responsible* party, while the principle of sanctuary understands the offender also as a *vulnerable* party.

The laws of restitution insist on accountability: the offender must "arrange for the full recovery" of a physically injured party (Exod 21:18f.), and is responsible to restore (or double) equity to a victim of property crimes (Exod 21:33ff.).[32] The principle articulated in Leviticus 24:17ff. is one of proportional reparation: "life for life." "Biblical law is primarily concerned not with punishment of the thief," summarizes Joseph Telushkin, "but with gaining restitution for the victim" (1997: 448).

The laws of sanctuary (Exod 21:12) go further back, to one of the oldest stories in the Bible: Cain's murder of Abel. The ancient cosmology encoded in this etiological tale is that the earth itself is in solidarity with the victim of violence, illustrated through wordplay in the Hebrew:

> And the Lord said, "What have you done? Listen; your brother's blood (Heb *dam*) is crying out to me from the ground (*'adamah*)!" (Gen. 4:10; similar wordplay occurs in Gen 2:7)

Cain immediately realizes that by acting violently he is now targeted for blood vengeance: "I shall be a wanderer on the earth, and anyone who meets me may kill me!" (Gen 4:14). He straddles liminal space: he is an actual offender, yet also a potential victim.[33] But the divine voice intervenes in order to halt the spiral of retributive violence before it can commence:

> "Not so! Whoever kills Cain will suffer a sevenfold vengeance." And the Lord put a mark on Cain, so that no one who came upon him would kill him. (Gen 4:15)

Christendom has still failed to grasp fully the implications of this ancient, archetypal "tattoo of taboo." Justice will *not* be served by killing the killer. The mark of Cain represents a warning to any would-be vigilantes that any act of retribution will reignite the logic of vengeance, which will inevitably spiral out of control until all are consumed by it. We in modernity are facing the consequences of this logic, as manifested in death penalty policies, protracted ethnic feuds, and wars on real and perceived enemies. Seduced by the myth of redemptive violence, "we've started a fire we can't put out."[34]

YHWH's solution to the problem of Cain's violence is, counterintuitively, to protect the one who "should" be punished. The idea of sanctuary for a killer is ancient, found across many cultures, most commonly associated with the sanctity of an altar.[35] It was institutionalized in Torah through the establishment of "cities of refuge" for those guilty of manslaughter. Six are named, three on either side of the Jordan, thus close enough for perpetrators to flee to (see Num 35:13-15; Deut 19). These villages were designated both to offer asylum while the offender was awaiting trial and to offer hospitality as long as they had to live in exile. This does not negate the principle of restitution; it does, however, remind us that the offender must not be "collateral damage" in the prosecution of justice.

French philosopher and Talmudic scholar Emmanuel Levinas (1994) reflects profoundly on why Torah and Talmud were so concerned to provide cities of refuge:

> We are all man-slaughterers. The man-slaughterer is the one who is half-guilty, since he has killed, and half-innocent, since he did not mean to kill. We all participate in structures of oppression—this makes us guilty—but we participate for the most part unwittingly—this makes us innocent.

The idea that in a very real sense we are all both victims and perpetrators is especially true for those of us who are citizens of social systems that routinely do violence to individuals and communities. And because we are complicit *and* wounded, we all have a stake in a justice process that will demand both accountability and mercy. This is the meaning of the central parable of Matthew 18.

The first half of Jesus' teaching emphasizes three crucial tasks:

- examining how power is distributed among us communally and socially, and standing in solidarity with the marginalized;
- being vigilant about not abusing whatever power we have, especially as we relate to those who are vulnerable; and
- making it a priority to seek out the wounded offender.

Jesus has taught that the "least" should be at the center of the church's concern, and the "lost" regained as part of the beloved community. But how do we attend to both? This is the subject of the next section: mobilizing the community to practice victim-offender dialogue.

3D. Jesus' Model of "Community Conferencing" (18:15-22)

Matthew 18:15-20 describes a demanding, victim-led process for bringing offenders back into community. It is presented as an alternative to the dominant criminal justice system of the first century C.E.—and beyond. Though this passage has been widely ignored in Western Christendom, the Peace Churches (particularly Anabaptists and Brethren) have taken the process of "confronting the errant sister or brother" seriously as a guide for ecclesial practice. And this text has rightly been important to modern Christian practitioners of restorative justice, since it outlines all four quadrants of the "peacemaking spectrum": negotiation, mediation, arbitration, and community resistance (see vol. II, 2B).

But those who have embraced this so-called church-order text have tended to understand it in too limited a way. For one thing, these five verses are usually taken apart from the rest of Jesus' analysis in this section of Matthew, thus missing (or avoiding?) crucial teaching about social power.[36] For another, the passage is viewed rather narrowly as a method for resolving interpersonal clashes in the church, and has often been used to legitimate practices of "shunning" problematic or nonconformist individuals or groups. But Matthew 18:15-20 addresses concrete acts of injustice, not mere differences of opinion or doctrine.

It is important to note at the outset that these instructions are directed toward the violated party: "If your brother/sister sins against you . . ."

(18:15a; see Lev 19:17). This process does not give license to engage in freewheeling policing or "correction" of others' behavior (Paul has a great deal to say about that in, e.g., Rom 14-15). The text appeals not to moral *authoritarianism* but to the moral *authority* of the victim. This is a key component to restorative justice, yet is easily misunderstood, with dire consequences. The victim is being invited to make the first step; this is not, however, a *demand*. Too often in church circles, for example, abused wives have been exhorted to "just forgive" their husbands, which only functions to perpetuate the cycle of violation. Victims should not be encouraged to take the initiative if they are not ready, or if it is not safe to approach the offender, or if the process will likely entail revictimization.

On the other hand, *if* and *when* victims feel able to press their case for justice and accountability, Jesus says, the support and accompaniment of the whole community should be marshaled. For when the moral authority of the violated party is mobilized, it carries a transforming and redemptive energy. Rightly handled, the process of victim initiative is inherently empowering because she is prosecuting her own case on her own terms, not for purposes of retribution, but of restoration. As these verses make clear, *she* decides when her story has been "heard," and what is needed to make things right.

"Arise," says Jesus, "and confront the offender." The first verb (Gk. *hypage*) is frequently used in Gospel healing stories (e.g., Matt 8:4, 13, 32). Matthew also uses it in his earlier, parallel exhortations to offenders (5:24) and victims (5:41; above, 3A). The second verb (Gk. *elegchō*) appears only here in Matthew, and has several connotations in wider New Testament usage. In Luke 3:19 John the Baptist "confronts" Herod for his suspect political alliances through marriage. In John's Gospel it means "to expose" (John 3:20) and "to convict" (John 8:46).[37] In the Pastoral Epistles it means to "reprove" errant members of the community, suggesting that Jesus' process was employed widely (1 Tim 5:20; 2 Tim 4:2; Titus 1:9, 13). And it also describes how believers are themselves "chastened" by the Lord (Heb 12:5; Rev 3:19). But perhaps most relevant to Matthew 18:15 is how *elegchō* is used in Ephesians to mean "unmasking" the works of darkness with the light (Eph 5:11, 13; see below, 4E).

This first attempt, if successful, helps the offender save face through a private approach: ". . . just the two of you alone." Without the shaming dynamic that comes from the presence of peers, the offender may be able to respond more sincerely. In mediation theory this is called the strategy of "negotiation," in which the parties work things out themselves. The goal is to "regain" the offender—"*if* he listens" (Matt 18:15b). Paul seems to allude to such a situation in the Corinthian congregation (2 Cor 2:5-11). The offending person has apparently repented, and Paul, participating in the process from a distance, pronounces his forgiveness and urges the community to follow suit and embrace the man again. He does this for two pastoral reasons: so that the penitent offender "might not be overwhelmed by excessive sorrow" (2:7), and to prevent Satan from exploiting an environment of resentment in the community (2:11).

If the offender is not, however, "won over" (Gk. *kerdainō*, Matt 18:16a), the violated party can pursue a series of steps that steadily increase community pressure on the offender:

- v. 16: If he does not listen (Gk. *ean de mē akousē*) . . .
- v. 17a: If he refuses to listen to them (Gk. *ean de parakousē autōn*) . . .
- v. 17b: If he refuses to listen even to the church (Gk. *ean de kai tēs ekklēsias parakousē*).

In each case, the victim alone determines whether or not she has been truly "heard."

The first recourse is to "bring along with you one or two others" (18:16b). The standard of "two or three witnesses" established by Deuteronomy 19:15 is then invoked, anchoring this process in the judicial tradition of Israel (see John 8:17). "Every word" (presumably of both victim and offender's testimony) must be confirmed (Matt 18:16c). As we have seen, Deuteronomy 19 warns vehemently against the crime of false testimony. The exhortation of Matthew 5:33-37 to speak the truth plainly is clearly assumed in this process.

The next step implies a certain degree of resistance or hard-heartedness on the offender's part: "He *refuses* to listen" (Matt 18:17a).[38] The entire community is thus invited into the process, an exercise in loving but firm, nonviolent coercion. Often the peer pressure of family, neighbors, colleagues, and church members will provide the needed push to a stubborn offender. Recent experiments in "community justice conferencing" are rediscovering the power of a strategic gathering of stakeholders, including victim and offender, to adjudicate for the common good. Paul captures the tone of such an ecclesial process in Galatians 6:1, including the important admonition not to become retributive: "If anyone should be overtaken by any trespass, you who are spiritual should restore (Gk. *katartizete*) such a one in a spirit of gentleness. Look to yourself, lest you too be tempted."[39]

These first two steps are approximated today in practices of "victim–offender dialogue." An important aspect of this facilitated process is the practice of paraphrasing. Often the offender is asked to summarize what the victim is saying, until the latter feels the former understands the consequences of the offense. Then the victim summarizes the offender. In this way the stories of both victim and offender are told twice, which in many instances represents the beginning of healing for both. We outline some of the prospects and pitfalls of victim–offender dialogue in volume II, 3B and 4A.

The worst-case scenario is that the offender "dismisses" the pain of the victim and the testimony of the whole church, which has gathered to stand with the victim but also to "bring back" the offender as a "lost sheep" (Matt 18:17b). In this case, the offender does not want to be found. The phrase "let that one become to you as a Gentile or tax collector" implies that such a person must now necessarily be redefined as an outsider, having chosen not to be accountable to the community.[40] This is not a strategy of punishment, but rather a change in the community's approach to the offender. Tactical exclusion of an intransigent offender can certainly be punitive, as has too often been the case with Anabaptist practices of "shunning." But it can also be a nonviolent strategy of defending against a predatory person (this may be what Paul is alluding to in 1 Cor 5:5). And, ironically, disconnection can be a strategy of *engagement* with the friend-turned-adversary, analogous to how, in the political arena, a strike or boycott is designed to pressure the target group to change its behavior.

In fact, the revaluation of the offender as a "Gentile or tax collector" is far from being a categorical rejection.[41] Quite the contrary. In this story, Jesus is accused of being "a *friend* of tax collectors and sinners" (Matt 11:19). Matthew also cites Isaiah 11:10: "In His name the Gentiles hope" (Matt 12:21). Elsewhere Jesus retorts that tax collectors will enter the Kingdom *before* the chief priests and elders (21:31f.). So in 18:17, the strategy toward wayward members is to reestablish the special relationship that Jesus had with the socially excluded, reaching out to them and proclaiming the good news anew. The recalcitrant offender needs to be evangelized.

As in 18:5-6, Jesus underlines the seriousness of this teaching with another doublet that offers a warning (18:18) and a promise (18:19f.). To "bind and loose" connotes the legal authority to take a prisoner into custody, or to release him from prison.[42] According to Andrew Overman,

> Authority depicted in this way within the Matthean community would appear as a challenge to those existing structures and authorities outside the community, and would create inevitable conflict . . . The community has drawn back from the existing civil structures and replaced them with its own . . . [which] constitute both a challenge and a substitute for those processes already established in the civil realm.[43]

As we have seen in our treatment of Matthew 5:23-26, two convictions lie behind Matthew's alternative process of adjudication. One was strong skepticism regarding the ability of Christians to receive basic justice in the hostile rabbinic or Roman courts. The other is Jesus' vision of relational justice which seeks to heal the wounds of violation rather than punish, and to restore equilibrium to the victim, offender, and whole community.

Instead of justice being determined by the powerful, Matthew proposes an ethos of dialogue, accountability, and consensus. There is no prosecutor, judge, or jury, nor even professional mediators. This is a community process to be used by any and all. The focus is on the moral agency of the victim, rather than prosecution by the state. The goal is to end violation and restore relationship and communal solidarity rather than uphold the law. A contemporary analogy to Matthew's strategy in the context of Roman Antioch might be a First Nations tribal court. Recognizing racial discrimination in the dominant criminal justice system, it seeks to adjudicate intratribal conflict in an alternative, culturally appropriate way. The offender is understood to be wounded or sick, needing healing, not punishment. A "sentencing circle" invites community elders, the victim and her family, and the offender and his family, to determine how to make things right (see vol. II, 3B). Similar indigenous approaches are found in African *Ubuntu* or Hawaiian *ho'oponopono*.

This teaching empowers and commissions the church to be an advocate for both offender and victim, pressing for accountability, repentance, justice, and restoration. Those who are "liberated" by this process are truly free, but the implication of Matthew 18:18 is that if we fail, and resort to the traditional solution of retribution, this too stands "in heaven." It is a sobering note, anticipating the concluding parable of 18:23ff., which warns that the "alternative to the restorative alternative" is to be swallowed up in the spiral of vengeance.

It is precisely because this is such difficult and consequential work that Jesus guarantees divine accompaniment in any and every community-justice conference (18:19f.). The promise is twofold. Verse 19 echoes the earth/heaven rhetoric of 18:18: if "two of you" (referring to victim and offender) "agree on any case" (Gk. *pantos pragmatos*), God joins the consensual decision![44] Verse 20 is the famously misunderstood phrase we noted at the outset of this chapter. Jesus will be "in our midst" when we engage in the challenging but redemptive process of supporting victims to take moral initiative, and holding offenders accountable, for the health of the whole discipleship community.

The rhetorical device of "diminutive numbering" functions as a unifying theme throughout the whole of Matthew 18:

- A *single* coin can subvert the empire's stranglehold on conscience (17:27).
- A *single* child challenges our internalized hierarchy of social value: "whoever receives *one* such . . . receives me" (18:2-5).
- To live in solidarity with the "little ones" is to be "defective," but "better to enter life with *one* eye than with two eyes to be thrown into Gehenna" (18:9).
- We should seek the *one* lost member of the community and celebrate her restoration, for God wills not *one* to perish (18:12-14).
- Violation should be resolved if possible by "you and the offender *alone*"; if not bring "*one* or *two* others" and confirm the story with "*two* or *three* witnesses" (18:15f.).
- If "*two* of you agree on any case" God will concur (18:19).
- Where "*two* or *three* are gathered" Jesus will be present (18:20).

Matthew's minority ethic needs only a handful of committed disciples. This is heartening, since so few seem willing to embrace the vision of restorative justice. Yet upon the moral imagination of this minority hangs the fate of the world.

This section ends by returning to the focus on the agency of the victim. The happy case in which the violator is "regained" as a sibling (18:15, 17) implies that some sort of forgiveness has occurred. This is tricky in contemporary practice, as noted, since a restorative process can never *demand* that a victim forgive. But presumptive pardon is not the point of the exchange with Peter in 18:21f. The issue is our vision of, and capacity for, forgiveness. Matthew understands that disciples harbor deeply rooted, socially conditioned preconceptions about the boundaries of grace—and the ultimately retributive nature of the universe.

Peter, as is so often the case in the Gospels (e.g., 14:28-31; 15:15; 17:24), voices what we all think privately: "Surely there are *some* things that cannot be forgiven—there *must* be limits to restorative justice" (18:21)! His incredulous "how often?!" unmasks our own skepticism about and resistance to the process just proposed.[45] Seven represents, for Matthew's Jewish audience, the symbolic limit of perfection (there may be an allusion here to the atonement ritual of Lev 16:14ff. in which blood is sprinkled on the altar seven times). Though Peter appears to be looking for a loophole, on the lips of a real victim of serial violation this sort of incredulity is surely understandable.

Jesus' answer (18:22) alludes not to an abstract ethical principle but to the legacy of Cain and God's attempt to stem the tide of vengeance. Lamech, one of Cain's progeny, mocks the divine taboo in a curse that vows massive revenge: "If Cain is avenged sevenfold, then Lamech seventy-sevenfold!" (Gen 4:24). This sentiment surely resounds in our world and our hearts. Lamech represents the archetypal logic of retributive justice: only the threat of superior retaliation will deter those we fear or mistrust. But this is specifically repudiated by Jesus, who exhorts us to pursue forgiveness with the same intensity that Lamech pursued revenge: "seventy times seven" (literally, "times seventy-seven," citing the Septuagint translation of Gen 4:24). A teaching that has been woven with the thread of small numbers now culminates with an extravagant figure that symbolizes infinity! Jesus understands that only an absolute commitment to restorative justice can hope to undo the spiral of retribution that Lamech's curse has wrought in our history.

Conversely, if we abandon restorative efforts and thus "bind" God's grace, we are consigning ourselves to the equally infinite narrative of vengeance. The alternative to Jesus' restorative alternative is a collective death sentence of our own design. This cruel world is now described in the parable that concludes the discourse of Matthew 18.

3E. "No Future without Forgiveness": A Warning Parable (18:23-35)

The closing parable stands in structural parallel with the opening object lesson of the child (18:1-5) but represents a mirrored opposite: it models how *not* to be. It is a difficult story, for two reasons. One is our persistent tendency to read parables of this genre as theological allegories that identify God with the king or landowner, an interpretive tradition that has had lamentable theological and social consequences.[46] Another is the fact that this story describes a world in which the main character gets *one* chance at grace—but thereafter, the hammer! This abruptly contradicts the imperative to show unlimited grace that Jesus has just pressed on his disciples (Matt 18:21f.)! If we allegorize this parable as a teaching about God's ultimate justice, the entirety of Matthew 18 becomes incoherent.

This story is consequently ignored by most who read Matthew 18 as a text of restorative justice. But we must read texts whole. Moreover, Matthew *means* this parable to flow directly from Jesus' teaching about forgiveness. It is firmly linked to the previous section by the introductory phrase: "Because of this . . . " (Gk. *dia touto*, 18:23a). As William Herzog puts it, many interpreters

> freely admit that the social picture in the parable is murky to the point of unintelligibility while maintaining that the parable's mean-

ing is crystal clear. This could be the case only if the social scenario were either incidental or irrelevant to the meaning of the parable, whose center of gravity would then lie in some form of hypothetical universal human nature . . . The parable's figures would be ciphers for the clash of abstract ideas (mercy, forgiveness, goodness) . . . (1994: 135)

But the social context is not irrelevant. This parable makes sense as a cautionary tale that grounds the consequences of not forgiving in the real world of ancient "predatory lending." As such it represents an emphatic conclusion to Jesus' teaching: our failure to practice restorative justice means that the imperial system's logic of retribution remains intact—and we will *all* inevitably become its victims.

Our approach demands time and attention, and requires that we hold the traditional allegorizing interpretation at bay long enough to enter into Matthew's social world. This is admittedly difficult, since parables are routinely literalized or spiritualized in our churches, as we have noted. So let us begin with a reminder about the role of metaphor. Daniel Berrigan, in a poem entitled "A Visit to the Book of Kells and a Walk in the Park" (1998: 217), writes:

> Under glass, in Met museum/this day I saw
> a bird of paradise/outspread
> the grandiose, grotesque/book of Kells.

He does not literally mean that the book is a bird of paradise; nor is he spiritualizing it (both referents are concrete). Rather, the simile is a figure of speech meant to illumine the illuminated manuscript, inviting us to *see it differently.*

Jesus, too, was on a mission to help us apprehend the world differently: "Do you have eyes, yet fail to see . . . ?" (Mark 8:18; see Mark 4:10-12). His pedagogic purpose was twofold:

1. to unmask illusions his audience harbored about the social status quo and their place in it (both rich and poor); in order
2. to open their hearts and minds to the alternative—what he called the Kingdom of God (itself a metaphor).

In contemporary parlance we might call this "deconstructing" and "reconstructing" consciousness. Jesus employs two basic kinds of parables: those that attempt to unmask and critique the way the world really is (e.g., "there was a certain rich man . . . and a certain beggar . . . ," Luke 16:19f.); and those that offer a vision of the world transformed (e.g., "the Kingdom of Heaven may be likened unto a mustard seed . . . ," Matt 13:31-33). Matthew 18:23ff. is an example of the former: it paints a dark portrait of the real world ruled by powerful but capricious royal moneylenders who end up cannibalizing their own. But why would Jesus illustrate the need to forgive *sin* with a story about the endgame of economic *indebtedness?*

Luke does this very thing with different material, wrapping the story of a "sinful" woman (Luke 7:36-40, 44-50) around a parable about forgiveness of debt (Luke 7:41-43). In Aramaic (the probable idiom of Jesus), debt was the primary metaphor for sin. In Greek both words are governed by the same verb (*aphiēmi*), such that they sometimes seem to be interchangeable in the New Testament.[47] But to assume, as do many scholars, that the terminology of debt was intended merely as a metaphor for the spiritual or moral "economy" of sin is to ignore the socio-economic context of such semantics.

First-century Roman Palestine was fundamentally characterized by a political economy of debt that kept rich and poor polarized. The vast majority of the population groaned under the oppressive burden of direct levies on land, crops, and persons, as well as numerous indirect tolls, duties, and market taxes. Imperial tribute obligations and local structures of taxation were both "designed to assert elite control over agrarian production," explain K. C. Hanson and Douglas Oakman (1998: 115f.). They functioned to redistribute up to *two-thirds* of the wealth upward, from the peasant and artisan classes to the aristocracy. This is why throughout this period, advocates of political reform focused on tax relief, while local armed insurrections often targeted centralized debt records for destruction—most famously after the liberation of the Temple from Roman rule in 66 C.E. (see Rhoads, 1976: 94ff.). The social consequences of widespread economic marginalization driven by protracted debt, then and now, include banditry, crime, and interpersonal violation among the poor (see Horsley, 1987). This is why the debtor class was widely perceived by elites as "sinners," as illustrated by Luke's story of the penitent woman.

The upper-class male host of the dinner party automatically assumes that the uninvited woman is a "sinner" (Luke 7:39). This is a dismissive social label, analogous to "gang member" or "welfare queen" or "illegal immigrant" in our context; indeed, most middle-class people today assume the same equation between low socio-economic status and immorality or criminality. To be sure, Luke has already identified her euphemistically as a "woman of the city" (Luke 7:37), but Jesus' parable implies that she was *driven* into prostitution because of her debt-fueled impoverishment (7:41f.). He then goes on to challenge her social invisibility and radically reverses the status in the room by shaming the male company by his public criticisms of the host (7:44-47), while addressing her as "daughter" and embracing her "love" (7:48, 50). Jesus understood that moral dysfunction and social injustice are profoundly intertwined, and taught that transformative strategies must address both persons *and* the political-economic terrain they inhabit. This is crucial background for a proper understanding of our parable (and others in the gospels), because these tales intentionally conflate interpersonal and social relationships.

Matthew's opening phrase—"the Kingdom of Heaven may be compared to . . ." (Matt 18:23a)—is ambiguous, and immediate cause for confusion. The verb (Gk. *hōmoiōthē*) is used by Matthew in three other major "Kingdom of Heaven" parables, each of which is *also* a warning tale:[48]

- the wheat and the tares (13:24-30);
- the king's wedding banquet (22:2-14);
- the bridesmaids (25:1-12).

Given our habit of reading such parables as theological allegories, it is important to recognize that this introductory phrase does *not* set up a simple, positive analogue. These four parables represent *negative* (or at best ambiguous) scenarios. Their purpose is to instruct us to "stay awake" so that we do not make mistakes as do the characters in these stories (25:13).

In our case, we have a political folktale drawn from the social world of tribute and tax. While there is still some scholarly debate about exactly how the political economy functioned in the eastern empire, we know that politically subservient nations (such as Herodian Palestine) paid annual tribute to Rome, and that "tax farming" was the primary mechanism for the extraction of domestic wealth:

> Native entrepreneurs (sometimes cities) contracted with the Roman administration to collect local taxes. Such individuals were required to pay the tax allotment in advance and then organize collection in the contracted district in hopes of turning a profit. Evidence indicates that such ventures were risky, open to abuse, and often far from profitable . . . The tax collectors familiar in the Synoptic tradition were for the most part employees of the chief tax collector and were often rootless persons unable to find other work. (Malina and Rohrbaugh, 1992: 82)

Since the great households controlled the tax-lease franchises, Matthew 18:23ff. offers a realistic, if parodied, portrait of this plutocracy, including:

- "a king who wished to settle accounts" (an allusion to the Herodians, who operated at the political favor of Rome while growing rich on the backs of their own subjects);
- a gesture of amnesty to a high-ranking but hopelessly indebted functionary (a common political strategy when it was determined that policies of bleeding the country dry with taxes had crippled the economy);
- and a dramatic internal struggle for survival and advancement within the rigid hierarchy among the "retainer" (bureaucratic) class that oversaw the work of buying and selling debt.

This is a story, in other words, about the real world of the elites.

The narrative is composed around two key semantic fields: "to be in debt/debtor" (*opheilō/opheiletē*) and "to pay up" (Gk. *apodothēnai*), both of which appear in all three scenes. The plot structure, as is typical of ancient storytelling, is repetitive and concentric:

Verse 23: introduction

> **Scene I** *(vv. 24-27)*
> > a. king's "accounting"
> > b. indebted servant's plea
> > c. king's amnesty
>
> **Scene II** *(vv. 28-30)*
> > a. servant's "accounting"
> > b. indebted co-servant's plea
> > c. co-servant's punishment
>
> **Scene III** *(vv. 31-34)*
> > a. co-servants' counterprosecution
> > b. king's response
> > c. servant's punishment

Verse 35: conclusion to story

The ruler is introduced as a "man-king," (Gk. *anthrōpō basilei*), a Semitism with a hint of disrespect for the widely despised Herodian royalty. This moniker helps us apprehend this "lord" in human terms instead of as a metaphor for the divine.

The scene opens on a sinister tone: he is "settling accounts with his servants."[49] Herzog outlines the hierarchy of an ancient royal tribute and tax-farming franchise:

Retainer bureaucrats can be divided into three levels . . . the *illit-terati* (porters, gaolers, etc.), the *litterati* (scribes, lawyers, accoun-tants), and possessors of *dignitates* (high royal positions). The highest level retainers were operatives in the royal court, often the heads of the largest bureaucratic agencies; the middle level bureaucrats were the record keepers. Often stationed in the same department and post for many years, the latter group schemed to gain the lowest titles held by the highest bureaucrats, to maintain and if possible increase their emoluments, and to protect their honor . . . Because the entire system was fueled by endemic feuding, mistrust, and "honest graft," the ruler frequently changed department heads to keep corruption and ambition within reasonable bounds. (1994: 137)

Given the intrigues of the modern corporation and bureaucratic state, such dynamics are not too difficult for us to imagine. Against this sociological background, Matthew's parable narrates the tense relationships between a king who means to clean house, a high-ranking servant who is failing to meet his obligations, and rival *litterati* who rat out their immediate supe-rior in order to advance themselves.

We can assume that the "one brought to him" (v. 24) is near the top of the franchise pyramid (hence, having *dignitas*) by the amount of the debt. Ten thousand talents equaled approximately sixty *million* denarii.[50] This absurdly large amount signals that we are in the realm of a kind of political cartoon, but without some sense of its relative value, the hyper-bole is lost on us. K. C. Hanson's illuminating work on the economy of aristocratic imperialism in the advanced agrarian society of Roman Pales-tine puts this amount in perspective: "Josephus estimates the annual rev-enue of Herod Antipas from his tetrarchy [as] 1.2 million denarii" (1997: 105). The most any Palestinian king of the first century extracted from his subjects in one year was Agrippa I, at two thousand talents—but Mat-thew's story stipulates *five times* that amount! This is clearly a parody of the oppressive economics of "foreign debt" and the cynical policies of elite managers of the tributary regime—as opposed to a morality tale about the ethics of interpersonal lending. Nor is it, as pious commentators often claim, merely a fantastic exaggeration to make a theological point about our fathomless "debt" to God.

The cruelty of this system surfaces in 18:25. By failing to produce the revenues demanded by the king, the high-ranking servant is compromising (or even challenging) royal honor. He must be made an example of, and so he and his entire family are to be sold into slavery.[51] This fall to the abso-lute bottom of the social ladder was an eminently plausible consequence of such default in the Roman system, though ironically selling someone into slavery was a punitive practice eschewed by Jews. The strange reversal that occurs next (18:26f.) can be explained by the adversarial but symbiotic relationship between the king and his "CFO." In fact, the king depends on this retainer to run his franchise. Herzog posits that the ten-thousand-talent debt signals the first servant's "location at the highest levels of the bureaucracy and his attendant power, prestige and wealth" (1994: 142). He portrays this as a "conflict between a ruler and a powerful, trusted bureaucrat" over tribute collection.

The question is whether the default represents an act of defiance by the retainer, or whether he is honestly representing a bankrupt populace that cannot accommodate this stratospheric tribute obligation. While the story is narrated more in terms of a personal struggle, the latter scenario makes more sense in the socio-political context. There are many examples in antiquity of kings agreeing to limited debt amnesty, because: (1) the economy was teetering on bankruptcy because of the tax/tribute burden; (2) exploited classes were on the verge of revolt; and/or (3) to gain special favor from his subjects. Conversely, we know of many instances in which high-level delegations from subject peoples petitioned rulers for debt relief, including notable examples from Roman Palestine. The genuine plight of the retainer's hard-pressed clients would provide plausible explanation of both the retainer's plea for patience and the king's "pity."

On the other hand, if this is a challenge, the king's severe and summary sentence signals to the upstart retainer that he will not succeed.

Realizing his mistake, the servant reverts to form and does obeisance; he falls on his knees at the king's feet and implores him like the supplicant he now is . . . The servant does not simply repent, but promises to make good on the contract for the tribute. His plea indicates that he can very well cover a good deal of his debt. (Ibid.)

Whether this is a personal or political negotiation, the convicted retainer's desperate plea and promise function to restore honor to the offended patron and earn him a dramatic reprieve: "The Lord of that servant freed him and forgave his debt."[52] In the wider political context, this gesture has little to do with grace, and everything to do with the king's assessment that he has put a dissident retainer back in his place and/or averted long-term economic disaster through this one-time special amnesty. In either case, his position of absolute patronage is strengthened. The ruler's unilateral decisions, first to destroy his lieutenant, then to forgive him the debt when he does penitent homage, "followed the logic of the absolute and ruthless tyrant, who gives and takes away at will."[53]

The second scene in the parable, however, confirms the chief retainer's poor judgment. He immediately goes to his "co-servant" (Gk. *syndoulos*), who owes one hundred denarii, "seizes him by the throat" in order to choke him (an act of intimidation), and demands that he pay up (18:28). The amount noted here could realistically represent the obligation of a street-level tax-farmer:

> A loan of one hundred denarii was not small. It represented one-half of a Roman legionnaire's annual salary and more than a full year's wages of a day laborer. Few peasants would see one hundred denarii in a lifetime. The size of the debt signifies the relative social location of the middle-level bureaucrat in relation to the top-echelon official . . . As the king is lord over the high-level bureaucrat, so the servant is lord over the middle-level bureaucrat. (Ibid.: 143)

Verse 29 is almost an exact repetition of verse 26: the second-tier retainer prostrates himself, petitions for patience (again, Gk. *parekale*; see 18:32), and promises to repay. But unlike the first scene, this plea is summarily rejected (18:30), and the underling is cast into prison (Gk. *eis phylakē;* see 18:34).

If the chief tribute-collector was shamed and put back in his place by his patron, this act of domination may be his play to reassert his position and power over his subordinates. If he was given a reprieve on behalf of his wider clientele, this act is even more egregious, suggesting that he is simply rapacious with no conscience. Meanwhile, the king's attempt to restore economic equilibrium through amnesty goes for naught because of his own minion's heavy hand. In either case, the parable clearly portrays this as a horrific act of duplicity. This brings us to the third scene, and the "payoff" of the parable.

We are told that some lower-level retainers (Gk. *syndouloi*) are "profoundly distressed" (Gk. *elypēthēsan sphodra*) by their superior's actions, and decide to "expose" (Gk. *diesaphēsan*) him to the king (18:31). This represents an unusual and risky act of going over the head of their boss, but a gamble which, if successful, also holds potential for their own advancement. The deceitful chief tribute collector is again "summoned" (Gk. *proskalesamenos*, v. 32), and again reproached: "You wicked slave; I forgave you everything because you petitioned me (Gk. *parekalesas me)."* He is told that the mercy (Gk. *eleēsa*) he received should have been reciprocated to his own subordinates or clients (v. 33). This is, of course, the obvious "moral" to the story. But the king's "mercy" evaporates in a rage, and the duplicitous tribute collector is delivered to "torturers" until he should pay up the *entire* debt (18:34).[54] This withdrawal of amnesty and restoration of the original punishment demonstrates the freedom of the king to suspend or apply "the law."

At the conclusion of the story, the royal tribute franchise has become even more oppressive than before, and everyone in the system lives in greater fear of the king. Seeing this outcome, the reader is caught trying to get a foothold on slippery moral ground. The story condemns the failure of the tribute collector to reciprocate tax amnesty, but there is more to this parable than stating an obvious principle of fairness. Moreover, in the real world of imperial tax collecting, arbitrary decisions at various levels of the bureaucracy were commonplace, and a peasant hearer would hardly have been surprised at such shenanigans. The only difference here is someone high up got caught.

The "payoff" is how we get sucked in to the story. We, like the underling retainers, feel outrage at the central character's duplicity. But in so doing, we have unwittingly identified with those who "rat" in order to send competitors to oblivion, and sided with a king who just as well could turn and crush us. Bernard Brandon Scott comments:

> There is then a gap between story and kingdom . . . The outcome is of the hearer's own doing, for by joining forces with the fellow servants in calling on a higher authority, a hearer is enticed into a threatening world whose boundaries and guidelines begin to dissolve. A profound irony in this parable is that the accounting is supposed to set things aright. By appealing to the hierarchical structure to bring right order, the servants have instead brought chaos . . . The narrative leads to a parabolic experience of . . . systemic evil. (1989: 279f.)

At the political level, this story portrays a world captive to the logic of retribution. Temporary amnesty from above, no matter how dramatic or seemingly magnanimous, won't change the system, which is predicated upon domination, not mercy. As Herzog puts it, "even if a king of messianic stature forgave debt of unimaginable proportions, he could not transfer that mercy to the bureaucratic system that encased his rule. The functionaries had internalized the system to such an extent that they were creatures of it" (ibid.: 148).

At the personal level, listeners/readers become complicit in the desire to punish those who don't forgive! But this is hardly restorative justice as defined by Jesus' teaching in the preceding section. So the parable forces us to examine how we ourselves are deeply mired in the logic of retributive justice, unwilling, like the king, to forgive more than once. In both the political and personal realms, this story warns us that the alternative to

Jesus' alternative is a world still hostage to the whims of the king, a world of intrigue, subterfuge, and, ultimately, torture. It leaves us with a portrait of Lamech's cold world.

"Even so" (Gk. *houtōs kai*), the parable concludes, "my heavenly Father will do to you if you do not forgive (Gk. *aphēte*) your brother or sister from your heart" (18:35). This puzzling Matthean ending seems to undermine our "political" reading, and to assert precisely the theological allegory we are trying to overturn![55] Must we concede that there lies a cosmic hammer at the culmination of history? If the cosmos is ultimately retributive, then why are we bothering with the difficulties of restorative justice? Again, however, this verse, like the parable as a whole, must be interpreted in the context of the whole of Matthew 18; otherwise, the discourse is non-sense.

What we see here is wholly in keeping with judgment motifs in the Hebrew Bible. The consequences of human misbehavior are often articulated as positive divine action: "If you do or do not do X, God will do Y." In a monotheist universe, God is the "true lord" of history. This means that what happens is what God "allows" to happen. So while we may be reaping what we have sown, the rhetorical tradition of both Torah and the prophets portray God as "doing it to us."[56] This coheres with the powerful assertion of Matthew 18:18f.: God is "bound" by our decisions to liberate, but also to lock down. The implication of 18:35 is that God will not save us from the consequences of *not* interrupting the spiral of vengeance. To invoke retribution on others is to invoke it on ourselves—this is not just moral cause and effect, but a historical ultimatum!

Two weeks after Martin Luther King was gunned down in 1968, an article he had prepared for *Look* magazine appeared posthumously. Reflecting on the urban rioting that had characterized each of the previous four summers around the United States, Dr. King reaffirmed his commitment to nonviolence. But the piece also issued a sober indictment from beyond the grave:

> There is an Old Testament prophecy of the "sins of the Fathers being visited upon the third and fourth generations." Nothing could be more applicable to our situation. America is reaping the harvest of hate and shame planted through generations of education denial, political disenfranchisement and economic exploitation of its black population. Now, almost a century removed from slavery, we find the heritage of oppression and racism erupting in our cities, with volcanic lava of bitterness and frustration pouring down our avenues ... White America has allowed itself to be indifferent to race prejudice and economic denial. It has treated them as superficial blem-

ishes, but now awakes to the horrifying reality of a potentially fatal disease . . . All of us are on trial in this troubled hour, but time still permits us to meet the future with a clear conscience. (Washington, 1968: 71)

King's words reiterate the truth of Torah, the prophets, and the parable of the "unforgiving servant": namely, that sooner or later, we *will* "reap the harvest of hate." King's appeal rings like an altar call, insisting that we do not have "a choice of continuing in the old way." Like the apostle Paul, he insists that "now is the time" to embrace the ministry of reconciliation, because if we do not cooperate with divine grace, it becomes "empty" (2 Cor 5:16-6:2; above, 1B).

The great New Testament scholar Amos Wilder described parables as a "war of myths," in which Jesus and the early church pitted their "liturgy" (by which he meant "lifestyle, action and ethic") against the "liturgies" of empire (1982: 103). In the second half of Matthew 18, Jesus has put the "seventy-times-seven restorative justice liturgy" of disciples, who live in solidarity with the least, side by side with the "retributive justice liturgy" of the rich and powerful, who live in a fearful, dog-eat-dog cosmos. The choice is ours. The point of the entire discourse is to persuade us that only restorative justice can free us from the curse of Lamech.

Or, as the motto of the South Africa Truth and Reconciliation process put it: "Without truth, there will be no healing, without forgiveness, no future."[57]

4

"...AND ABOLISHED ENMITY"

Jesus' Cross and the Peacemaking Vocation
of the Church (Ephesians)

The explanatory power of Jesus' Death is much greater than we realize, and Paul's exalted idea of the Cross as the source of all knowledge is anthropologically sound.
>—René Girard, *I See Satan Fall Like Lightening* (2001: 3)

There was a time when the church . . . was not merely a thermometer that recorded the ideas and principles of popular opinion; it was a thermostat that transformed the mores of society . . .
>—Martin Luther King, Jr., "Letter from Birmingham City Jail"
>(Washington, 1986: 299)

The U.S.-Mexico border fence, erected the same year the Berlin Wall came tumbling down, poignantly symbolizes the social architecture of division that defines our world. It stands up to twenty feet tall and runs for hundreds of miles, bright with floodlights by night, thick with Border Patrol officers by day.[1] But it cannot stem the flow of undocumented immigration, because when barriers are built by the strong and wealthy to keep out the vulnerable and the poor, they will always be transgressed by those desperate to survive. Yet there is a cost, as a memorial built by the parishioners of Nuestra Señora de Guadalupe church in Altar, Sonora, Mexico, attests. There, hundreds of crosses have been erected to commemorate those who have died trying to cross the desert borderlands to find work to feed their families—and to do labor that most U.S. citizens refuse to do.

The border wall reminds us that there have always been two Americas: one of inclusion and one of exclusion. The former has found expression in the ideal of "liberty and justice for all," and has been realized whenever Indian treaties were honored, civil rights embraced, "huddled masses yearning to be free" welcomed, or child labor laws passed. The latter was articulated in a Constitution that originally enfranchised only white landed males, and has been consolidated through land grabs, Jim Crow segregation, Guilded Age economic stratification, restrictive housing covenants, and laws precluding gay marriage. These two visions of America continually compete for our hearts and minds, not least in our churches. The America of inclusion is the only hope for democracy; the America of exclusion, as Lincoln's ultimatum about a "house divided" warned 150 years ago, is unsustainable.[2]

Essayist Annie Dillard writes:

> You hammer against the walls of your house. You tap the walls, lightly, everywhere . . . Some of the walls are bearing walls; they have to stay, or everything will fall down. Other walls can go with impunity; you can hear the difference. Unfortunately, it is often a bearing wall that has to go . . . It cannot be helped. There is only one solution, which appalls you, but there it is. Knock it out. Duck. Courage utterly opposes the bold hope that this is such fine stuff that the work needs it, or the world. (1989: 4)

Dillard's metaphor refers to her struggle to write, but it also describes eloquently the task facing First World Christians today in a world constructed upon division. The difficult business of tearing down walls that divide in our *own* house—whether we understand this image in terms of a local city, a large institution (such as our denominations), a nation, or our globalized but increasingly rickety civilization as a whole—is the most urgent demand facing those committed to restorative justice and peacemaking.

Admittedly, we Christians do not usually think of our vocation in terms of a radical "remodeling" project. Quite the contrary: our churches have tended to prop up existing institutions. Indeed, when social movements throughout American history have challenged dividing walls—women's suffrage, labor justice, civil rights—it has often been our *churches* that become a house divided, unable to reach consensus about change. But true peacemakers must figure out how to dismantle structures, policies, and cultural practices that threaten the integrity of the house—even if they appear to be bearing walls.

This is why Jesus transgressed the prevailing social boundaries of his culture (above, chapter 2), and why he urged his disciples to repair fissures between them (above, chapter 3). It is why he protested the way in which

YHWH's "house for all peoples" had become a "den of thieves" (Mark 11:15ff.). And it is why shortly thereafter he called for the Temple system to be "overthrown" (Gk. *katalythē*; Mark 13:2). Such revolutionary rhetoric was used to convict Jesus in court for treason—understandably, from the authorities' point of view (14:58). Yet, as Jesus expired on the executioner's cross, Mark reports that "the curtain of the Temple was torn in two, from top to bottom" (15:38). This apocalyptic "sign" infers, to borrow Dillard's language, that even the most culturally sacred "bearing" wall was "knocked out" by God's work in Christ—however "appalling" this prospect might have been to first-century Jews, and to us. The extraordinary claim that on the cross something cosmic happened that has somehow "overthrown" the rule of the Principalities and Powers became a foundation of New Testament faith. And its meaning is most thoroughly explored in the Epistle to the Ephesians.

4A. The Mystery of God's Will Made Known: Paul's "I Have a Dream" Speech (Ephesians 1)

In the middle part of the twentieth century, during the darkest period of the Cold War, the Epistle to the Ephesians, with its emphases on peace and overcoming division, was a favorite text of three notable social movements: international ecumenism, disarmament, and civil rights. In the last thirty years, however, it has fallen into disfavor in mainstream Christian circles, and is widely avoided today. Many New Testament scholars dismiss Ephesians as a derivative, late deutero-Pauline work that exhibits too much so-called early Catholicism. Particularly odious, they claim, is its spiritualizing "realized eschatology" and its patriarchal household code. While such scholars raise important (though not undebatable) questions and concerns, we think they too often end up throwing the proverbial baby out with the bathwater.[3] We believe that the central character of this epistle as a manifesto of peacemaking is too important to ignore, and we want to reclaim it for the work of restorative justice and peacemaking.[4]

The authorship and date of Ephesians have long been a matter of debate. We join with the majority opinion that the epistle probably dates from the late first century, authored by someone (or group) belonging to a "Pauline school."[5] This hypothetical author takes on the task of summarizing the social character of the apostle's theology for a new generation of Christians, a quarter century or more after Paul's death. Some scholars even feel that the epistle may have served as an introduction to a collected corpus of Paul's letters.[6] Though tradition attached this letter to Ephesus, it is probably a circular letter sent around to churches throughout Asia Minor.

Indeed, a map of the ancient Mediterranean world shows Ephesus in the geopolitical middle, roughly halfway between Jerusalem and Rome, and we know it was the hub of early Christianity in the region. Thus we find it helpful to consider Ephesians as the first "encyclical" in the history of the church.

The letter is addressed to communities, not individuals—only first person plural pronouns are used. Its elegant Greek is characterized by lofty, extravagant, sometimes redundant and even mystical vocabulary, which can make it easy to miss its tough-minded perspective on real-life issues. The tone is often liturgical, with formulaic prayers, baptismal motifs, and catechetical fragments. The encyclical reflects concerns of a fourth generation ecclesiology, in particular a changing demographic situation in which the Jewish roots of the church are in danger of being forgotten by the emerging Gentile Christian majority. This epistle recontextualizes Paul's argument for inclusion (articulated, e.g., in Romans) by inverting it—challenging Gentile Christians to treat Jewish Christians as equals in a wider social context where enmity between them was assumed and enforced.

The apostle Paul, like Jesus, wagered his entire ministry on the double task of *deconstructing* the "divided house" and *reconstructing* it on a foundation of race, class, and gender equality: "There is no longer Jew or Greek, slave or free, male or female; all of you are one in Christ" (Gal 3:28). Ephesians honors that legacy by offering a treatise on how to realize God's great plan for the "reunification" of all things (Eph 1:10). It focuses on the great conflict, at once both cosmic and terrestrial, within salvation history between Christ's inauguration of peace and the Powers' perpetuation of enmity. At the center of this struggle stands the church, which has inherited the messianic vocation of peacemaking, but is persecuted because of it. This letter is a handbook for a community of "peace-warriors."

It should not be a surprise, then, that in the middle of the epistle, like a fulcrum on which the entire argument balances, comes a stark reality check: "Because of all this I, Paul, a prisoner for Christ Jesus on behalf of you Gentiles . . ." (Eph 3:1; see 4:1; 6:20). This lofty epistle of peace is written not in an ivory tower, but from a dungeon, by a political prisoner of empire (see below, 4D). This reminds us that the imagination igniting historic peace and justice movements has never "trickled down" from the privileged classes of society. Rather, it has welled up from the social vision and moral authority of people who know violence and oppression first hand. They draw on deep wells of suffering, yet maintain profound convictions that, as Dr. King put it, "the universe bends toward justice"— despite all appearances otherwise.

Dr. King's two most famous public discourses—both written during the eventful year of 1963—offer compelling analogies for the spiritual energy and social location of Ephesians. The first half of the epistle, articulating a vision in which the social realities of apartheid have been dismantled, can justifiably be compared to King's "I Have a Dream" speech. The second half of Ephesians, focusing on the philosophy and "tactics" of nonviolent struggle, can be read fruitfully through the lens of King's "Letter from Birmingham City Jail" (below, 4D). Because we are clearer about the issues underlying King's movement than we are about those surrounding Ephesians, let us turn to the epistle's argument to see why it landed Paul in jail.

The "thesis statement" of the epistle is found in the middle of a long, run-on opening prayer (1:3-14; try holding your breath while reading that verse!). It answers the perennial question of individuals and churches alike: What is God's will for me/us?

1:8b   . . . with all wisdom and insight
1:9   God has made known to us the mystery of God's will, according to God's good pleasure set forth in Christ,
1:10   as an administration for the fullness of time, to gather up all things in Christ, things in heaven and things on earth . . .

Citing the Hebrew tradition of "Lady Wisdom" (Gk. *sophia*, reiterated in 1:17), the author announces that this longstanding "mystery" (Gk. *mystērion*) has been made manifest in Christ.[7] It consists of four assertions:

1. The cosmos is under a "new administration" (Gk. *eis oikonomian*).
2. This has happened in "the fullness of time" (Gk. *tou plērōmatos tōn kairōn*).
3. The "policy" will be "to gather up" (Gk. *anakephalaiōsasthai*, literally to "reorganize" under Christ's leadership)
4. *all* things (Gk. *ta panta*) spiritual and terrestrial.

The suspense of this announcement—"when the time is full"—has all the drama of Jesus' inaugural proclamation in Mark 1:15 (there the Greek phrase is similar, *peplērōtai ho kairos*). There it was the imminence of the Kingdom of God; here it is God's desire and intention to reunify everything that has been alienated—to overcome all division, to bring all beings back into communion, to heal every wound.

This is, by any account, a remarkably big vision for a small movement just four generations old—and raises the uncomfortable question whether our big churches nurture only small visions! The fact that the writer repeatedly stresses this program as a "mystery" throughout the epistle (see 3:3-6, 9; 6:19) testifies to his realism. After all, human history has long defied the hope for lasting, comprehensive peace. God's "wisdom" in the Pauline tradition, however, specifically opposes the conventional thinking of Mother Culture:

> Among the mature we impart wisdom, though it is not the wisdom (Gk. *sophian*) of this age or of the rulers of this age, who are doomed to pass away. Rather, we impart a mysterious (Gk. *en mystēriō*) and hidden wisdom of God, which God decreed before the ages for our glorification. None of the rulers of this age understood this; for if they had, they would not have crucified the Lord of Glory. (1 Cor 2:6-8)[8]

Caesar was unable to destroy God's dream of reconciliation by executing Jesus, who has been raised up to "administer" the new order, and placed far above the Principalities and Powers (Eph 1:20f.).

The closing words of the opening prayer introduce a second key theme of the epistle, and ground this program in the concrete social terrain of the writer. We read the following equation:

1:12a **We** who first hoped in Messiah . . . +
1:13a In Messiah **you** also, who have heard the word . . . =
1:14a The Holy Spirit is the guarantee of **our** inheritance.

Our author was, like Paul, a Jewish Christian ("we"). The audience being addressed ("you"), on the other hand, consisted of non-Jewish Christians, who had "heard the word of truth . . . and believed" (1:13). The latter's ethnic "otherness" is clearly expressed in 2:11f: "Remember that at one time you Gentiles in the flesh, called the uncircumcision by what is called the circumcision . . . were separated from Christ, alienated from the commonwealth of Israel and strangers to the covenants of promise."

Because this joint "inheritance" of both Gentiles and Jews (1:14) is not just spiritual but concretely social in character, deep cultural and political segregation must be overcome. The dream of God, therefore, stands or falls on the creation of a new "people," who will be tested upon the historical fact of human alienation, indeed upon a "worst-case" example. In Hellenistic antiquity the cultural, economic, and political conflict between Jew and Gentile was considered to be the prototype of all human hostility (see Dix, 1953). These two communities were in a protracted, intergenerational war—not unlike the legacy of American apartheid, or Israelis and Arabs today, or Protestant Unionists and Catholic Republicans in

Northern Ireland. We know from Galatians 1:6-9 that Paul's entire missionary project threatened to founder more than once on the reality of this "institutionalized enmity."

This "we/you" discourse is a strong reason for assuming a later dating of this epistle, reflecting a time in which Gentiles had become the demographic majority in the church. Apparently they were beginning to marginalize Jewish Christians and the religious-cultural roots of the faith—a direction carried to disastrous extremes in later Christendom. This prompted the writer to reverse Paul's argument in Romans concerning the right of Gentiles to be equal partners in the faith. He believes that Paul, if he were alive, would insist that now, with the "shoe on the other foot," it is up to Gentiles to remain in solidarity with Jews, who remain "first" in salvation history. Just as it was difficult for a minority community to throw open its doors to accept converts from the dominant culture during Paul's time, so now, two generations later, it was a challenge for the majority group to remain hospitable to and mindful of the increasingly dwindling numbers of Jewish Christians. But "reverse discrimination" was not acceptable. We should recall that during the civil rights era in the United States, *both* Black and white "integrationists" were pressured by their respective racial/ethnic communities to abandon their "radical social experimentation"—think of Bayard Rustin and George Houser during the Journey of Reconciliation in 1947 (see above, conclusion to chapter 1).

This is why the author prays in 1:17-19 that Gentile disciples might receive God's wisdom and "revelation" (Gk. *apokalypseōs*) to be "enlightened in eyes and heart" (a possible allusion to Isa 6:9f.). Above all, they need the "immeasurable greatness (Gk. *hyperballon megethos*) of God's power (Gk. *dynameōs*), according to the energy of God's powerful strength" (Gk. *energeian tou kratous tēs ischyos autou*). This remarkable sentence, which piles up no less than four synonyms for power, is aptly paraphrased by a contemporary definition of nonviolence as "A Force More Powerful."[9] This "force" is what "energized" the Risen Christ to sit at the right hand of God (1:20), and will be necessary for anyone seeking to "live the dream" in a world of enmity.[10]

Ephesians' prolegomenon concludes in 1:21-23 with a portrait of Christ as *Pantokrator* (another beloved image in the Eastern Church). He is

1:21   far above all rule and authority and power and dominion, and above every name that is named, not only in this age but also in the age to come.

1:22   God has put all things (Gk. *panta*) under his feet (see Ps 8:6), has made him head over all things (Gk. *panta*) for the church,

1:23   which is his body, the fullness of him who fills all in all (Gk.
        ta panta en pāsin).

The Principalities and Powers (Gk. *archēs kai exousias kai dynameōs kai
kyriotētos*) represent another important cast of characters in the drama
of Ephesians (1:21). Walter Wink's work (1984, 1986) has helped us
recover the meaning of this New Testament semantic tradition referring to the personal and political forces that perpetuate enmity and
division in history. With them the church must do battle, as the epistle
will argue (3:10), possibly because the *Pantokrator* is "above" their rule.
He is also "head" of the church, but this should not be understood in
a hierarchical sense. The Greek *kephalē* is the root of the complex verb
anakephalaiōsasthai in the thesis statement (1:10), so we should think
of Christ as the "animator" of the community (in modern parlance we
might say, "the brains of the outfit"). The author, in a mystical turn,
then refers to the church as "the fullness (Gk. *plērōma*) of the One
who fills (Gk. *plēroumenou*) everything!" The repeated refrain of
"everything" (Gk. *panta*) stresses that God's plan is cosmically comprehensive.

The epistle's introduction thus strikes a momentous tone. It calls to
mind Dr. King standing before the Lincoln Memorial in 1963, addressing
what would "go down in history as the greatest demonstration for freedom
in the history of our nation" (Washington, 1986: 217). King called on
America to "make real the promise of democracy," while exhorting his followers to "conduct our struggle on the high plane of dignity and discipline
. . . we must rise to the majestic heights of meeting physical force with soul
force" (ibid.: 218). Then he intoned his famous "I have a dream" refrain,
imagining overcoming segregation in order to sit together at "the table of
brotherhood," and transforming the "heat of oppression" into an "oasis of
freedom and justice." Finally, King invoked the great Isaianic vision: "The
crooked places shall be made straight and the glory of the Lord will be
revealed and all flesh shall see it together" (ibid.: 219; see Isa 40:4f.). "At
that moment," Coretta King famously said later, "it seemed as if the Kingdom of God appeared" (ibid.: 217f.). The civil rights movement was still
small in 1963; but it had a big vision—just like the author of Ephesians.

4B. Cross as Abolition of Enmity,
Church as Reconciled Community (Ephesians 2)

A precondition for the realization of God's dream is the conversion of a
people to embody it. So the first ten verses of Ephesians 2 offer a medi-

tation on the journey from death to life in Christ (2:1). In apocalyptic fashion, the author describes the spirit of violence that prevails in history, because humanity, "the children of wrath by nature," follows the "prince of the power of the air" (2:2f.). We might paraphrase this to say: human beings are inured to violence and division because it surrounds us "like the air we breathe." But in Christ we have been "raised up" out of this swamp of oppressive "normalcy." The language here is baptismal (2:6). In consummate Pauline fashion there is a careful dialectic: the gift of salvation is not "*because* of our works," yet is for the express purpose of *practicing* good works (2:8-10). Whenever we move from "walking" in sin (2:2) to "walking" in this new way of life, we represent "God's work of art created in Christ Jesus" (2:10).

The next verses articulate the concrete social formation of alienation: the political antagonism that Gentiles throughout the Mediterranean world maintained toward Judaism (and vice versa!). In 2:11f., Gentile Christians are exhorted (twice!) never to forget that they remain deeply indebted to the minority culture of Judaism:

> Remember that you were at that time separated from Christ,
> alienated from the commonwealth of Israel,
> strangers to the covenant of promise,
> having no hope and without God in the world. (2:12)

This is a stinging indictment of a people politically, religiously, and psychologically bereft, calling to mind Paul's rant in Romans 1-3 (see above, 1A). It functions to deconstruct the sense of "natural entitlement" that a majority culture always presumes, particularly as they had been socially formed by Roman propaganda of imperial superiority. An analogy to this stern "reminder" in our context might be an African American theologian challenging white Christians about our ignorance of the tradition and history of the Black Church, and insisting that we must never forget the long, terrible history of racism that has characterized all our institutions, not least our churches![11]

"But now in Christ Jesus . . . " (2:13a). This hopeful phrase brings us to the theological heart of Ephesians. The author launches into an extended midrash on Isaiah 57:19 ("Peace, peace to the far and the near, says the Lord; I will heal my people"), cited twice in verses 13 and 17, which bracket a poignant description of what transpired on Christ's cross, the great moment of cosmic peacemaking. Note the elegant concentric structure of this section:

A 2:11-12: you Gentiles separated from the commonwealth
    B 2:13: you who were far off have been brought near . . .
        C 2:14-16: Christ is our peace . . .
    B' 2:17f.: preached peace to those far and those near
A' 2:19: you are no longer strangers, but fellow citizens

Isaiah's promise has been realized "in the blood of Christ" (2:13b), which is less a cultic image than a reminder of the cost of Jesus' discipleship: execution at the hands of the Roman state.

The author now offers a litany, in the form of a series of participial clauses stacked on top of one another, as if he is searching for different ways to communicate this magnificent but incredible assertion. Christ embodies peace because he has "in his flesh" (2:15a) deconstructed and reconstructed the world of hostility in *all* its aspects:

• made us both one	= *cultural*
• broken down the dividing wall of enmity	= *spiritual/ psychological*
• abolishing the law consisting of commandments and statutes	= *legal*
• creating in himself one new humanity from the two	= *social/ anthropological*
• thus making peace	= *political*
• in order to reconcile both, in one body, to God through the cross	= *theological*
• thereby putting to death the enmity in himself (2:14-16).	

Let us examine a few of these important images.

In the semantic universe of the author, the "dividing wall" may allude to several traditions simultaneously. One is Ezekiel 13:14, where a "whitewashed" wall represents the false prophets who proclaim peace when there is no peace. Another is undoubtedly the five-foot wall that separated the Outer Court of the Gentiles from the rest of the Jerusalem Temple. Paul had, after all, at least once been legally charged for bringing a Gentile past that barrier into the Temple courtyard (see Acts 21:28f.). A third allusion may be to Torah itself, which was often referred to as a "fence" around Israel. Above all, however, the wall symbolized the institutionalized enmity between Jew and Gentile, enforced by a complex matrix of statutory regulations, cultural prejudices, and institutionalized imperatives, of outer structures and inner attitudes—much as apartheid or Jim Crow were constructed in our own time. This "bearing wall" has been dismantled in Christ.

There are two more remarkable notions here. One is an image fraught with irony. The cross was, in the first century, the symbol of Roman public terrorism, the executioners stake on which all political dissidents were hung. Yet the author claims that the cross *itself* "put to death" all these deep-seated hostilities (2:16b). This is tantamount to saying today that "the electric chair killed the death penalty." It defies logic. Here, however, the work of René Girard is illuminating. In his comments on the parallel passage in Colossians 2:14f., Girard contends that the cross unmasks the scapegoat myth, which ultimately lies beneath every justification for officially sanctioned violence:

> The Crucifixion reduces mythology to powerlessness by exposing violent contagion, which is so effective in the myths that it prevents communities from ever finding out the truth, namely, the innocence of their victims . . . Though ordinarily the accusation nails the victim to a cross, here by contrast the accusation itself is nailed and publicly exhibited and exposed as a lie. (2001: 138)

Then and now, the majority culture believes that the state's use of violence "when necessary" is rational, noble, and just (think of the popular support today for the death penalty and foreign military interventions). But "by depriving the victim mechanism of the darkness that must conceal it so it can continue to control human culture, the Cross shakes up the world"; it "discredits once and for all the untruth of the Principalities and Powers" (ibid.: 142). The power of nonviolent love has undone the love of power in a world of domination (see below, 4C).

This brings us to the second extraordinary idea: Jesus has built a bridge on his back between adversaries, who are *together* reconciled as "one new humanity" to God (2:15b-16a). The order of the assertions here is unambiguous: making peace with our social enemies is a *precondition* to reconciliation with God! This wreaks havoc on the long tradition of pietism that imagines we must first "get right with God" if there is ever to be any social change. As Markus Barth puts it, "to confess Jesus Christ is to affirm the abolition and end of division and hostility, the end of separation and segregation, the end of enmity and contempt, and the end of every sort of ghetto" (1959: 45).

Peace has thus been declared as gospel, and the gospel as peace (Gk. *euēngelisato*, 2:17; see 6:15). The result, stated in almost Trinitarian fashion, is that in Christ both formerly alienated groups now "have access in one Spirit to the Father" (2:18). This peace is neither a sentimental feeling, nor the absence or suppression of conflict, nor a truce in which adversaries tolerate one another, but the abolition of the deepest justifications for enmity. "Accordingly" (Gk. *ara*, 2:19a), those who abide by this unilateral declaration of peace represent a "third force" in history—the desegregated community of the church (2:19-22).

The church is described in frankly political terms, drawing again on the image of a "house" (as did Jesus, above, 2D). The formerly alienated status of Gentiles has been reversed:

- 2:12: you were . . . excluded from citizenship (Gk. *politeias*) in Israel and strangers (Gk. *xenoi*) to the covenants of promise;
- 2:19: you are no longer strangers (Gk. *xenoi*) and "outside the house" (Gk. *paroikos*), but are "fellow citizens" (Gk. *sympolitai*) with the saints and "members of the household" (Gk. *oikeioi*) of God.

The writer now moves to an elaborate description of this "undivided house." The apostles and prophets are the "foundation" and Christ the "keystone"— not the cornerstone, as is often translated, but the stone at the top of a Roman arch (2:20; literally, "lying at the extreme angle," the final stone that keeps the structure in place). Three different verbs with the Greek root *oikos* are used: "The whole structure (Gk. *oikodomē*) is joined together in Christ and grows into a holy Temple in the Lord, in whom you also are built (Gk. *sunoikodomeisthe*) into it for a dwelling place (Gk. *katoikētērion*) of God in the Spirit" (Eph 2:21f.). The suggestion here is that brick and mortar has been replaced by an organic, *living* Temple (Gk. *naon*).[12]

Members of this "church without walls" cannot, by definition, cooperate with any of the myriad social constructions of enmity—nation, gender, class, race, or sexuality. Despite the fact that walls still exist in the world, Christians should live as if they have been torn down. This means having to rethink some of our most fundamental assumptions, as the Jewish writer to the Ephesians did concerning the "Law." How, for example, is the "structural integrity" of our undivided house compromised by the wall at the U.S.-Mexico border? Or the second-class citizenship of gay and lesbian persons in the church? Or the social architecture of our cities that still insulates rich from poor by the "thin blue line" of police discrimination and the "thick red line" of economic apartheid? If we are not involved in defying these walls of division—even if they are bearing walls—the church is not being the church, no matter what it calls itself.

4C. Metaphors of Atonement and Restorative Justice: A Theological Interlude

To reflect on the meaning of the cross inevitably takes us into a minefield of Christological contestation. It is appropriate, therefore, to venture a brief theological interlude. From the perspective of the history and tradition of Constantinian Christendom, there are two main objections to our nonviolent reading of the New Testament. The first arises from the long-standing hegemony of atonement theory: the belief that the violence of the cross was somehow necessary to satisfy the justice of God. The second is the eschatology of final judgment: the belief that even if violent retribution is not allowed for Christian disciples, room must be left for God's ultimate vengeance. These theological trajectories continue to prevail in modern churchly culture, especially among conservatives. And the two are intimately interrelated in the popular notion that only the former (the death sentence of Jesus' sacrifice) can save us from the latter (our death sentence by God's final judgment). Theologians of nonviolence, in turn, are challenging these powerful and influential ways of thinking.

Our objection to "satisfaction" atonement is that it sacralizes the violence of Jesus' death, placing it at the *center* of salvation history (and deep in the heart of God). If the murder of God's child was necessary to redeem the world, then violence is not an aberration in the cosmos but lies at its core. The satisfactionist paradigm contradicts both Paul's theology of the work of reconciliation by God-in-Christ (above, 1B) and Ephesians' vision of the cross as the divine work of disarmed peacemaking, just examined. Needless to say, it also undermines a discipleship of nonviolence. Moreover, some feminist theologians have recently argued that satisfaction atonement can be likened to "divine child abuse," and has functioned historically to justify all manner of abusive behavior by the powerful against the marginalized (Brock and Parker, 2002). To posit that the problem of sin can only be solved by destroying (or substituting a victim for) the sinner turns God into an executioner, which is no solution at all.

Our objection to theologies of eschatological punishment, in turn, is that they give ultimate legitimation to the "myth of redemptive violence" (Wink, 1992a: 13ff.), placing it at the *culmination* of salvation history (and similarly, deep in the heart of God). If the lethal punishment of sinners is necessary to restore equilibrium in the cosmos, then justice is finally defined by retribution. And if behind every divine (or human) attempt to restore wholeness to both victim and offender stands the threat of retribution, then coercion, rather than love or solidarity, is the bedrock of being and history. Eschatological retribution makes a mockery of Jesus' seventy-times-seven ethos of forgiveness (above, 3D and 3E), and obviously undermines a discipleship of restorative justice. Moreover, the idea that the righteous have the right (and duty) to punish or destroy the sinner has functioned historically to justify making war, capital punishment, and genocidal conquest. To posit that the problem of violence will only finally be solved by superior violence is no solution at all.

We will not go into detail concerning the issues just outlined in bare summary, since they inhabit a vast and rocky terrain that deserves careful treatment which is beyond the scope of this volume. Fortunately there is a growing body of literature that tackles these issues well. In particular, we commend a half-dozen recent studies. The problem of violent atonement theory (and practice!) is examined historically by Anthony Bartlett (2001); theologically and biblically by J. Denny Weaver (2001); and anthropologically and psychologically by Girard (2001; see also Swartley, 2000; Williams, 1991). The problem of eschatological retribution and its influence on criminal justice practices is tackled by T. Richard Snyder (2001), Timothy Gorringe (1996), and most comprehensively by Christopher Marshall (whose painstaking analysis of the New Testament testimonies concerning "final judgment" is thorough, nuanced, and extremely helpful; 2001: 175ff.). We refer the reader to these important books for detailed exploration, and are content here to make just a few observations germane to our project.[13]

We believe that the significance of Christ's cross must always *first* be grounded in history: Jesus was executed as a dissident by the Roman Empire. The primary meaning of "Jesus died for our sins" is that he was killed *because* of a sinful humanity. From the New Testament point of view, Jesus' death was "necessary" (Gk. *dei*) not in terms of divine predestination, but rather as the *inevitable* consequence of prophetic practice in a world of violence and injustice (above, 2D). Any approach that severs Jesus' death from his life, as frankly most atonement theologies do, turns the cross into a cosmic cultic drama without political significance, and thus skirts close to docetism.[14]

While cross-as-consequence is primary, however, it is not by itself sufficient. The New Testament is clear that the martyrdom of Jesus is categorically different from that of other heroes of the faith, even before we reckon with the matter of the resurrection. The cross has "metaphysical" and Christological significance as well. Jesus died for our sins also in the sense of "on our behalf" and "in our stead." Here, however, we have to heed a crucial theological principle: *all talk of God is metaphorical.* Therefore, talking about what happened on the cross is also necessarily metaphorical.

The early Christians understood that the cross represented a "scandal" (1 Cor 1:23; Gal 5:11). Death by execution was the ultimate shameful fate in antiquity (Deut 21:22; Gal 3:13). Indeed, God seemed to be *absent* (or at least silent) at Golgotha, leaving the impression that Jesus was abandoned (Mark 15:34).[15] Nevertheless, the New Testament writers insist that the cross was *not* shameful, and that Jesus' Way was vindicated at the resurrection. But they acknowledge that this defies the logic of world rulers, and confounds the "wise and powerful" (1 Cor 1:18-25; 2:6-8). The counterpoint is the conviction that God was fully (if mysteriously) *present* on the cross, in an act of solidarity with Jesus and ultimately all victims of rape, torture, and ignominious death. God was *in* Christ on the cross, as we saw in our discussion of 2 Corinthians 5:17ff. (above, 1B). It represents the ultimate manifestation of redemptive nonviolence, that somehow "disarmed the Principalities and Powers and made a public example of them, triumphing over them" (Col 2:15).

There are a variety of other metaphors for how New Testament writers speak of the meaning of the cross, and each gives us part of the mysterious truth of salvation. Most of these metaphors are predicated on the symbolic, cultural, and linguistic universe of the Hebrew scriptures (and occasionally from that of the Hellenistic and Persian worlds). Let us name seven of the more prominent "semantic fields" through which the early writers reflect on the meaning of sin and salvation through the cross:

1. *Images from purity code and the sacrificial cult of Israel:* Sin imaged as stain or pollution. Salvation imaged as cleansing, covering or expiation. "Mechanism" imaged as sacrifice or "substitution" (in sense of a scapegoat). See, e.g., Matt 26:28; Rom 3:22-26; Heb 2:17f.; 9:11-14; 1 John 2:2.

2. *Forensic images (criminal justice):* Sin imaged as offense or lawbreaking. Salvation imaged as amnesty, exoneration, acquittal, or vindication. "Mechanism" imaged as restorative justice, justification, forgiveness. See, e.g., Rom 8:3f.; 1 Cor 6:11.

3. *Images of struggle against the Powers, death, Satan:* Sin imaged as captivity, addiction, or oppression. Salvation imaged as Exodus-type liberation, ransom, rescue, victory, escape. "Mechanism" imaged as the overthrow of Powers, victory over death/Satan. See, e.g., Rom 5:21; 6-7; 1 Cor 1:18-2:8; 5:7; Gal 4:3-5; Col 2:13-15; Heb 2:14f.; 1 Tim 2:5f.

4. *Images of Jubilee:* Sin imaged as debt and/or slavery. Salvation imaged as forgiveness, release, redemption, freedom, accounts reconciled. "Mechanism" imaged as redistribution, economy of grace, justice. See, e.g., Mark 10:45; 1 Cor 6:20; 2 Cor 5:18-6:2.

5. *Images of social alienation:* Sin imaged as violence, enmity, separation. Salvation imaged as reconciliation, reunification, restored kinship. "Mechanism" imaged as adoption, peace treaty, ceasefire. See, e.g., Rom 5:1-11; 2 Cor 5:14-17; Eph 2:11-18.

6. *Covenant images:* Sin imaged as infidelity, faithlessness, refusal of gift. Salvation imaged as covenant of the heart, gratitude.

"Mechanism" imaged as covenant renewed. See, e.g., 2 Cor 3:6-11; Heb 9:15.

7. *Anthropological images:* Sin imaged as corruption, fall, old Adam. Salvation imaged as new Adam, new creation, resurrection, eternal life. See, e.g., Rom 5:17-21; 8:21-31; 1 Cor 15:35f.[16]

Each of these metaphorical "strands" is illuminating, and each can be understood nonviolently. But each is also limited, and often misunderstood, particularly if taken literally. For example, in the cultic metaphor (1 above), Jesus might be compared to a "sacrificial lamb without blemish," but Pilate who executed him is certainly *not* comparable to a high priest presiding over the cult, so the analogy breaks down. Similarly, the idea of Jesus "taking our punishment" to appease an offended God (the penal substitution version of 2) is incoherent from a Trinitarian perspective.

Paul often mixed metaphors in the same argument, as in Rom 5:6-10:

- Verses 6-8: "While we were still weak, at the right time Christ died for the ungodly. One will hardly die for a just person, though perhaps for a good person one will dare even to die. But God shows love for us in that while we were yet sinners, Christ died for us." This uses the metaphor of heroic sacrifice, as on the battlefield (perhaps reflecting elements of 5 and 6 above). We might paraphrase this: "He took the bullet for us—and we weren't even comrades!"
- Verse 9: "Since therefore we are now justified by his blood, much more shall we be saved by him from the wrath of God." Paul now switches to blood imagery, but not in the sense of expiation. This image comes from the semantic field of Passover (3 above), in which the blood on the doorposts spares the people from God's judgment on empire.
- Verse 10: "For if while we were enemies we were reconciled to God by the death of his Son, much more, now that we are reconciled, shall we be saved by his life." This sounds very much like 2 Corinthians 5-6, and belongs to the relational metaphors (5 above).

A truly biblical approach, therefore, will draw on all of these (and other) metaphors, while absolutizing no one of them, enabling a rich and nuanced theology of the cross.

At the very least, this brief exercise shows that we are not beholden to substitutionary atonement as the only "orthodox" option. Still, if we wish to move away from that problematic but still dominant metaphor, we must nevertheless take seriously the problem it tries to solve: namely, that sinful human beings have wreaked unfathomable havoc on God's good creation, for which there must be accountability. God cares profoundly about our violation of all that is truly sacred and beautiful. Scripture tells us that YHWH is particularly attentive to "the blood of the innocent crying out from the ground" (see Gen 4:10), to the lament of the poor and oppressed (Exod 3:7; Deut 15:9), and to the groans of creation (Isa 14:7f.; Rom 8:19-23). It is in this context that we should understand the biblical notion of "the wrath of God"—as an *expression*, not *negation*, of love for our violent race. We would expect that caring parents would be anguished over the misbehavior of their children, proactive about the problem, not laissez faire. But the Compassionate One worries about *offenders* as well as victims—and ultimately, Paul reminds us, that is all of us (Rom 3:23).

The New Testament does take these issues seriously, but rejects the two logical solutions of Mother Culture. On the one hand, it refuses *retributive* justice, which sacrifices the offender through "redemptive violence." On the other, it cannot imagine *no* justice at all, since this would be to deny the existence of God. Inaction sacrifices victims; the only thing worse is to blame them. As we have seen (above, 1B, 3C), both Jesus and Paul believed that the "justice of God" is expressed as redemptive nonviolence and restorative justice. God models solidarity with the violated and relentless moral initiative toward the violator. On Jesus' cross, God dignifies the victim's suffering by *becoming* the victim—even while still reaching out to the executioner (Luke 23:34). As Reed Leverton says, citing Luke 23:43, "the last person to whom Jesus spoke was a convicted felon, and He did so to offer forgiveness and absolution" (2006: 1). Similarly, in Jesus' resurrection, God vindicates the victim, and the Risen One's first act is to reach out to those who betrayed him (Mark 16:7). The resurrection thus invites us into the process of

> winning back what God has created. That process is grounded in God's defeat of the estranging powers of death, and it lives from the conviction that the crucified Christ will be the measure and the purpose of history . . . By raising the crucified One from the dead, God wants to change history in the direction of justice here and now. (Lorenzen, 2003: 47, 80)

God-in-Christ, as the "injured party," insists on making things right, but understands that true healing and wholeness are bound also to the fate of the offender. The "justice of God" is found not in punishment but in truth, reparation, accountability, and changed behavior. The goal of the Cross is to redeem both victims and offenders from their dehumanization and alienation, and to empower both to embrace restorative practices themselves.

But what about beyond the horizons of narrative and history? Paul certainly speaks about the "wrath and fury" of divine judgment that awaits those who persist in evil.[17] But is this a *lethal* response? At three key points in Romans, Paul appears to equivocate. He asks a classic theological question in Rom 3:5: "Is God unjust to inflict wrath on us?" But he then immediately adds parenthetically, "I speak in a human way," as if to caution us against assuming we know what God's wrath consists of. At a second point he asserts that divine mercy always seems to trump wrath (Rom 9:22f.). The third and most telling example comes on the heels of Paul's famous reiteration of Jesus' call to love our enemies (Rom 12:14-18). Paul counsels disciples never to practice vengeance but to "give place to the wrath (of God)" (12:19, citing Deut 32:35). But this is followed by an example of "alternative vengeance": feeding one's enemy in order to shame him, thus overcoming evil with good (12:20f.). This implies that God's "vengeance" might also have the same character—"heaping hot coals on our heads" (12:20c) by doing good to us, rather than retaliating in kind.

Jonathan Burnside argues that we should leave place for divine vengeance on those who utterly refuse to yield to God's grace, concluding that "human nature sets limits on the restorative ideal . . . the Bible wisely bears witness to the complex relationship between retribution and restoration" (2007: 144). We think, however, that Thomas Yoder Neufeld better catches the New Testament nuance when he points out that disciples' commitment to nonviolence

> does not preclude their participation in the divine outrage at injury, violence, and injustice, at crime, big and small. Indeed, not to be outraged is not yet to stand in solidarity with the victim . . . In Ephesians 4:26 we read these striking words: "Be angry, but do not sin!" (2003: 8)

If we are enjoined to rage-without-violence in our love for the enemy, then it seems likely that this is also the character of God.

As we have suggested (above, 3E), there is another way to understand "God's wrath" that is in keeping with certain traditions of the Hebrew Bible: God allows us to reap the lethal consequences of our own historic depravities. When we break taboos woven into the fabric of creation, we will live to see the disaster.[18] In our time such "judgment" looms in the end-game of our addictions or infidelities in the personal sphere, or of the arms race or environmental destruction in the collective sphere. From such consequences God indeed wishes to save us, which is why the biblical tradition repeatedly expresses the divine desire for our repentance (e.g., Rom 2:4).

We return, in conclusion, to the difficult notion of "redemptive suffering." Instead of postulating Jesus' suffering as payment to an angry God, the New Testament imagines a God who suffers in Jesus at the hands of an angry humanity. There is certainly tension in the idea that God does not want us to suffer, and therefore suffers with us and for us. But it *does* address the central question of theodicy. If God is *against* suffering, then God would not *inflict* suffering; however, God can *suffer* as a consequence of employing the "force more powerful" to stop those who *inflict* suffering. Nonviolent resistance to the point of absorbing the adversary's violence is the ultimate weapon of restorative justice, and it is ultimately efficacious because God absorbs the violence before us, with us, and for us. But Ephesians rightly calls this a "mystery."

In the end, our theological speculations on the shape of God's eschatological judgment should be modest, even perhaps agnostic. This is terrain beyond the metaphors, and we should tread there meekly. Marshall wisely concludes his thoughtful and important discussion of these issues by quoting Albert Camus: "You were speaking of the Last Judgment. Allow me to laugh respectfully. I shall wait for it resolutely, for I have known what is worse, the judgment of men" (2001: 195).

4D. Evangelizing the Powers: Paul's "Letter from Birmingham City Jail" (Ephesians 3)

We pick up the thread of Ephesians at 3:1, where, as noted, it is abruptly revealed that Paul is in jail. The phrase is incomplete, hanging over the whole of Ephesians 3 until it is reiterated in 4:1, which begins the formal *parenesis* (ethical instruction) of the epistle. The tendency of modern theologians (few of whom have been to jail) has been to romanticize Paul's prison experiences, as if he only endured brief stints in a civilized holding cell. Craig Wansink has shown, however, that the prisons of empire were brutal, marked by "suffering, beatings, chains, darkness and squalor" (1996: 33).

The incarcerated had no rights; then (as now) the prison population consisted either of poor people or dissidents (apparently Paul was both).[19] "Imprisonment might lead to death: either execution by the authorities or death resulting from disease, torture or the psychological trauma of imprisonment" (ibid.). The comment of Roman historian Sallust (86-34 b.c.e.) sums the matter up succinctly: "Some have been crucified, others thrown to wild beasts; a few whose lives were spared, in gloomy dungeons amid sorrow and lamentation drag out an existence worse than death" (ibid.: 31).

If Ephesians was penned in the last decade of the first century, there would have been strong resonance between the author's political situation and that of Paul. The apostle was jailed and executed during the first great systematic persecution of the church under Emperor Nero (64-68 c.e.). Ephesians most likely circulated during the next wave of imperial pogroms under Domitian (81-96 c.e.). The latter period, during which Jewish practices were outlawed and the emperor cult established, inspired the fierce apocalyptic rant of another political prisoner, John's Revelation.[20] We might well wonder whether the author of Ephesians, like his teacher three decades earlier, also experienced incarceration. In any case, the letter's "origins" in prison gives its grand vision of cosmic unity a distinctive realism. The Pauline tradition could indeed claim to have "lived within the monster and know its entrails."[21]

We have already noted some of the similarities between the ministries of Paul and Martin Luther King, Jr. (above, 1A). We have further suggested that the first half of Ephesians, with its grand vision of comprehensive peace, comes alive when read through the lens of King's "I Have a Dream" speech (above, 4A). This dream is not a pollyannish fantasy, however, but a social and theological imperative, which means that disciples must strategically and nonviolently engage the existing social architecture of division, whatever the cost. Thus, the second half of the Ephesian encyclical speaks from and to the context of engaged struggle—as does King's "Letter from Birmingham City Jail."

King's jail epistle was penned during a tough period in his struggle for integration and voting rights for African Americans in the South—his eight-day confinement as a result of civil disobedience in mid-April, 1963. Taylor Branch recounts:

> Furtively through the bars—because the jail rules allowed no material possessions to prisoners in solitary—King showed [his lawyer] Jones a copy on the *Birmingham News* that had been smuggled in on a previous legal visit. All around the margins, meandering from page to page, he was scribbling a passionate response to a small story headlined "White Clergymen Urge Local Negroes to Withdraw from Demonstration." Led by C. C. J. Carpenter, the Episcopal bishop of Alabama, an ecumenical group of eight religious leaders—all at least mild critics of segregation—had issued a statement calling King's Birmingham campaign "unwise and untimely" . . .
>
> King consumed precious visiting minutes demanding more blank paper to be sneaked in, and giving detailed instructions for stitching

together the piecemeal letter . . . He addressed the eight Birmingham clergy in dozens of voices—begged, scolded, explained, even
cooed to them, and conspired icily with them as fellow experts . . .
Outside the jail, the finished letter was typed neatly at a length of
twenty pages, then copied and distributed widely by hand and post.
(Branch, 1998: 46-48)

The letter was initially picked up by neither local nor national press,
appearing only in a Quaker journal, as many of King's white political
allies outside the South took an ambivalent stance toward the Birmingham campaign. Yet its eventual fame is more than justified as a brilliant
theological and political defense of nonviolent direct action. It remains
especially enduring for activists who face (as they almost always do) the
criticism of prominent leaders, who appeal for more time and less agita-
tion. This is why we have cited the letter often throughout this volume.

There are compelling parallels between King, appealing from jail to
white clergy for solidarity with his witness against American apartheid,
and Paul, calling on Gentile Christians from prison to support his challenge to the political-cultural system of social segregation between Jew
and Greek. Paul is locked up by the very statutes that Christ came to overturn in the interests of social reconciliation (2:15). Ephesians 3:1f. makes
it clear that he knows why he is there:

3:1   "I, Paul, a prisoner for Christ Jesus on behalf of you Gentiles
       . . ." (Gk. *hyper hymōn tōn ethnōn*)
3:2   ". . . assuming that you have heard of the stewardship of God's
       grace that was given to me for you . . ." (Gk. *eis hymas*)

The author could just as well have said "*because* of you Gentiles." And there
is another hint of ethnic tension in his sarcastic speculation about whether
or not they have heard about Paul's imprisonment—which of course they
had.

King's jailings were embarrassing to polite Southern society, and we
can assume the same was true of the historic Paul's imprisonments for his
Gentile colleagues. It may be that for Ephesians to invoke Paul's imprisonment (in full knowledge of his eventual martyrdom) by the Roman
authorities functioned as a warning to Gentile Christians not to be com-
placent citizens of that empire, particularly if the heat was again ramping
up under Domitian. The incarceration of persons of conscience always
serves as an unwelcome reminder that all is *not* well in society; ministers
being treated as criminals exposes the political problems that everyone
knows exist. This was precisely the strategy that King took from Gandhi:

using civil disobedience to provoke a crisis of conscience. King's letter argues that this tradition goes back to the Bible, "evidenced sublimely in the refusal of Shadrach, Meshach and Abednego to obey the laws of Nebuchadnezzar, on the ground that a higher moral law was at stake. It was practiced superbly by the early Christians, who were willing to face hungry lions and the excruciating pain of chopping blocks rather than submit to certain unjust laws of the Roman Empire" (Washington, 1986: 294).

King, a member of an oppressed and marginalized minority, was appealing directly to leaders of the Christian church who, as members of the majority culture, were also his historic adversaries, socially and politically speaking. He both defended his witness and challenged them to live up to their faith. This is exactly what the author of the Epistle to the Ephesians was doing: reminding his Gentile colleagues of the moral authority of the Jewish founders of Christianity, while also charging them to follow Christ by refusing to cooperate with the institutionalized segregation that kept Jews and Gentiles "separate and unequal." Both authors languished in jail *knowing* that good Christians were doing nothing about apartheid, taking comfortable refuge in their dominant culture privileges, and hiding behind pious rhetoric while avoiding real solidarity with their oppressed cousins in the faith.

King is candidly critical of his "white moderate" colleagues:

> You deplore the demonstrations that are presently taking place in Birmingham. But I am sorry that your statement did not express a similar concern for the conditions that brought the demonstrations into being . . . So we had no alternative except that of preparing for direct action, whereby we would present our very bodies as a means of laying our case before the conscience of the local and national community . . .
>
> I have almost reached the regrettable conclusion that the Negro's great stumbling block in the stride toward freedom . . . is the white moderate, who is more devoted to "order" than to justice; who prefers a negative peace which is the absence of tension to a positive peace which is the presence of justice; who constantly says: "I agree with you in the goal you seek, but I cannot agree with your methods of direct action"; who paternalistically believes he can set the timetable for another man's freedom; who lives by a mythical concept of time and who constantly advises the Negro to wait for a "more convenient season." Shallow understanding from people of good will is more frustrating than absolute misunderstanding from people of ill will. (Ibid.: 290f., 295)

With similar frustration, the author of Ephesians points out that Paul inhabited an imperial dungeon because of his commitment to Gentiles.

The claim that Paul was an "administrator of God's grace" (Gk. *oikonomian tēs charitos tou theou*) was bold, since it is Christ who is the "administrator" of God's vision in Ephesians 1:9. But that is precisely the point just made in Ephesians 2:19-22: disciples are called to embody the peace Christ has declared. The "we/you" discourse of Ephesians 1-2 is now personalized in a refrain of "*me*/you" (second person plural):

3:1   *I* Paul, a prisoner for Christ Jesus on behalf of *you* Gentiles—

3:2   assuming *you* have heard of the administration of God's grace that was given *me* for *you,*

3:3   how the mystery was made known to *me* by revelation, as *I* have written briefly.

3:4   When *you* read this you can perceive *my* insight . . .

Paul challenges, as King would later, his colleagues to fully embrace both the gospel *and* their responsibilities in the historical moment. And both do so from behind bars of the system they are seeking to overturn.

The vision of reconciliation is a tall enough order; all the more so when broadcast from such an obscure, vulnerable space in the entrails of empire. This is why the author now returns to the notion of God's will as a "*mystery*" (3:3, 4, 9; see 1:9). The prospects for transformation are not at all evident to the rational or the powerful—nor, for that matter, are the personal prospects of those trying to "enlighten everyone as to the plan of the mystery" (Gk. *hē oikonomia tou mystēriou*, 3:9). But this counterintuitive truth has been "revealed by the Spirit" to Paul, as an apostle in the prophetic tradition (3:5). The Greek verb here is *apocalyptō* (literally, "to unmask"), because the Dream of God requires a different way of seeing. Modern Christians have trivialized apocalyptic literature by obsessing over (or ignoring) it as some sort of coded map for navigating the end times. Rather, we need to recover apocalyptic consciousness as the practice of "double vision": on the one hand, seeing the realities of injustice that are being denied; on the other, glimpsing possibilities of a world transformed (see Myers, 1994: 396ff.). In Ephesians, the first is articulated in its exposition of the fact of enmity, the second in the repeated annunciation that Gentiles have been fully embraced into salvation history (3:6).

As peacemakers both King and Paul stressed repeatedly that members of the very group that had historically oppressed their people are welcome as full members in the movement. This was not easy for nationalists in their respective contexts to accept, and certainly both men were accused of being "race traitors." Nor was their advocacy of nonviolence widely embraced. Why should the already marginalized suffer *more* in the struggle to wrest justice from the dominant culture? And should not the oppressors be punished? Violated people, too, assume justice should be retributive (as illustrated in the book of Jonah). But both Dr. King and Paul understood that in a situation of systemic injustice, it is actually the privileged majority who stand in deepest need of redemption. The oppressed minority, by struggling for freedom, is offering a healing gift—though it is rarely perceived that way by those with power.[22] This gift lies at the heart of restorative justice—but the work behind it is incredibly demanding. So we can understand why the author of Ephesians repeatedly emphasizes Paul's dependence on the transformative "energy" of divine grace: "Of *this* gospel I was made servant, according to the gift of God's grace, given to me according to the energy (Gk. *energeian)* of God's power" (3:7).[23]

The three goals of Paul's mission are summarized next, which he identifies with the "eternal purpose of God as realized in Christ" (3:11):

1. to proclaim the gospel to the "other side" (i.e., Gentiles, 3:8);
2. to illuminate *all* people concerning the "mystery hidden for the ages," already identified as the overcoming of social enmity (3:9); and
3. to animate the church "to make known the wisdom of God (Gk. *sophia tou theou)* in its rich variety to the rulers and authorities in the heavenly places" (3:10).

It is this third aspect that sets his vocation firmly in a political context. Paul is in jail because he is an evangelist for the gospel of peacemaking in a world of hostility and division, and because he proclaimed it to the highest authorities—the very architects of social enmity (see Acts 23-26).

This same concern for the unavoidably *public* vocation of the church marks King's jail letter, though stated more negatively. After commending some "notable exceptions," King launches a scathing indictment of the white church's lack of support of the civil rights movement. Speaking as "one who loves the church," he laments that whereas he had hoped that religious leaders in the South would be "some of our strongest allies . . . instead, some have been outright opponents, refusing to understand the freedom movement and misrepresenting its leaders; all too many others have been more cautious than courageous and have remained silent behind the anesthetizing security of the stained-glass windows" (Washington, 1986: 299). King was looking for the churches of Birmingham to help as a

"channel through which our just grievances would get to the power structure," and expected leaders to put morality before the law. But

> in the midst of blatant injustices inflicted upon the Negro, I have
> watched white churches stand on the sideline and merely mouth
> pious irrelevancies and sanctimonious trivialities. In the midst of a
> mighty struggle to rid our nation of racial and economic injustice,
> I have heard so many ministers say, "Those are social issues with
> which the gospel has no real concern." (Ibid.)

King abhorred the church's failure to preach the gospel to the Powers, and
upbraided it as a community "largely adjusted to the status quo, standing
as a taillight behind other community agencies rather than a headlight
leading men to higher levels of justice" (ibid.). King and Paul could not
be more explicit, yet modern Christians still imagine that our churches
should "stay out of politics"—as if that were possible! The question is only
what *kind* of politics the church should embody.

The author concludes his meditation with a long, pastoral prayer for the
very Gentile Christians who are not too sure about the appropriateness
of his witness (3:14-21). Reminding them that witnessing to the Powers
comes with a cost, he asks them to pray that he will "not lose heart over
my suffering" (3:13), which is redefined as *their* glory! This is no doubt
intended ironically (as was so much of King's letter), since it will be his
audience's response that determines whether or not Paul loses heart! The
epistle as a whole will close with a similar petition for solidarity—especially for the political prisoner Paul to continue to speak truth to power
(6:19f.; below, 4E).

He goes on to pray that they will be "strengthened in the deepest part
of them" (3:16), that they will be "grounded in love" (3:17), and that they
will "comprehend the big picture" of this love (3:18f.)—a sort of "keep
your eyes on the prize" exhortation. In a final summons for these citizens
of empire and disciples of Jesus to transcend their entitlements and their
domesticated fears, a benediction invokes "the One who is able to do far
more with us than anything we might ask or think" (3:20). King also
concluded his letter with a similar tone, after apologizing if he may have
offended anyone (!):

> I hope this letter finds you strong in the faith. I also hope that cir-
> cumstances will soon make it possible for me to meet each of you, not
> as an integrationist or a civil rights leader but as a fellow clergyman
> and a Christian brother. Let us all hope that the dark clouds of racial
> prejudice will soon pass away and the deep fog of misunderstanding

will be lifted from our fear-drenched communities, and in some not too distant tomorrow the radiant stars of love and brotherhood will shine over our great nation with all their scintillating beauty. (Ibid.: 302)

In both cases, the authors' pastoral concern makes no attempt to hide their hope that these ambivalent colleagues will become true partners in the faith.

4E. "Put on the Whole Armor of God": A Call to Nonviolence as a Way of Life (Ephesians 4-6)

It is ironic but instructive that Ephesians' "peace manifesto" concludes with a "nonviolent call to arms," which will be the focus of this last section. First, however, we will make a few summary comments about Ephesians 4:1-6:9. The second half of the epistle begins with Paul summoning his audience to discipleship: "I beg you (Gk. *parakalō*), as a prisoner of the Lord, to walk (Gk. *peripatēsai*) in the calling to which you have been called" (4:1).[24] There is a sobering rhetorical resonance between the "one in *bonds*" (Gk. *ho desmios*, 4:1) exhorting the audience to "maintain the unity of the Spirit in the *bond* of peace (Gk. *en tō syndesmō tēs eirēnēs*, 4:3).

The author now commences a virtual catechism of nonviolence as a way of life. It is first articulated positively, emphasizing the community-as-body seeking to live in unity while celebrating a diversity of gifts (4:3-16). This section concludes with a reiteration of 2:19-22: the church is an organic, growing body, with Christ as the head, forming a "building of love" (*eis oikodomēn heautou en agapē*, 4:15b-16). Then come sharp warnings, underscored as a solemn "witness" (Gk. *martyromai*): "You must no longer walk (Gk. *peripatein*) as the Gentiles walk" (4:17). This is a pointed challenge to those being addressed to stop conforming to imperial culture—tantamount to an African American pastor telling a white congregation to renounce its skin privilege. The author pulls no punches: this culture is futile, without understanding, alienated from life, ignorant, hard of heart, callous, and greedy (4:18f.). But the tone gets still tougher, repeating the barb of 3:2: "*This* is not what you learned in Christ—assuming you have heard and were taught about him!" (4:20f.). We are still in the rhetorical orbit of "Paul's Letter from Birmingham City Jail."

There is clearly doubt in the author's mind as to the integrity of the faith of these dominant culture Christians. Thus, the rhetoric turns baptismal (typical of New Testament catechetical traditions), inviting them to renewed commitment: "Take off your old human nature . . . and put on the new, which is truly created after the likeness of God in justice and holiness" (4:22-24). Nonviolence requires us to examine our lives each day, to make conscious choices to forsake old habits large and small, and to embrace new practices of nonaggression, noncompetition, compassion, and solidarity. The author continues with practical advice, again as both affirmations and warnings (4:25-5:5). "Be angry but do not sin" is a perfect job description for nonviolent resistance to injustice, while "do not let the sun set on your anger" speaks of the need to keep short accounts within the community (4:26). The exhortations of 4:29-32 contain strong echoes of the "community conferencing" ethos for dealing with violation, which we examined in Matthew 18 (above, 3D).

The audience is reminded too of the economic dimensions of violence: the command to "stop stealing and engage in honest manual labor!" was (and is) as relevant to the wealthy exploiter as to the street hustler (4:28).[25] Sexual fidelity is also important to maintaining healthy, trusting, and non-exploitive relationships (5:3-5; something activists today would do well to take more seriously). We might think of these exhortations as "evangelical disciplines" of nonviolence, in which the ends and means are congruent, as Gandhi put it. The church cannot possibly stand for peace in the world if it is unable to resolve its own internal conflicts and face its own abuses of power. In all of this, disciples are urged to "imitate God, as beloved children, and walk in love, as Christ loved us"—high standards indeed (5:1).

In 5:6ff. the epistle takes on a distinctly defensive tone, with a warning about the deception that constantly swirls around us. Our response should be twofold. On the one hand we are to *disassociate* ourselves from those who would perpetuate hostility and domination (5:6f.), instead trying to "learn what is pleasing to the Lord." "Take no part in unfruitful works of darkness" (5:10f.) uses a verb that implies "noncooperation" (Gk. *synkoinōeite*). This is a longstanding tool of nonviolent activists, from conscientious objection and war tax resistance to the many ways oppressed people actively and passively noncooperate with authority, refusing to give up their dignity in the face of dehumanizing conditions (see J. Scott, 1987).

On the other hand, "Instead, expose them. For it is a shame even to speak of the things that they do in secret; but when anything is exposed by the light it becomes visible" (5:11b-13). We are to exercise an "offensive" ministry of unmasking lies as well, especially in the public sphere. As noted (above, 3D), the verb here is the same one used in Matthew 18:15 to start the process of victim-offender dialogue. Here, however, the connotation is more political than interpersonal. King addresses this need to expose the injustice to the light in his letter:

We who engage in nonviolent direct action are not the creators of tension. We merely bring to the surface the hidden tension that is already alive. We bring it out in the open where it can be seen and dealt with . . . Injustice must likewise be exposed . . . to the light of human conscience and the air of national opinion before it can be cured. (Washington, 1986: 295)

This kind of truth telling is difficult, and demands profound personal discipline. But it includes some of the most creative nonviolent actions in recent history, such as the symbolic disarmament actions of the Plowshares movement.[26] This section concludes with a call to "conscious living" that resists addictive and compulsive behavior (5:14-20), staying awake to the times "because the days are evil" (5:16).

Delightfully, the author includes a reminder to celebrate with song as much as possible (5:19). This brings to mind the venerable old Shaker hymn, which resonates powerfully with both Ephesians' and King's epistles as a song of faith and justice from the darkness of a jail cell:

> My life goes on in endless song
> Above earth's lamentations,
> I hear the real, though far-off hymn
> That hails a new creation.
> Through all the tumult and the strife
> I hear its music ringing,
> It sounds an echo in my soul.
> How can I keep from singing?
> While though the tempest loudly roars,
> I hear the truth, it liveth.
> And though the darkness round me close,
> Songs in the night it giveth.
> No storm can shake my inmost calm,
> While to that rock I'm clinging.
> Since love is lord of heaven and earth
> How can I keep from singing?
> When tyrants tremble in their fear
> And hear their death knell ringing,
> When friends rejoice both far and near
> How can I keep from singing?
> In prison cell and dungeon vile
> Our thoughts to them are winging,
> When friends by shame are undefiled
> How can I keep from singing?

Music was indeed the spiritual sustenance of the civil rights movement, as the great African American musician and musicologist Bernice Johnson Reagon has chronicled (2001: 100ff.).

The final part of the catechism is the admittedly problematic "household code" of 5:21-6:9. Many scholars believe that this parenetic form—in which wives are instructed to be subordinate to their husbands, children to their parents, and slaves to their masters—originates from secular Hellenistic patriarchal manuals on household order. This passage grates on modern ears, and with its long and lamentable history in Christendom of being used to suppress women and persons of color, would seem to qualify as a "text of terror," to use Phyllis Trible's phrase (1984). Does it in fact relegitimize the very divisions between groups that the whole epistle has heretofore tried to overturn? If so, then the author of Ephesians was being distressingly inconsistent at best, and incoherent at worst. We hold out the possibility that, properly understood, this Ephesian version of a traditional Hellenistic code may not be as regressive as many contend. To argue this would take us well beyond the scope of this volume; but we do offer one line of inquiry for further reflection.[27]

The introduction and conclusion are surely keys to interpreting the code:

5:21   "Be subordinate (Gk. *hypotassomenoi*) to one another out of fear of Christ."
6:9   "Know that the One who is both their Lord and yours is in heaven, and has no partiality."

The initial emphasis on mutuality would seem to be subversive in a cultural context of highly structured social roles. Invoking the "fear of Christ," who seemed to pay little attention to hierarchy, may underline this.[28] The writer goes on to address *both* parties in each of the three household relationships, urging them to be respectful of each other.[29] This was *not* the case in the secular codes, which were addressed only to the *paterfamilias*, because subordinates were not deemed worthy of ethical instruction. Any putative hierarchy is further undermined by the radical "leveling" effect of the closing reminder in 6:9.[30]

Also of interest is the fact that the empirically "less powerful" party is addressed *first* in Ephesians. There is no anthropology of inferiority here, and there may be an echo of Matthew 18's notion of the moral agency of the victim (above, 3B). To push this further, the parties are exhorted to subordinate themselves not because the "superior's" station demands it, but

5:22   "as if to the Lord" (wives);
6:1   "in the Lord" (children); and
6:5   "as to Christ" (slaves).

But what if "obedience to Christ" demands "noncooperation" or even "exposing works of darkness" (Eph 5:11)? If following Jesus entails resisting oppression—including in the dominant ethos of urban Hellenistic culture—then the above qualifiers are substantial. Might they actually be trying to nurture an ethic of nonviolent transformation from below?

To be sure, this code does not clearly advocate egalitarianism, as modern, rights-oriented readers would wish. But it does stress mutuality, and it is at least possible that the author may have believed that if each party took its part of these instructions seriously, domination would disappear. After all, even today, the "rules" of intimate affiliations tend to be different than those of the workplace or public square. Healthy family dynamics routinely put relationships before rights and allow love to trump power. This suggests that a *consistent* ethic of mutual subordination may be how nonviolent community is best built and maintained. But of course these texts have not been employed consistently, but instead used to justify "Christian" patriarchy and class/race superiority. Given such traditions of interpretation, the household code is treacherous terrain to navigate. If we can't abide its rhetoric for our context, however, we still have to figure out how to live *respectfully* with our intimates, and how to resist *nonviolently* those who treat us or others as socially inferior.

This brings us to the final section of Ephesians, which catalogues an arsenal of nonviolent weapons of resistance (Eph 6:10ff.). Here again we have to ask: Do its unabashedly military metaphors contradict the peaceable tone of the rest of the epistle? This is only the case in the theological tradition of American pietism, which has mishandled this text as it has the household code. One tendency is to spiritualize the metaphors of "God's armor," taking them far out of the realm of politics or even conflict, and driving them inward. Another is to see Eph 6:10ff. as a precise protocol for "spiritual warfare." These are strange interpretive strategies for traditions that otherwise have no principled objections to war. There are, of course, those who believe that these metaphors provide tacit or explicit justification for Christian participation in war. The image of the model religious soldier is well attested in patriotic symbolics—classically portrayed by General George Washington kneeling at prayer in the snow at Valley Forge.[31] These traditions are not wrong in imagining a spiritual warrior. But they have missed the point by removing the text from the broader narrative of Ephesians, which is about the *abolition* of enmity. Because peace is defined as social reconciliation in a world of hostility, and because the church is called to speak truth to the Powers, it stands to reason that disciples must learn the art of nonviolent resistance. This text seems to ask the same question as the motto of Christian Peacemaker Teams today: "What would happen if Christians devoted the same discipline and self-sacrifice to nonviolent peacemaking that armies devote to war?"[32]

Ephesians' military images function rhetorically in two ways. One is shock value: they disabuse us of the notion that there are polite transfers of power in the real world, or that justice trickles down, or that if we just present a rational proposal with proper diplomacy, the Powers will work with us. Such are fantasies of middle-class politicians and liberal social reformers, but the poor know better, and so does the Bible. Transformation involves intense struggle—the only question is what kind of weaponry we wield. The logic of Ephesians 6:10ff. is precisely that whoever would remain in the peace of Christ must be prepared to wage *satyagraha* with the forces of violence and oppression in the world.

The other function is to offer a midrash on Isaiah 59, where the divine warrior Yahweh "goes to battle" against a people which has forsaken the ways of peace and justice:

> Their deeds are sinful; they commit violent crimes. They are eager to do evil, quick to shed innocent blood. Their thoughts are sinful; they crush and destroy. They are unfamiliar with peace; their deeds are unjust. They use deceitful methods, and whoever deals with them is unfamiliar with peace . . .
>
> YHWH sees that there is no advocate; is shocked that no one intervenes, so takes matters into her own hands; YHWH's desire for justice drives her, she wears it like a breastplate; the desire to deliver is like a helmet on God's head. God puts on the garments of vengeance, and wears zeal like a robe. (Isa 59:8, 15a-17)

Ephesians, too, hears the cry of victims of violence as a call to militance.

The first in a string of verbs in the imperative mood commands us to "be empowered" (Gk. *endynamousthe*) in the "strength of God's might" (6:10; Gk. *kratei tēs ischyos autou*, the same phrase as in 1:19). Here is another reminder that we will need the divine "force more powerful" to contend with the brute force of the domination system. This was a core conviction of Gandhi:

> The only weapon of the Satyagrahi is God . . . without Him the Satyagrahi is devoid of strength before an opponent armed with

monstrous weapons. Most people lie prostrate before physical might. But he who accepts God as his only protector will remain unbent before the mightiest earthly power. (2001: 95)

Nonviolence is not passivism, as it is so often mischaracterized, but an alternative form of potent engagement.

Ephesians' catechism gets the "troops" dressed for battle. Again, however, it is not an individual soldier being equipped, but a *community* of resistance—the verbs are still in the second person plural. Once more we encounter the baptismal language of "putting on" (Gk. *endysasthe*; 6:11a). We need "the *whole* armor (*tēn panoplian*) of God"; nothing less will enable us to withstand "the tactics of the devil."[33] Those committed to restorative justice and peacemaking are forever struggling with the seductive logic of domination, especially the temptation to sacrifice the opponent in order to "win," or the pressure to join the armed cause of one's kinsfolk. The author stipulates at the outset that this is a "struggle" (Gk. *palē*, used only here in the New Testament). The word connotes wrestling—the most intimate form of adversarial combat. Yet he immediately clarifies that this "hand-to-hand combat" is not ultimately "against enemies of blood and flesh, but against the Principalities and Powers, against the world-rulers of this present darkness, against the spiritual hosts of wickedness in the highest places" (Eph 6:12). This represents a sort of taxonomy of the "domination system," which is in a protracted struggle with God over history.[34]

This is a specific rejection of the summons to eschatological battle against "flesh-and-blood enemies" advocated in the Qumran scrolls (e.g., the War Scroll, 1QM 12:11f.). And, we might add, promoted by modern Christian millenialists and holy warriors, including the religious ideologues of the presidential administration of George W. Bush. Instead, this exhortation is about standing one's ground, being centered, and maintaining equilibrium in the face of the propaganda of redemptive violence. Rationalizations for retribution are always rooted in the worst-case scenarios of murder, attack, or severe oppression, as we have seen in the wake of the attacks of September 11, 2001.[35] In the light of Christ's peacemaking work on the cross, Ephesians calls for resistance to enmity itself: the ideology of alienation wrought by oppressive and toxic power, and spread through systems, technologies, and worldviews of superiority and domination. We should not overpersonalize the struggle (imagining the problem is defined by Sadaam Hussein or George Bush), nor depersonalize our adversaries, for they are also part of the beloved community. But it is surely sobering to realize that peacemakers—whether a victim-offender dialogue facilitator, a protestor crossing the line at a military base, or a civilian peacekeeper standing between hostile parties—are in fact taking on this entire cosmology of institutional and ideological hostility.

For a second time, we are told to "take up" the whole armor, now not as clothing but as a defensive instrument (6:13). There is a keen emphasis on "standing against" (Gk. *antistēnai*) and "standing" (Gk. *stēnai*)—battlefield metaphors used by Roman foot soldiers (6:14a; we still refer to "standing" or "falling" in combat). Now we come to the elements of "divine armor":

1. The "belt of truth" resonates with Gandhi's conviction that at the core of nonviolence is *satyagraha*, "experiments with truth." It is an allusion to the Septuagint version of Isaiah 11:5. This is part of the larger "stump of Jesse" oracle concerning messianic redemption (Isa 11:1), which has been so important to Christian theology. There we are told that "with justice God's representative will judge the poor and decide with equity for the meek of the earth" (11:4). The very next verses famously envision the peaceable kingdom in which predator and prey "lie down together" (11:6-9).

2. The "breastplate of justice" (6:14b) and the "helmet of salvation" (6:17a) invoke Isaiah 59:17. But the prophet's reference to "vengeance" is omitted by Ephesians.

3. Footware is the readiness to proclaim the good news of peace (6:15)—yet another allusion to Isaiah: "How welcome on the mountain are the feet of the one heralding peace" (Isa 52:7). This oracle refers to the duty of the noble warrior to know when to cease struggle and come to the negotiation table. In the social context of the Roman Empire, official messenger-runners would carry declarations of a cease-fire directly into the field of battle. But according to Ephesians, Christ has already declared peace "unilaterally" on the cross.

4. "And besides all these," says the writer in the midpoint of his litany, we must "take up the shield of faith, to quench all the flaming arrows of the evil one" (6:16). This time the allusion is to Psalm 91:4: "God's faithfulness is a shield." While the defensive aspect is obvious, Roman centurions also used huge shields to advance against archery assaults in laying siege to cities—thus the metaphor has *offensive* connotations as well. Yoder Neufeld interprets the image as a call to use our disarmed bodies to intervene between hostile parties (2002: 302).

5. "The image of grasping the helmet of salvation," says Yoder Neufeld, "is meant to place on the church the task of bringing

liberation to those in bondage by imitating the God of Isaiah 59"
(ibid.: 303). One might think here, by way of analogy, of United
Nations Peacekeeping forces, referred to around the world as the
"Blue Helmets," as a violence reduction strategy.

6. Finally, we take up the "sword of the Spirit, which is the word
of God" (see 2 Cor 6:7; Heb 4:12; Rev 1:16; 2:12). Even as we
nonviolently resist with our bodies we must use the power of the
word to persuade our opponents. Dr. King was the consummate
example of an orator's ability—and responsibility as a constituent
part of the overall struggle—to win hearts and minds.

The section closes with a last, twofold exhortation to prayer (6:18-20).
The audience is to pray "at every moment" (Gk. *panti kairō*), petitioning on
behalf of "all the saints" (6:18). The addition "to that end stay awake with
all perseverance" gives this a distinctly apocalyptic tone, urging vigilance
in the darkness of a historical moment of persecution, which as we have
seen is the context of this epistle.[36] In that mode, they are to pray specifically for Paul to have the courage to

> open my mouth boldly (Gk. *parrēsia*)
> to proclaim the mystery of the gospel
> for which I am an ambassador in chains
> so I might declare it boldly. (Gk. *parrēsiasōmai*; 6:19f.)[37]

The message of Christ's abolition of enmity is not warmly received by
those in authority. The image of an "ambassador in chains," as Wansink
points out, represents an ironic expression of status confusion (1996: 161).
It also echoes Paul's exhortation in 2 Corinthians 5:20 (above, 1B), com-
pleting the circle of this volume's scope.

The great sixteenth-century leader of the Radical Reformation, Menno
Simons, once tried to explain the nonviolence of his Anabaptist colleagues
to European lords in this way:

> These people know no other weapons than patience, hope, silence
> and God's Word . . . Our weapons are not weapons with which one
> destroys cities and countries, smashes walls and gates or spills human
> blood like water, but they are weapons with which one destroys the
> kingdom of the devil . . . we neither possess nor recognize any other
> weapons . . . Our fortress is Christ; our defense is patience; our
> sword is God's Word, and our victory is an open, firm clear belief in
> Christ Jesus. We leave iron, metal, pikes and swords to those who

unfortunately consider human blood to be worth no more than the blood of pigs. (Goertz, 1996: 153)

It rings with an Ephesian tone. But the efficacy of these alternative weapons is never obvious. Gandhi insisted that "the spinning wheel is my sword," and that it "alone will solve, if anything will solve, the problem of the deepening poverty of India." But this lowly tool of economic self-sufficiency and spiritual centering did not seem too formidable to Britain's imperial military machine—until the spinning wheel became the symbol of India's successful struggle for independence.[38]

"The master's tools will never dismantle the master's house." So wrote Black lesbian poet activist Audre Lorde, in a famous essay about how to deconstruct practices and systems of domination (1984). It sums up a core conviction of nonviolent faith: building a "new creation" is dependent upon a community that abides in the peace of the cross and which is fully equipped with the "whole armor of God." From beginning to end, Ephesians means to ignite our imagination to search for these alternative tools of transformation, and to experiment with them in the real world of conflict and hostility.

Believing that Christ has dismantled the bearing wall of American apartheid and armed with the "whole armor of God," Dr. King "stood firm" in the face of hatred and opposition, even from members of his own faith. He was a magnificent "ambassador of reconciliation," though this vision took him to prison and ultimately to the cross, as it did Jesus, and as it did the apostle whose vision is enshrined in the Epistle to the Ephesians.

We end this last chapter where we began: at the wall. It is a few nights before Christmas. A small group of us are singing thinly, clutching candles against a chilly drizzle. We make our way slowly up a muddy hill. Below us an orange glow floats like fog above the border checkpoint at San Ysidro, California. "*En nombre del cielo, les pido posada. Pues no puede andar mi esposa amada*" ("In the name of Heaven I beg you for lodging, for my beloved wife cannot walk"). We have come to this barren hilltop on a *posada* march. This traditional Mexican liturgy is celebrated throughout the Catholic Southwest during the last nine days of Advent, a kind of public ritual theater. People accompany statues of the Holy Family from house to house around the *barrio*, waiting to be recognized and allowed in so that the Christ child may be born. But this *posada* has intentionally relocated to a "door" that is closed and heavily guarded: the U.S.-Mexican border. For the last fifteen years, it has been organized by immigrants' rights groups to protest the abuse and criminalization of undocumented immigrants.

Holding aloft three large *piñatas* representing Mary, Joseph and the innkeeper, we are a congregation gathered on both sides of this menacing border fence. The metal wall was donated to the U.S. Border Patrol by the Pentagon after Desert Storm, one war's surplus bolstering another war's front lines. To Joseph's petition for shelter, sung by a group of catechists, priests and community workers on the Tijuana side of the border, we on the U.S. side intone the response of the innkeeper: *"Aquí no es mesón; sigan adelante. Yo no puedo abrir; no sea algún tunante"* ("This is not an inn, so keep going. I cannot open, for you may be bad people"). For as far as we can see, the border is bathed by floodlights and buzzing with Border Patrol vehicles and helicopters. These "innkeepers" spend millions of taxpayer dollars in an effort to reduce illegal entries across this, the world's most heavily used border crossing. Their mission is, ironically, to keep out the very ones who, a century earlier, were expressly invited *into* the United States by the extraordinary verse of the immigrant poet Emma Lazarus that is inscribed on the Statue of Liberty: "Give me your tired, your poor, your huddled masses yearning to breathe free . . . Send those, the homeless, tempest-tossed to me; I lift my lamp beside the golden door."

Joseph pleads his case: *"No seas inhumano; tenos caridad. Que el Dios de los cielos te lo pagará"* ("Don't be inhumane; have mercy on us. The God of the heavens will reward you for it"). We sing the litany back and forth across the wall, hearing but not seeing one another. To symbolize our solidarity, green ribbons are passed through small holes in the fence. "We pray that the day will come when we can have a *posada sin fronteras* (without borders)," the auxiliary bishop of San Diego tells the gathering. "If we reject the poor, we are rejecting Jesus Christ himself." Turning up the collar of our coats against the cold, we marvel at this liturgy of hope, celebrated along a wall that runs right through the heart of this congregation.

"Ya se pueden ir, y no molestar," threatens the innkeeper. *"Porque si me enojo les voy a pegar"* ("Better go on, and don't bother us. For if I become angry, I shall beat you up"). Behind us a knot of Border Patrol officers keep a watchful eye. *"Dichosa la casa que abriga este día,"* sings the Mexican side, *"Dichosa esta casa que nos posada"* ("Blessed is the house that today offers protection; blessed is this house that gives us shelter"). As the liturgy finishes, doves are released on both sides of the fence and fly off, defying the barrier. Candy showers us, launched over from the Mexican side. Roberto Martinez, a farmworker's son turned legendary immigrant rights activist, and a beloved colleague, addresses the gathering. He has often toured us around this border war zone, and into the canyons of northern San Diego county, where farmworkers live in caves and plastic tents, just yards away

from affluent trophy homes. Roberto tirelessly works to document Border Patrol abuses, seeing hundreds of violations each year, small (verbal abuse, illegal confiscation of documents, deportation of legal residents) and large (maimings, rapes, deaths in pursuit or custody). His compassion for the "least" is palpable.

As we leave in the thrumming rain, we look back on this barren terrain. It is the only place where First and Third World stand adjacent, a free fire zone in the war against the poor and refugee, the neoliberal global economic order's Berlin Wall. It brings *posadas* painfully alive. Like the gospel story it enacts, this liturgy poses a hard challenge to North American Christians who are stuck with the role of the "inhospitable innkeeper." In the words of Ephesians: "You did not learn this in Christ—assuming that you were taught the truth of Jesus!" (Eph 4:20f.). This border may be sacred to many in our nation-state, but it represents a theological dilemma for a church that is supposed to be an undivided world house. The gospel of Ephesians is unequivocal. In Christ this wall cannot stand.

CONCLUSION

The Lorraine motel in Memphis, Tennessee, where Martin Luther King spent his last night, has been (after a protracted community struggle) turned into the National Civil Rights Museum. Just below the balcony where he was gunned down is a memorial plaque, inscribed simply with the taunt of Joseph's scheming brothers: "Behold, here cometh the dreamer . . . Let us slay him . . . and we shall see what will become of his dreams" (Gen 37:19-20). Indeed, the question of what will become of King's dream hangs over our nation and our churches like an unresolved chord.

This volume has tried to show that the vision of restorative justice and peacemaking lies at the heart of the New Testament witness, articulated variously in 2 Corinthians 5-6, Mark 1-3, Matthew 18, and Ephesians. We have also offered the work and words of Martin Luther King as a foil, since he represents the greatest North American embodiment of this biblical faith and practice. This vision was embraced by most Christians prior to the fourth century C.E. "An enemy must be aided, so that he may not continue as an enemy," said Clement of Alexandria (ca. 150–211); "for by help, good feeling is compacted and enmity dissolved" (Roberts et al., 2.370). "We who formerly murdered one another now refrain from making war even upon our enemies," agreed Justin Martyr (100–165; ibid., 1.176).

This way of discipleship became increasingly marginalized after the church made its fateful pact with empire during the time of Constantine. Nevertheless, the biblical vision has continued to animate "ambassadors of reconciliation" throughout the history of Christendom, from St. Benedict to St. Francis, from Menno Simons to John Woolman, and from Harriet Tubman to Sojourner Truth. In our era, too, we can name exemplars: Catholics such as César Chávez, Dorothy Day, Oscar Romero, and Dorothy Stang; Protestants such as Dietrich Bonhoeffer, Clarence Jordan, and Julia Esquivel; and the Peace Church traditions (Quakers, Mennonites, and Brethren), from whom came our most recent martyr, Tom Fox. Unfortunately, these represent the exception, not the rule, in Christian history. Indeed, far more church members have earned their reputations in the military or the criminal justice system than in forging restorative alternatives to them. Among North American denominations today, those engaged in trying to end the scourges of war, the death penalty, or the violence of poverty are still in a minority. Instead, most of us act like unwitting ambassadors of the *Pax Americana*—despite the fact it was constructed upon and is maintained through military domination, social oppression, and ecological destruction.

But there are notable and inspirational exceptions, and some of their stories are the subject of volume II of this project. There we relate the testimonies of nine contemporary North American disciples who represent diverse expressions of restorative justice and peacemaking. These ordinary people doing extraordinary work come from different denominational backgrounds, diverse geographical and generational contexts, and represent distinct modes of nonviolent engagement for justice and peace. Lawrence Hart and Nelson Johnson have responded to Paul's call in 2 Corinthians to "cooperate with Christ" in their attempts to bring truth and reconciliation to the painful legacy of historical violations. Elizabeth McAlister and Jim Loney follow the Jesus of Mark's Gospel in their work and witness for nonviolent direct action. Marietta Jaeger, Joe Avila, and Harley Eagle work with victims and offenders in the restorative justice spirit of Matthew 18. And Myrna Bethke and Murphy Davis have embraced Christ's abolition of enmity in Ephesians to defy dividing walls and build community with "enemies" abroad and those languishing on death row at home. These colleagues are, in our opinion, exemplary "ambassadors of reconciliation," from whose lives we have much to learn.

Volume II will also explore more deeply some of the conceptual and practical questions that arise out of this reading of the New Testament. Taking our cue from Jesus' reversal of Lamech's curse (above, 3D), we examine the dynamics of the spiral of violence in human society and history in order to identify the roots of violation (vol. II, 1). Inspired by Ephesians' vision of "taking up the whole armor of God" (above, 4E), we offer a model of holistic, "full-spectrum" peacemaking, and encourage practitioners to overcome the functional balkanization that has grown between various expressions of restorative justice and peacemaking (vol. II, 2B). And mindful of the way that our New Testament witnesses advocated transformation from below, we look at ways of mapping social power, so that our practices of mediation or nonviolent action can be more cognizant of dynamics of privilege and marginalization (vol. II, 3A).

It is important to study the New Testament in order to recover Jesus and the apostolic movement as visionary peacemakers—and peace disturbers. And we do well to honor an undomesticated Martin Luther King, a child of the church and a prophetic treasure to the nation, who followed the

New Testament story in life and death. But the challenge implied on his memorial stone remains: what will become of the dream of King, indeed, of the dream of God, in a world ever more captive to the "giant triplets" of racism, militarism, and poverty? May the testimonies of these "ambassadors of reconciliation" ancient and modern serve to inspire, instruct, and compell us to embrace ever more deeply a discipleship of restorative justice and peacemaking.

NOTES

Introduction

1. Web sites that offer overviews of literature and resources are www.non violence.org; www.peacejusticestudies.org; and www.gradschools.com/programs/ peace_studies.html. Three of the best overviews of nonviolence theory and practice in the North American context are Chernus (2004); Lynd and Lynd (1995); and Cooney and Michalowski (1987).

2. Swartley (2006) gives a comprehensive biblical overview of the concepts of *shalom*/peace, though with few practical correlations. Dear (2000) gives a popular portrait of Jesus as a nonviolent activist. The most comprehensive and significant effort to analyze restorative justice from a biblical perspective is Marshall (2001). Two briefer summaries in the same vein are Burnside (2007), who articulates a moderate Calvinist view, and Yoder Neufeld (2003), who expresses a thoughtful Anabaptist perspective. Recent theological explorations of nonviolent readings of the Christian doctrine of atonement are also important (overviewed below, 4C), as is the work of René Girard (2001; see Swartley, 2000).

3. The "socio-literary" methodology and hermeneutic analysis that also undergird these studies are articulated in Myers (1988).

4. Liberation theologians speak about the dialectical process of "practice and reflection" (see, e.g., Segundo, 1976). Ched took a similar approach of reading ancient text and contemporary context synoptically in his popular reading of Mark's Gospel (Myers et al., 1996).

5. In the fall of 1999, the King family, long convinced that Martin's convicted assassin James Earl Ray did not act alone, brought a civil suit to the Circuit Court of Shelby County, Tennessee, 30th Judicial District in Memphis, in order to discover the real facts of Martin's murder. The family statement on December 9, 1999, in the wake of the jury's verdict, read in part:

> 1. We initially requested that a comprehensive investigation be conducted by a Truth and Reconciliation Commission, independent of the government, because we do not believe that, in such a politically-sensitive matter, the government is capable of investigating itself.
>
> 2. The type of independent investigation we sought was denied by the federal government. But in our view, it was carried out, in a Memphis courtroom, during a month-long trial by a jury of 12 American citizens who had no interest other than ascertaining the truth.

3. After hearing and reviewing the extensive testimony and evidence, which had never before been tested under oath in a court of law, it took the Memphis jury only 1½ hours to find that a conspiracy to kill Dr. King did exist. Most significantly, this conspiracy involved agents of the governments of the City of Memphis, the state of Tennessee and the United States of America. The overwhelming weight of the evidence also indicated that James Earl Ray was not the triggerman and, in fact, was an unknowing patsy.

4. We stand by that verdict and have no doubt that the truth about this terrible event has finally been revealed.

The story of this trial and its stunning verdict was virtually ignored in the U.S. press. It is told however in Pepper (2003). For complete trial transcripts, see http://thekingcenter.com/news/trial.html.

1. "Ambassadors of Reconciliation"

1. The story of this strike and King's role is best told in the 1993 documentary directed by David Appleby, Allison Graham and Steven Ross, *At the River I Stand*. After King's death the SCLC launched the multiracial "Poor People's Campaign," which culminated in a tent city in Washington, D.C., in 1968 (on this see Chase, 1998.) For a good overview of King's work and its enduring meaning, see Harding (2008).

2. The phrase "beloved community" appears to have been coined by California-born philosopher Josiah Royce (1855-1916), who saw it as the ideal communion between those fully dedicated to the cause of loyalty, truth, and reality—and which was closely embodied by the Pauline church! Marsh (2005) gives a good account of the evolution of this idea in King, and compares it with other contemporaneous currents of faith-based social change, such as Clarence Jordan. Marsh also compares King's and Jordan's metaphors for the Kingdom of God.

3. For more on the evocative parallels between the jail epistles of King and Paul, see below, 4D.

4. Friesen (2004: 359) challenges the middle-class lens through which the past generation of scholars studied Paul's social context, from Meeks (1983) and Theissen (1982) to Meggitt (1998) and Theissen (2003). "Twentieth-century mainstream interpretation that Paul's assemblies contained a cross-section of society," Friesen argues (358), has exhibited powerful capitalist biases in "ignoring the silent majority of the inhabitants of the Roman empire when reconstruct[ing] Roman imperial society" (337). His conclusion that most Pauline Christians were "living near or below the level of subsistence" (323) is based on more reliable economic and sociological modeling, and has stimulated renewed scholarly debate.

5. The Greek geographer Strabo (writing just before the time of Paul's ministry) attests: "Corinth is called 'wealthy' because of trade, since it is situated on the

Isthmus and is mistress of two harbors, of which the one leads straight to Asia, and the other to Italy. It facilitates the exchange of goods between these far-distant lands. Just as the straits of Sicily were difficult to sail long ago, so too was the sea . . . It was a welcome alternative to traders from Italy and Asia to avoid the voyage to Malea and to land their cargoes here" (*The Geography*, 8.6.20).

6. On the question of the date of the epistle, and whether 2 Corinthians represents one or a collection of two or more letters, see Witherington (1995: 328ff.). For much more detailed social descriptions, see the relevant chapters on Corinth in two anthologies edited by Richard Horsley on Paul and the Roman Empire (1997, 2000).

7. See 1 Thess 2:9; Hock (1980). Paul acknowledged that he had a "worker's right" to receive support for his ministry from his congregation, as he details in 1 Cor 9. However, he did not want economic dependence to compromise his credibility among the poor, so determined to offer "the gospel free of charge" (1 Cor 9:18) in order to "win the weak" (9:22).

8. An analogy comes to mind. Some years ago our colleague J. Herbert Nelson, a fourth-generation minister and national leader among Black Presbyterians, left an affluent and prestigious African American pulpit in Greensboro, North Carolina, to take on a tiny, struggling mission congregation in an economically devastated part of Memphis, Tennessee. Few of his colleagues could understand the choice, nor was the denomination willing to help fund the venture. "Liberation Community Church" has nevertheless found a way to self-sustain its ministry to the poor of Memphis.

9. The Greek term for grace (*charis*) appears no less than seven times in 2 Cor 8, functioning almost like a refrain. See Myers (2001a: 54ff.) for a fuller discussion.

10. The conversation within the Black community about how to overturn white supremacy is longstanding and complicated. It is trivialized when reduced to a putative debate between "Malcolm and Martin." On this see Cone (1992) and Bennett (1994).

11. Both verses begin with the Greek *hōste*, "therefore," which in Pauline rhetoric is "resumptive," meaning that these ideas follow necessarily from what Paul has been asserting in the epistle up to this point.

12. This misconstrual of the meaning of *sarx* lies behind a long history of Christian gnosticism and docetism, expressed both through ancient asceticism and modern spiritualism. It has been particularly hard on women, and all somatic and sensate ways of knowing.

13. ". . . though we once knew (Gk. *ginōskō*) . . ." alludes to what we might call "cultural epistemology"—how we know what we know in a given context. Paul most fully argues this issue in Rom 8, where *sarx* appears fourteen times.

14. The literature on apocalyptic symbolism and the New Testament is voluminous. For good introductions, see Myers (1988: 388ff.); Howard-Brook and Gwyther (1999: 46ff.); Beker (1982).

15. Each of our testimonies in vol. II, part 2 involves such conversion, whether it is Joe Avila deciding to take personal responsibility for having killed a young

woman in a drunk-driving accident (II, 4A); Marietta Jaeger's "wrestling with
God" to change her hatred toward the man who murdered her daughter (II, 4B);
or the journey of Nelson Johnson from political rage to truth and reconciliation
(II, 7B).

16. For a critique of this popular heresy, see Barbara Rossing's *The Rapture
Exposed* (2004); Howard-Brook and Gwyther (1999: 3ff.).

17. Alternatively, Swartley suggests a chiastic structure for vv. 17-20. "Each
unit of the chiasm includes some form of the word "reconcile" (2006: 202f.):

    a God reconciled us . . .
        b gave us the ministry of reconciliation . . .
           c God was in Christ, reconciling . . .
        b' entrusting the message of reconciliation to us . . .
    a' be reconciled to God!

18. We will explore the problem of "substitutionary atonement" theologies
below, 4C. For now it is enough to say that we understand God as "victim" in at
least two respects: 1) a loving creator is victimized when the creation is destroyed
or exploited; and 2) the originator of right relations is victimized when people are
dehumanized by violence, as a parent is victimized when a child is violated.

19. Young and Ford write:

> The Spirit is called a "down payment" or "deposit" (1:22). Paul's work as an
> apostle is called a *diakonia*, meaning "ministry" or "service" such as that of
> a slave who waits at table or acts as a messenger, a common form of labor
> in the economy of the time; and he sees himself as a poor man who makes
> many rich (6:10). The Gospel, as summed up in 4:5-6, is called "this trea-
> sure" (4:7) and chapters 8-9 show the connection between "real" economics
> and the gospel's "economy of God." (1987: 169f.)

They add that in 12:14f. Paul uses the metaphor of his ministry as an inheritance:
he will gladly be "spent" for the sake of his "children." Opponents of the gospel,
on the other hand, "huckster the Word of God" (2:17) and "cheat" in their work
(11:13).

20. For a thorough and applied discussion of this crucial theme, see recent
work on the biblical Jubilee and "Sabbath economics": Lowery (2000); Kinsler
(1999); and Myers (2001a).

21. G. Bornkamm calls it a "solemn official term": "The ambassador legally
represents the political authority which sends him . . . In the Roman period
presbeutēs is the Greek equivalent of *legatus* . . . commonly used for the imperial
legates" (*Theological Dictionary of the New Testament*, 6:682). Legates were usually
appointed by the emperor, and included legionary military commanders and foreign consularies (our word "delegation" is etymologically related). *Legatus* could
be synonymous with "governor" of an occupied territory, as Quirinius is called in
Luke 2:2. Luke uses the term *presbeia* ("embassy," meaning an official delegation)
twice, both in clearly political contexts (Luke 14:32; 19:14). These words derive
from *presbeutēs*, "elder," hearkening back to traditional societies in which wisdom

and diplomacy were seen always as a function of age and experience rather than of hierarchical rank or patronage (this is probably also Paul's meaning in Philemon 9). For a more detailed discussion, see Wansink (1996: 157ff.).

22. See, for example, Rom 12:1ff. and Eph 4:1ff. (below, 4E). An excellent explication of this hortatory style is found in Furnish (1968: 208ff.).

23. A parenthetical story is germane to our subject. The Greek imperative here (*katallagete*) was the moniker for an occasional theological journal that arose out of the civil rights movement in the mid-1960s. It was published by the "Committee of Southern Churchmen" and led editorially by Will Campbell and James Holloway, who described the naming in an article in 1978:

> It was 1964 and a few of us were sitting in a cheap hotel in Nashville talking about starting a magazine. We were women and men, black and white, young and old, Protestant and Catholic. There were a few things we had in common. We were involved, one way or another, in what was then called the Civil Rights Movement . . . We began to understand that the mission of reconciliation we were seeking to accomplish by *our* designs—well, that reconciliation had already been wrought, not by our efforts and schemes but in Crucifixion and Resurrection. We had been trying to effect reconciliation where reconciliation already *is*, by God's act in Christ. So what would we name a magazine trying to say *that*? We kept coming back to a word Paul had used in one of his letters to his friends, fellow sufferers and believers in Corinth: *Katallagete*.

This grassroots but influential magazine provided a forum for progressive social thought on race, violence, and economic justice in and beyond the South, and included many notable (though mostly white and male) contributors, such as Thomas Merton, William Stringfellow, Daniel and Philip Berrigan, Vernard Eller, Jacques Ellul, W. H. Ferry, Duncan Gray, John Howard Griffin, Fannie Lou Hamer, Joe Hendricks, Jim Herndon, Christopher Lasch, Julius Lester, John Lewis, J. Louis Martyn, Reinhold Neibuhr, Walker Percy, and Robert Penn Warren. *Katallagete* was published sporadically through 1990 (there are now attempts to resurrect it: www.katallagete.org/). On this history, see Miller (2004) and the archives: www.olemiss.edu/depts/general_library/files/archives/collections/guides/latesthtml/MUM00249.html.

24. For example, Jim Loney's prayers on behalf of his captors in Iraq (II, 5B); Peace Chief Lawrence Hart embracing the grandsons of those who killed his ancestors (II, 7A); Myrna Bethke's decision to stand with victims of U.S. bombing in Afghanistan (II, 5A); and Nelson Johnson reaching out to the Klansmen who murdered his colleagues (II, 7B).

25. This powerful realization is what brought Marietta Jaeger to a new understanding of the man who murdered her daughter (II, 4B), and motivated Murphy Davis to reach out to the poor on Georgia's death row (II, 6B).

26. The Greek participle is *synergountes*, a verb rare in the New Testament (see Rom 8:28; Jas 2:22). The noun "co-workers" (Gk. *synergos*) is almost always used by Paul to describe his companions in mission (Rom 16:3, 9, 21; 2 Cor 8:23;

Phil 2:25; 4:3; 1 Thess 3:2; Phlm 1, 24); only here and in 1 Cor 3:9 does it carry the implication of "co-worker with God." Paul is urging what Girard calls the "mimetic" response: reproducing in one's own life what one has observed in that of another (see Robin Collins, 2000).

27. The Greek *kenos* means "empty"; see also 1 Cor 1:17. Paul's stern caution is not unlike Jesus' warning parable in Matt 18:21ff. (below, 3E).

28. "Look! Now!" is repeated in Paul's Greek:

idou nyn kairos euprosdektos
idou nyn hēmera sōtērias

The Septuagint (Greek version) of the Isaiah text uses almost identical phrases: "acceptable time" (*kairō dektō*) and "day of salvation" (*hēmera sōtērias*).

29. This is the second of three such litanies in 2 Corinthians: see also 4:8-11 and 11:23-27.

30. Similarly, Myrna Bethke and Jim Loney practiced "unauthorized" peace diplomacy—indeed, solidarity with their country's "enemy"—when they traveled to Afghanistan and Iraq respectively in the wake of the terrorist attacks of September 11, 2001 (II, chapter 5).

31. Greek: *en thlipsesin, en anangkais, en stenochōriais*. The first and third are found together also in Rom 2:9 and 8:35. The middle word can mean "necessity" and/or "suffering."

32. Paul here invokes traditional "virtue lists" found in catechetical traditions such as Gal 5:22f.; Phil 4:8; Col 3:12-15; and Eph 4:1-3. The "weaponry of the Spirit" is a favorite metaphor of Paul, and he reiterates his "nonviolent warrior" identity in 2 Cor 10:3-6. See also 1 Thess 5:8; Rom 13:12; and especially Eph 6:13-17 (below, 4E).

33. Washington (1986: 226). This view also animates Elizabeth McAlister's struggle against the omnipotence of nuclear weaponry, and undergirds her embrace of nonviolence as a way of life both in prison and in daily community living (II, 6A).

34. Gk. *stenochōreisthe*, "to confine" or "crowd." Could this allude to the Hebrew Bible's metaphor for Egypt as *Mizraim*, the "narrow, restricting space" of imperial captivity? Or, literally, to restricted quarters? Paul was placed under house-arrest more than once by the imperial authorities (see Acts 21:31-33; 28:16ff.), and his "rap sheet" would have been an embarrassment to Roman citizens in his Corinthian church (below, 4D).

35. The introduction of a new topic in 2 Cor 6:14 signals the beginning of a new section of the epistle. Its abrupt change of tone has led many interpreters to see 2 Cor 6:14-7:1 as a fragment of another correspondence that has been inserted here. Witherington argues rather that it reflects the rhetorical style of a "digression" (1995: 402), one that reminds the Corinthians that restorative justice does *not* mean conformity with dysfunctional imperial culture. "It is doubtful that 6:14 is referring to marriages. Verse 16 suggests that Paul is referring here to spiritual profligacy in the form of attendance at idol feasts in pagan temples"

(ibid.: 404). As noted above, Paul has already addressed that issue in 1 Cor 8 and 10.

2. "A House Divided Cannot Stand"

1. John Raines (1984) gives the account: "On March 25, just ten days before he was killed, King had met with the annual Rabbinical Assembly in the Catskill Mountains of New York. The rabbis gave him a special greeting that evening, singing 'We Shall Overcome' in Hebrew. An old friend and ally, theologian Abraham Heschel, introduced him to the assembly, saying: 'Martin Luther King is a voice, a vision and a way . . . I call upon every Jew to hearken to his voice, to share his vision, to follow in his way. The whole future of America will depend upon the impact and influence of Dr. King.'"

2. For the text and audio excerpt, go to www.drmartinlutherkingjr.com/beyondvietnam.html, or see Washington (1986: 231ff.). For an analysis of this speech in its historic context and its meaning for today, see Harding (2008: 66ff.).

3. For a brief biography of this remarkable person, see www.wagingpeace.org/menu/programs/youth-outreach/peace-heroes/lawson-jim.htm.

4. For a representative sampling of such debates over the last half-century see, e.g., Merton (1968); Marty and Peerman (1969); Yoder (1972); Brown (1973/1987); Wengst (1987); Horsley (1987); Swartley (1992); and Swartley (2006). The lack of interaction between historians and ethicists of the Bible, on the one hand, and King's movement, on the other, again attests to the ongoing gulf between the seminary, the sanctuary, and the streets.

5. For a detailed consideration of the date and historical context of Mark's Gospel, and of the generalizations made here about its social setting, see Myers (1988: 39ff.). Theissen agrees that both internal and external evidence support a provenance for Mark "marked by the proximity of war . . . probably after the capture of the temple in August 70 and before all military activities and events in the immediate aftermath of the war had ceased" (1991: 271).

6. For a detailed discussion of how a narrative world can provide testimony about historical social conditions, see Myers (1988: 21ff.).

7. Crossan stresses the essential collaboration between John's and Jesus' movements in their resistance to the intensifying Roman colonization of Palestine in the first three decades of the first century c.e. under Herod Antipas (2007: 115). Crossan points, for example, to Jesus' defense of John's ministry in Luke 7:24-27, which contrasts the Baptist with Antipas, the king he criticized, "who dresses in soft robes, puts on fine clothing and lives in luxury in royal palaces." Josephus, himself among the Judean elite, criticized Antipas as "a lover of luxury" (*Antiquities* 18:245).

8. We were visiting professors at Memphis Theological Seminary in Spring 2003, during the outbreak of the second Gulf War. We immediately began using

King's Riverside speech in our organizing and preaching against the war, aston-
ished by its resonance in our different context. Because of this message, however,
we were iced out of most of the city's white churches, even as we were warmly
received into Black churches. See Myers (2006b).

9. In Mark 6:3, the hometown crowd at Nazareth wonders about Jesus: "Is
this not the carpenter . . . ?" The Greek *tektōn* can mean skilled or unskilled construction worker. Perhaps the first modern theologian to propose that Jesus lived
in the shadow of Sepphoris was the African American mystic Howard Thurman
in his 1949 classic *Jesus and the Disinherited*. "It is utterly fantastic to assume that
Jesus grew to manhood untouched by the surging currents of the common life
that made up the climate of Palestine" wrote the great mentor to M. L. King
(Thurman, 1996: 18; see below, n. 18).

10. The lake (also called Sea of Genneseret, Lake Kinneret, or Lake Tiberius) is fed by the Jordan River, which flows in from the north and out to the
south. Some 209 meters below sea level, it is the lowest freshwater lake on Earth.
Due to this low-lying position in a rift valley, the sea is prone to sudden violent
storms, as attested in the Gospel stories.

11. Migdal's Greek name was Tarichaeae, which Hanson (1997) translates
as "processed fish-ville." It is situated on the northwest side of the sea. Crossan
calls it "the most important town on the lake before Herod Antipas built Tiberias
around 19 C.E. . . . [its] Hebrew name comes from *migdal*, a tower, presumably a
lighthouse" (2007: 98). It was likely the village of Mary "the Magdalene" (Mark
15:40).

12. Upon the death of Herod the Great in 4 B.C.E., Antipas had been passed
over as sole heir to the kingdom. Caesar Augustus instead divided up Palestine
between him and his brothers Archelaus and Philip. Antipas hoped to demonstrate to the new emperor, therefore, that he was the best candidate to intensify
Romanization of the region by establishing a rebuilt Sepphoris and then Tiberias
as Hellenized administrative and military centers.

13. The remnants of a first-century fishing boat, discovered in 1985 under the
Sea of Galilee, symbolizes the hard life of peasant-fishermen. The 27- x 7-foot
boat had both oars and a sail, and could hold up to thirteen persons. It evidenced
having been rebuilt at least five times from seven different kinds of wood in
all manner of patching, indicating cannibalization of other boats. Indeed, all
reusable material had been removed from this boat before it was finally jettisoned
into the sea, no longer reparable. This remarkable artifact, possibly from the time
of Jesus, indicates the marginal existence of the fishermen (see Crossan, 2007:
121f.).

14. For popular accounts of Gottwald's important and influential understanding of the history of early Israel, see Ceresko (1992: 99ff.) and Pixley (1981:
19ff.). For an overview of the debate concerning Israel's origins, see McDermott
(1998) and McNutt (1999).

15. Fictive kinship is an anthropological term connoting relationships in
which non-blood-related persons practice the kind of social solidarity usually

reserved for kin (e.g., sharing of wealth, cooperation, or hospitality). As a social strategy, it was practiced in the early church, as Bartchy has shown (2003).

16. In addition to the ones examined in this chapter, Mark narrates these healing or exorcism stories and themes: the story of the Gerasene demoniac (5:1-20; Roman occupation); Jairus and the two females (5:21-43; socio-economic disparity within Israel); the Syro-Phoenician woman (7:24-30; ethnic exclusion); the deaf man (7:31-37; ethnic inclusion); the blind man at Bethsaida (8:22-26; discipleship); the deaf and mute boy (9:14-29; the need to confront one's inner demons); and Bartimaeus (10:46-52; discipleship). For a full exploration of healing as socio-symbolic action, see Myers (1988: 141ff.). For anthropological consideration of the "two bodies," see Myers (1994: 84ff.).

17. This was a constant issue of concern for King, who was repeatedly the victim of FBI-choreographed "disinformation" campaigns. A notorious case was the billboard that appeared in Alabama with a picture of a young King sitting in a seminar labeled a "Communist Training School." It was in fact a photo from the venerable Highlander Folk School in Tennessee, which trained Rosa Parks and many other civil rights organizers, and whose work continues today. On this, see Branch (1998: 188-192); on FBI director J. Edgar Hoover's attempts to assassinate King's character, see ibid.: 708ff.

18. King was planning to spend an extended time of retreat with the Trappist monk Thomas Merton after the Poor People's Campaign, but by the end of 1968, both spiritual leaders were dead. Raboteau (1996: chapter nine) explores the fascinating connections between the two. The influence of Thurman was more direct on King; he was a family friend, having attended Morehouse College with King's father. After studying with Quaker mystic and Fellowship of Reconciliation leader Rufus Jones in the 1920s, Thurman began to develop seminal notions of Negro nonviolent resistance. In 1936, Thurman led a delegation of African Americans to meet Gandhi, where the latter said that Blacks could have a special role in spreading nonviolence to the world. Thurman's book *Jesus and the Disinherited* (1949) deeply influenced King and other leaders of the civil rights movement. King reportedly always kept a copy with him.

19. For background on cultural definitions of disease and cure from the perspective of medical anthropology, see Pilch (2000: 19ff.).

20. For the significance of this apocalyptic title, see Myers (1988: 155, 243f.). For more on the purity code and the debt code, see ibid.: 152ff.

21. Worship is suggested by the verb *doxazein*, "to glorify." The Greek verb *existasthai* could be translated as "unsettling astonishment." It literally means to "stand outside oneself," and in Mark it is used either as a euphemism for having "lost one's mind" (3:21) or to connote an extreme, liminal experience of consternation (5:42; 6:51).

22. Literally, Mark's distinction in 2:17 is between the "strong" (Gk. *hoi ischyontes*, which in 3:27 is a metaphor for those who rule) and those who "have it badly" (Gk. *hoi kakōs echontes*).

23. For background on this, see Myers (1988: 157ff.). It needs to be emphasized again that the struggle between Jesus and the Pharisees was an internecine

conflict over proper understanding of Torah and Sabbath practice, *not* "Christian vs. Jew" or "grace vs. Law," as it has too often been understood in the long Christian history of supercessionism.

24. See Exod 23:11f.; Lev 23:22; 25:35, 37. The "sojourner" in the Hebrew Bible refers to what we would today call an "undocumented immigrant laborer": someone who has been forced by economic conditions to leave one's own land just to find a livelihood. The Torah "principle of the remainder" serves as a warning against the temptation to extract for our own benefit every last ounce of produce or profit from the land we exploit. From the true Owner's perspective, a measure of the earth's fruits always belongs by right to the disadvantaged, not as charity, but justice. For more on this Sabbath dispute, see Myers (1988: 159ff.) and Meier (2004).

25. Queller is currently finishing this material as a dissertation at the University of Idaho. Citations used with author's permission.

26. Queller stresses that Jesus' version substitutes active *doing* of good or evil (Gk. *agathapoiein, kakopoiein*) for Deuteronomy's more abstract choice between good and evil (Gk. *agathon, kakon*). This may allude to the refrain of Deut 30:12f: ". . . so that we may hear the word and *do* it." The purpose of Sabbath lies thus not in what we refrain from, but in what we *do*.

27. Queller goes on to wonder whether Mark's story might be something of a midrash on Deut 29:18f., which cautions that sins of silent complicity will destroy the innocent and the guilty alike. This, he thinks, may explain the strange expression that Jesus is "brought to grief with them" (Mark 3:5, Gk. *synlypoumenos*). Jesus seems to understand that the ruling class's failure to change a system that is headed for disaster will result in the demise of many innocent people as "collateral damage." The plot in 3:6 suggests that foremost among them will be Jesus himself.

28. Queller recognizes that later in Mark Jesus commends the woman who anoints him for "doing a beautiful thing" (Mark 14:6). The next verse cites Deut 15:11: "The poor will always be among you, and whenever you want you can do good for them" (Mark 14:7; Gk. *eu poiēsai*). The issue of redistribution of wealth is addressed directly in Mark's story of the rich man, who refuses to give to the poor, and its epilogue concerning the disciples, who "released" their assets into a communitized "family" of mutual aid and abundance (Mark 10:17-31; see Myers, 1988: 271ff.; 2001a: 30ff.).

29. On this campaign, see Jesudasan (1984: 99). For an analysis of Gandhi's economics of *swaraj*, or self-reliance, and how it was subsequently developed in India, see George and Ramachandran (1992).

30. Horsley (2001: 137) contends that behind Mark's verb "to silence" (Gk. *epitimaō*, 1:25; 3:12; 4:39; 9:25) lies the Hebrew *ga'ar* from traditions such as Ps 9:6; 68:31; 78:6, where it connotes "conquering." However, *epitimaō* is also used in Mark for struggles within the discipleship community (8:30-33; 10:13).

31. Peter (8:32) and the other disciples (10:35ff.) imagine that following Jesus will bring them personal prestige and power, and the crowds imagine a trium-

phant king (11:9), while the authorities convict Jesus of heresy (14:55ff.) and taunt him about his "titles" as he is tortured and executed (15:18, 32).

32. Mount Pisgah is the end of Moses' journey, from which he looks over the Promised Land and delivers his lengthy farewell address to the Israelites (Deut 3:27; 34:1). Of course, Deuteronomy has numerous references to Moses' sojourn "up" and "down" Mount Sinai/Horeb, beginning with Deut 4:11, and especially 9:9-15 and 10:1-5.

33. The disciples are later sent out to practice exorcism and to preach (6:7ff.). That episode, like this one, is also "regenerative" of the discipleship narrative after a synagogue rejection story (6:1-6). That mission is closely knit in Mark's narrative to the flashback account of John the Baptist's fate at the hands of Herod, serving as a sobering reminder of the cost of discipleship (6:13-30). In that vein, it is portentous that the list of the Twelve concludes with "Judas Iscariot, who betrayed him" (3:19a). The Gospel will climax with the sad account of how not only Judas but *all* those who were commissioned on the mountain end up abandoning Jesus when the authorities come to arrest him (Mark 14:43ff.). Mark's story seeks to be transparent about how participation in this movement will have serious social and political consequences.

34. This matter is, of course, broached in the infancy narratives of Matthew (1-2) and Luke (1-2). The historical data for the constitution of Jesus' blood family are obscure, and given the pious tradition in Christendom about both Mary and Joseph, the question is highly contested. For an interesting analysis of the textual evidence, see van Aarde (2001). He notes that "given the importance of the father in Mediterranean culture, the cancellation of the role of an earthly father is inexplicable," and argues we must consider the possibility that Jesus was abandoned by his father. This would explain (better than Joseph's early death) several things: 1. Jesus' tension with his family; 2. his defense of the fatherless; 3. his censure of divorce as an abandonment of women (and children); and 4. calling upon God as his Father (ibid.: 116). Ultimately, we can only speculate on this question; any hypothesis must, however, like van Aarde, take into account the silences in the New Testament concerning Jesus' domestic family life and upbringing, and avoid the romanticizing of churchly tradition.

35. Bartchy summarizes his important findings:

> The historical-Jesus traditions and the writings of Paul both share and emphasize the same radical reversals of core traditional cultural values, including these:
>
> —The rejection of patriarchal authority and domination, and of the traditional obligations of filial piety;
> —The invitation to become members of a surrogate family not based on blood ties yet expressive of the inter-personal values of sibling kinship;
> —The redefinition of the basis for attaining honor: serving rather than competing;
> —The demonstration of authentic power that now was characterized by empowerment rather than by control of others.

Paul continued the historical Jesus' vision of the surrogate kinship of "brothers and sisters" according to which kinship based on blood ties was rejected in favor of relationships rooted in the personally chosen, intentionally embraced and shared commitment to the will of God. (2003)

36. Malina and Rohrbaugh call this "deviance labeling" (1992: 199f.). See also Horsley (2001: 136).

37. The prophet, like Jesus here, uses a story to make the guilty party condemn himself—the king's betrayal of Uriah and adultery with Bathsheba (2 Sam 12:1-15). For an ancient parabolic parody of kingship, see Judg 9:8ff.; for other prophetic parables critiquing empire, see Isa 5; Ezek 17; and the important study of Weisman (1998).

38. See Myers (1988: 164ff.). Here and elsewhere in Mark, *Kingdom* symbolizes the state (see 6:23; 11:10; 13:8) and *house* its symbolic center, the Temple (see 11:17; 13:34f.). Horsley speculates that the "ransacking" of Mark 3:28 may allude to the Judean rebels' looting of the imperial armory at Sepphoris in 4 B.C.E., who according to Josephus, "'made off with all the goods that had been seized [from people's houses and taken] there' (*Ant.* 17.271). Similarly the popular 'king' Simon burned the royal palace at Jericho and plundered 'the things that had been seized [and taken] there' (274). Just as these popular kings are taking back from the royal fortresses what the oppressive king Herod's soldiers had taken from the people, so Jesus is taking from Satan's house" (2001: 273f.).

39. In drawing these parallels between King and Jesus we do not want to be understood as arguing that the latter was "just" a nonviolent martyr, or that the former was messianic. King was a disciple of the Master. And there is more to the New Testament meaning of Jesus' life, death, and resurrection than what we have focused on here (see below, 4B and 4C). We are simply arguing that there are significant aspects of Jesus' ministry as portrayed in the Gospels that are more intelligible to us if viewed through the lens of the nonviolent activism embodied by King—aspects that are routinely overlooked by theologians and churchgoers.

40. "This note [i.e., the Constitution] was the promise that all men, yes, black men as well as white men, would be guaranteed the unalienable rights of life, liberty and the pursuit of happiness" (Washington, 1986: 217f.).

3. Reversing "Lamech's Curse"

1. In this introduction to the matrix of Matthew, we will draw significantly on the work of Warren Carter (2000, 2001).

2. Overman (1990: 2). He offers a good summary of issues related to Matthew's struggle with "formative Judaism," which have been central to Matthean studies for some time. The scholarly debate continues as to whether in the late 80s C.E. there was a formal effort by synagogues to expel Jewish Christians (based upon the hypothetical "Council of Javne" and the disputed meaning of one of the "Eighteen Benedictions," the *Birkat ha-Minim*, or prayer against heretics). It is

clear, however, that "formative Judaism, as J. Neusner has shown, was a precursor of the eventually dominant authorities within Judaism in late antiquity, rabbinic Judaism" (ibid.). Thus, Matthew's Gospel provides a glimpse into a fateful historical moment in which "synagogue" and "church"—both of which were in formation—began the painful and consequential process of divergence.

3. See the similar refrain in Matt 6:2, 5, 16. The Greek term *hypokritai* referred to actors in the Hellenistic theater. It was, to be sure, a slight, given that Jewish culture eschewed the pagan dramatic tradition. But it did not connote disingenuity or fraudulence, as in modern usage. The frequency of this term in Matthew (fifteen times vs. five times in the rest of the New Testament) suggests the influence of the theater in Antioch.

4. See recent discussions of these critical historical questions and attempts to recover a Jewish-Christian conversation by Bruteau (2001) and Levine (2006).

5. W. Carter cites demographic estimates that there may have been only between twenty and one hundred Christians in Antioch at the time of Matthew! (2000: 28ff.).

6. Another analogy for Matthew's "double marginalization" might be helpful. We became friends with Rev. Robert Two Bulls, an Oglala Lakota Episcopal priest, when he was Native American Ministries Coordinator for the Diocese of Los Angeles. Rev. Two Bulls was part of an urban Native American community which, as less than 1 percent of L.A. county's population, had to battle constantly against prejudice, invisibility, and discrimination. At the same time, as an Episcopalian, he was a tiny minority of this already-fractional demographic, and sometimes had a hard time gaining a hearing from traditionalists in the area who felt that he and other Christians weren't "real Indians." Bob strove to be a loving advocate for justice for his people while also defending his faith against their antagonism.

7. It is important to emphasize that Jesus is not opposing his teaching *to* Torah, as presumed by Christian supercessionists; rather, he is contrasting *his* interpretation of Torah with those of other teachers of the Law at the time. His pedagogic strategy here is quite straightforward: he acknowledges the prevailing moral orthodoxy that guides majority behavior on crucial issues, names it, and then asserts a specific counterteaching designed to wean us off it.

8. The anger named here is not the righteous fury of the prophets but an act of public insult (5:22), which in the honor culture of antiquity was the severest form of disrespect short of physical blows (see Malina and Rohrbaugh, 1992: 142). The Greek verb *diallasomai* ("reconcile") appears only in 5:24 in the New Testament. It is related to *katallassō*, which as we saw is Paul's preferred vocabulary (above, 1B).

9. "Accuser" (Gk. *antidikos*) is a protagonist in a lawsuit (see Luke 18:3; 1 Pet 5:8). To "pay back" (Gk. *apodidōmi*) suggests debt," and is used thus eight times in Matt 18:23-30, which gives a sobering portrait of debtors' prison, as we shall see (below, 3E). The "penny" (Gk. *kodrantēs*, a Latinism referring to a *quadrans*, equal to two *lepta*) further indicates a social location of poverty, as in Mark 12:42, the only other time this coin appears in the New Testament.

10. The word appears four times in Matthew's closing "parable" alone (25:36-44). Only Acts uses it more frequently in the New Testament, reflecting the prison experience of Paul and others (see Rosenblatt, 1995).

11. In 1 Cor 6:1-9 Paul expresses horror that conflicted Christians are taking one another to secular court. On the one hand, he cannot imagine why "saints," who are supposed to be preparing for cosmic justice, are unable to settle smaller "life issues" (Gk. *biōtika*) among themselves (6:2f.). On the other hand, Paul assumes that Christians will not encounter fairness in the Roman courts, which he notes are run by the "unjust" (*adikoi*) and presided over by those considered "of no account" by the church (6:4).

12. The race/class divide in American cities can, for example, be defined by the advice teenagers are given by their mothers if they find themselves in trouble: white youth are told to go to the police for help, while Black and Latino youth are exhorted *not to*. Many Native communities have rehabilitated their own tribal courts to resolve community issues, rather than perpetuating their second-class citizenship in the dominant system (see vol. II, 3B). For an analysis of racism in the U.S. justice system, see Gilligan (1997).

13. Significantly, this severe metaphor reappears in Matt 18:8f. (below, 3B). By equating the "lustful" male gaze on a married woman with predatory behavior, Jesus conflates the prohibition of both adultery and covetousness in the Decalogue (Exod 20:14 and 17). In the first century, the influential rabbinic school of Hillel interpreted Deut 24:1-4 liberally, allowing a husband to "dismiss" his wife for a wide variety of real or imagined failures. Jesus is here taking the side of the more conservative school of Shammai, which recognized only adultery as grounds for divorce, as a way of protecting the woman against male power. For feminist readings of Matthew, see Wainwright (1998) and Levine (2001).

14. See above, introduction to chapter 2. We position nonviolent resistance in the "fourth quadrant" of our model of full spectrum of peacemaking as the strategy of "last resort" (see vol. II, 2B).

15. See, e.g., Matt 13:36; 26:6. Crosby (1988: 70f.) views Matt 18:1-19:15 as a household code of sorts, in which teaching regarding church-order (18:7-35) and marriage (19:3-12) are bracketed by object lessons with children (18:1-6 and 19:13-15).

16. The *didrachma* (17:24) refers specifically to the Temple tax paid annually in March by every adult Jewish male (see Exod 30:13). After the failed Judean revolt, as already noted, this tax was expropriated by Rome to pay for the Temple of Jupiter Capitolinus in the imperial city. The text further refers to "tolls" (Gk. *telē*) and the *kēnson*, which could mean the census tax or the imperial tribute. The double entendre contrasts the empire's "children" (i.e., Roman citizens), who do not have to pay the taxes of subject peoples, with the "children of Israel," who do. Part of the (bitter) irony here is the fact that most of the native Palestinian aristocracy was also exempt from imperial taxes, earning further resentment from the peasantry, who bore the vast burden of tax and tribute (see Freyne, 1998: 89f.).

17. W. Carter has made a careful study of this conflict story, arguing that it counsels Christians to pay the despised tax out of political necessity, even while delegitimating Caesar's sovereignty (2001: 130ff.). We find this to be overly subtle; if its purpose was to nurture outer obedience but inner repudiation, this could surely have been done far more straightforwardly. On the contrary, the tax collector's question (17:24) implies real doubt as to whether Jesus would pay this tax, while Simon's domesticated assumption that his master *would* comply seems to require further conscientization (17:25). We think it makes more sense to see the symbolic action in terms of political parody: working fishermen around Capernaum subvert Caesar's demand by making a "withdrawal" from the free bank of nature, and coins appear where fishhooks usually are (see our comments on the political economy of the ancient fishing industry on the Sea of Galilee above, 2A). For more on biblical political satire, see Weisman (1998). We agree instead with E. Carter's (2003) equally detailed exegesis of this text, which rightly draws parallels with Matt 22:15-22. That more famous dispute—in which Jesus similarly does *not* have the coin in question—ends with a riddle: "Give back to Caesar what is his" (Matt 22:21; see the comments on Mark 12:13-17 in Myers, 1988: 310f.). E. Carter notes that there the Pharisees are trying to "snare" (Gk. *pagideuō*) Jesus in his words (Matt 22:15), and thus argues that *skandalisōmen autous* in 17:27 must similarly refer to the disciples, not the authorities. To scandalize "has as its root meaning 'to jump up' or 'to snap shut.' The associated noun was originally the piece of wood that kept open a trap for animals" (ibid.: 424). Thus, 17:24-27 articulates Jesus' (or Matthew's) concern that disciples might be "entrapped" by the authorities on this question. As peasant humor, the story functions to relieve Peter's anxiety, while making it clear that Jesus feels no obligation to pay the tax.

18. Alternatively, if 17:24-27 is included, the narrative sequence would be bracketed by the discipleship community's arrival at (17:24) and departure from Capernaum (19:1). The outline would be similarly concentric:

> A 17:24-27: Internal dispute, parabolic action/satire with an economic
>   theme
>   B 18:1-10: Internal dispute, teaching on deconstructing social stratifi-
>   cation
>   C 18:11-14: Teaching parable on seeking least and lost
>   D 18:15-22: Teaching on restorative responses to violation
>   E 18:23-35: Parabolic satire with an economic theme

19. See the citation of Isa 40:4 in the preaching of John the Baptist (Luke 3:5). This connotation of restoring social equity (not reversing the disparity!) is found in the Gospels (Matt 23:12; Luke 14:11; 18:4); Paul (2 Cor 11:7; Phil 4:12); and even the Pastoral Epistles (1 Pet 5:6; Jas 4:10). *Tapeinoō* is also used in the famous Christological hymn of Phil 2:8. In 2 Cor 12:21 Paul indicates that he will have to humble himself before those in the congregation who have been impenitent; rather than assuming a stance of moral superiority, the apostle seeks to "serve" even those who ignore his appeals.

20. The Greek means "to embrace" or "extend one's hand to," and is the great hospitality verb in the New Testament, highlighting a crucial aspect of ancient Mediterranean culture. It is used in this way in Matt 10:14 and 40f., and more than a dozen times each in Luke, Acts, and Paul. *Dechomai* also is used in terms of "receiving the Word" (e.g., Acts 8:14; 1 Cor 2:14; 2 Thess 2:13; Jas 1:21)— which often was associated with offering physical hospitality to the messenger (e.g., Acts 21:7; 2 Cor 7:15; Col 4:10).

21. Each verse is in the aorist subjunctive: if x occurs, y will surely occur.

22. See the etymology in n. 17 above, which refers to a trap used in hunting (see, e.g., Rom 11:9). Matthew uses the verb a dozen times, more than any other New Testament writer.

23. In modern society "misbehavior" is defined by violation of the law, which often gives priority to property over people. For basic differences between restorative and retributive justice, see vol. II, 4A.

24. The parallel between these two traditions is further strengthened by the fact that Matt 24:41/Luke 17:2 and Rev 18:22 both also allude to a mill being abandoned in an apocalyptic moment, the only other time this vocabulary is used in the New Testament. The Exodus image of drowning appears to invoke an ethic of retribution, which is strengthened by two further resonances. The women of Thebez used a millstone to crush the head of the wicked, self-appointed tyrant Abimelech (Judg 9:53). And the Roman annalist Suetonius (ca. 120 c.e.) notes that Caesar used millstones tied around the neck to drown certain opponents (W. Carter, 2000: 364). But we must make room for hyperbole in this earnest warning. The allusion to God's judgment on empire suggests that it is *systems* of dehumanization, not persons, that need to be done away with. After all, the great crime of Egypt, Babylon, and Rome alike was to turn human beings into commodities (Rev 18:13).

25. The valley of Hinnom, south of the city, was where dead animals and other unclean refuse were burned, and reputed to be a site where children had been sacrificed to Moloch (2 Kgs 23:10). Matthew invokes Gehenna no less than seven times in his Gospel, more than the rest of the New Testament combined.

26. For theological reflections on sin and addiction, see Myers (2001b). See further his comments on amputation as a metaphor for being "defective" in relation to dominant culture imperatives (1994: 175ff.), and his notes on Mark 9:42-49 (1988: 262f.).

27. Verse 18:11 ("For the Human One came to save the lost") is omitted in most modern translations because of weak manuscript attestation.

28. Gk. *ti hymin dokei*. As noted, Jesus' response to Peter in 17:25 also begins with this phrase—as does a parallel conflict story over taxes in 22:17. The formula is also used in the parable of the two sons in the vineyard (21:28), which similarly articulates the revaluation of social status in the Kingdom. Elsewhere the verb connotes a "surmising" or "supposing" (3:9; 6:7; 22:42, 44; 26:53). For a historical-critical approach to this parable and its relationship to Luke 15:4-6 and *Gospel of Thomas* 107, see Collins (2003).

29. Note the several levels of irony in the character of David: the man who

was a real shepherd before he became the putative "shepherd" of Israel is exposed by a parable about expropriated sheep! For Matthew, he thus represents the archetypal "lost sheep."

30. The notion of offender as victim is strengthened by the ambiguity of the Greek verb *planaō* in the parable. In the active voice it means to "lead astray or "cause to err." First Peter 2:25 echoes our parable: "For you were as sheep going astray; but are now returned to the shepherd and bishop of your souls." It appears with the connotation "to deceive" four times in Matt 24, and frequently in the epistles (e.g., 1 Cor 6:9; Gal 6:7; 2 Tim 3:13; 1 John 3:7; and no less than eight times in Revelation). In Matt 18:12 we have the aorist subjunctive passive form (Gk. *planēthē*), which means "to wander." Thus, the semantics acknowledge that an offender has both wandered *and* leads others astray.

31. The best translation of *hina apolētai* here (aorist subjunctive middle) is "lost," in accordance with the phrase Matthew uses twice earlier, "the lost sheep of the house of Israel" (10:6; 15:24; Gk. *ta probata ta apolōlota oikou Israēl*). But *apollymi* can also mean juridical condemnation and death, specifically of Jesus (e.g., Matt 12:14; 27:20), as well as the power of the sword (Matt 26:52) and of Gehenna (Matt 10:28).

32. Restitution—"to make whole or right"—is repeated ten times in Exod 21:33-22:7. The Levitical version stipulates restitution of damage plus 20 percent, adjudicated through purity rituals of accountability and forgiveness (Lev 6:1-7; 5:20ff. in Heb.). These ancient statutes also, it must be pointed out, "count" slaves and women as property, similar to livestock. Jesus deconstructs this tradition in his healing of the "bent-over woman" (Luke 13:10-17).

33. This liminal space figures in the stories of both Joe Avila and Marietta Jaeger (vol. II, chapter 4). Avila reflects on having to come to terms with the reality of his incarceration, using the metaphor of a medieval passageway called the "bridge of sighs." Jaeger explains how she came to oppose the death penalty: her daughter died chained and defenseless, and she did not want to see another human being killed in that same, horrible way. This identifies the central problem with retributive justice in general, and capital punishment in particular: it turns offenders into victims, and victims into offenders.

34. This is the title of a song by the great Australian songwriter Paul Kelly, on his LP record album *Wanted Man* (Vanguard, 1994). For a detailed analysis of the "spiral of violence," see vol. II, 1B.

35. For example, Pu'uhonua O Honaunau, the site of a traditional Hawaiian city of refuge, is today a national park on the big island of Hawai'i. Some indigenous peoples are reclaiming the practice of temporarily exiling offenders, adjudicated through tribal courts (see vol. II, 3B).

36. A good example of this approach is Jeschke (1988). Two recent studies share our conviction that Matt 18:15-20 should be read in the context of the whole chapter's teaching on power: Gibbs and Kloha (2003) and Ramshaw (1998). The latter concludes: "Matt 18 keeps the issue of the nature of power front and center by beginning the discussion of intracommunal sin and reconciliation

with the question, 'Who is the greatest?'" For a historical-critical study of Matt 18:15-18 and its relationship to Q, see Catchpole (1983).

37. A variant reading of John 8:9 is of interest, since this story paints a scenario of "crime and punishment." Some manuscripts add that those who were about to stone the woman caught in adultery were "convicted in their own consciences" and backed down (see similarly Jas 2:9). While this whole episode may be a later addition to John, it gives an example of how the early church saw Jesus subverting the legal process of retributive justice. First Corinthians 14:24 offers a related but different scenario: prophetic truthtelling can "convict" nonbelievers into "accountability."

38. The Gk. *parakouō*, "to disregard," appears only here in the New Testament. See also Esth 3:8.

39. The verb *katartizō* is variously used in the New Testament to connote "to mend" (e.g., Matt 4:21) or to "perfect" (in the sense of completion; 2 Cor 13:11; Heb 13:21).

40. Again we hear echoes of this in the Pastorals, such as Titus 3:10f.: "As for the person who is factious [Gk. *hairetikos*, only here in the New Testament, from whence our word "heretic"], after admonishing him once or twice, shun him." This last verb (Gk. *paraiteomai*) is used by Luke as "excusing" (Luke 14:18f.), and in Timothy and Hebrews as "refusing" or "resisting" (1 Tim 4:7; 5:11; 2 Tim 2:23; Heb 12:19, 25).

41. The word *ethnikos* is used only by Matthew (also in 6:7). *Telōnēs* ("tax collector") on the other hand, appears nine times in Matthew, ten times in Luke.

42. This authority has already been invoked in Matt 16:17-19, where the term *ekklēsia* also appears (the only two places it is used in the entire gospel tradition). For parallels between these two traditions, see Matthew (1985) and Derrett (1983). John 20:23 invokes a similar authority to "forgive" or "maintain" sins, though using different verbs. W. Carter notes that "Hellenistic-Roman cities administered their affairs often through council/assemblies (or *ekklēsiai*; see 16:18), which exercised disciplinary power including exclusion (Sir 23:24; Acts 19:38-39; Josephus, *Ant.* 19.332)" (2000:367).

43. Overman (1990: 106). The verbs "bind" and "loose" are also found together in Matt 21:2 (referring to a donkey), 1 Cor 7:27 (marriage vows), and Rev 9:14 (the four angels of death). Every other appearance of the Greek verb *deō* ("to bind") in Matthew connotes either "tying up" (in the agricultural sense, 13:30) or being led to prison (12:29; 14:3; 22:13; 27:2). Eleven of twelve times in Acts it means incarceration or custody. Some exegetes argue that "binding and loosing" refers to a process of determining how scriptural commandments apply to ethical situations (Powell, 2003; Derrett, 1983; Hiers, 1985). But Basser (1985) shows that the vocabulary in both Testaments and the rabbis is specifically juridical.

44. The Greek term *pragma* often connotes a litigated case, as it does in Paul's parallel warning in 1 Cor 6:1 that Christians should not go to court against one another. It can also refer to a business matter (1 Thess 4:6, and perhaps Acts 5:4; Rom 16:2; Jas 3:16), suggesting that there may be a "reparation" function implied here as well. The claim that God is uniquely present in this process is not a small

one, given the backdrop of counterclaims in Matthew's time that the gods were immanent only in imperial temples or established institutions. W. Carter (2000: 369) suggests that there may also be a polemical edge directed to the synagogue in the phrase "wherever you are gathered" (Gk. *synagō*).

45. The Greek *prosakis* appears only here and in Matt 23:37/Luke 13:34. The latter, in contrast, is an expression of Jesus' long-suffering grace: "O Jerusalem, Jerusalem, you who kills the prophets, and stones them which are sent to you, *how often* would I have gathered your children together as a hen gathers her chickens under her wings, but you would not!"

46. See our comments above on Matt 18:12-14. A notorious example is another Matthean tale, the Parable of the Talents. See the discussion in Myers of that passage for background on many of the same issues that pertain to our parable here (2001a: 38-51). For an excellent study of the socio-economic context and detailed readings of both of these Matthean parables, see Herzog (1994: 131-70).

47. For example, Luke's version of the fourth petition of the Lord's Prayer reads: "Forgive us our *sins*, for we ourselves forgive everyone *indebted* to us" (Luke 11:4). He similarly equates "sinner" and "debtor" in Luke 13:2 and 4. The semantic equivalence of sin and debt in the Aramaic background of the New Testament (an equivalence not possible in Hebrew) is widely recognized among scholars (e.g., Anderson, 2002: 12f.).

48. This verb is related to the adjective *homoios* used in Matthew's Kingdom of Heaven similes (six times in Matt 13:31-52; see also the parable in 20:1). It is not, however, exactly equivalent, because the verb *homoioō* can have a similar sense as the English "to compare," implying either similarity *or* contrast. It is also used for human comparisons (6:8; 7:24, 26; 11:16).

49. Gk. *synarai logon meta tōn doulōn;* this same phrase is used again in Matt 25:19, a parable narrating an identical social scenario. Such a reckoning was the ruler's unilateral right, and though this may have been a routine audit, the tone suggests that all was not well in the franchise.

50. One denarius is generally considered to have been the average day's wage for a peasant worker; a talent (six thousand denarii) would thus have equaled roughly fifteen years' wages. Thus, the amount in question here equals, from a peasant perspective, "more money than I will ever see in three lifetimes"!

51. The Greek verb *pipraskō* with the accusative usually means "to sell someone into slavery" (as in Rom 7:14: "sold into sin"). Otherwise it means "to liquidate assets" (see Matt 13:46; Acts 2:45).

52. This is the most tempting point of the story to infer an analogy to the divine. The ruler has "compassion" (Gk. *splangnistheis*), a powerful gut-reaction attributed often to Jesus' encounters with the poor (see Matt 9:36; 14:14; 15:32). Moreover, the verbs here—"to free from prison" (Gk. *apelysen*) and "to forgive debt" (Gk. *aphēken*)—are specifically associated in the tradition with "Jubilee." As noted, the scenario may indeed infer some sort of declaration of royal amnesty, an ancient tradition on which the biblical Jubilee is to some extent patterned (on this see Lowery, 2000: 37ff.). This temptation to theological allegorizing should

be avoided, however, and this vocabulary instead seen as part of the parody of a king who acts capriciously on his whims. After all, this same ruler will ultimately deliver the servant "to the torturers" (Matt 18:33).

53. Herzog (1994: 140). The retainer's imploring (Gk. *prosekynei*) plea—"Have patience (Gk. *makrothymēson*) and I'll pay you everything"—echoes the scene in which David refrains from killing Saul (1 Sam 26:6ff.).

54. The Greek word *basanistais*, only here in the New Testament, is in other literature synonymous with "jailer"—which says something about ancient prison justice! It is often associated with interrogation used of slaves. Torture as a noun (Gk. *basanismos*) appears a half-dozen times in Revelation (Rev 9:5; 14:11; 18:10, 15), perhaps reflecting the traumatic experience of the political prisoner John of Patmos.

55. Herzog dismisses this verse as Matthew's attempt to allegorize the parable; he thus interprets the parable without this editorial "addition." But our socioliterary approach does not allow us to resolve an interpretive problem by exiling a troublesome passage that does not seem to "fit" our reading.

56. A classic example of this is found in the Levitical Jubilee. Leviticus 25 outlines the positive actions of debt release and slave manumission that are enjoined upon the community every fifty years, with the promise that obedience will bring prosperity (Lev 26:3-13). But Leviticus 26:14ff. outlines the consequences of *not* practicing Jubilee: God will withdraw fertility, allow Israel's enemies to prevail, and "lay the cities waste." Apropos, the refrain is, "I will in turn punish you myself sevenfold for your sins" (26:24, 28). This "threat" was realized in the Babylonian Exile, and it does not really matter whether Lev 25-26 was composed before, during, or after that traumatic event. The theologizing perspective on history is the same: If the people live on the land without practicing Sabbath, YHWH will see to it that sooner or later the land gets its Sabbath—without the people (26:34ff.)!

57. Archbishop Desmond Tutu has become a global ambassador of this great ultimatum since the South African Truth and Reconciliation Commission, as eloquently articulated in his 1999 book by this title. For an analysis of the phenomenon of "political forgiveness" in the South African Truth and Reconciliation Commission, see Daye (2004).

4. ". . . and Abolished Enmity"

1. As of August, 2008, the U.S. Department of Homeland Security had built almost 350 miles of fence, mainly in New Mexico, Arizona, and California, with construction under way in Texas. The walls stop and start, with areas in between monitored by a "virtual fence," which includes sensors and cameras. There have been more than five thousand migrant deaths along the Mexico-U.S. border in the last thirteen years, with thousands of cases of reported abuse by Border Patrol agents and detention facilities (see Molina, 2003). These issues

deeply impacted Ched during his years of work with the American Friends Service Committee (see the conclusion to this chapter; also Myers, 2006a; 1994: 318ff.). For a reliable online resource on immigrant rights, go to http://www.afsc.org/ImmigrantsRights/.

2. See above, conclusion to chapter 2.

3. A representative example is Katherine Grieb, an excellent scholar and friend who would be sympathetic to the other chapters in the present volume (2002b: 148ff.). An understandable stumbling block, particularly for women and African Americans, is the "household code" of Eph 5:22-6:9, with its apparent refusal to challenge slavery and patriarchy. This passage certainly presents thorny problems for our liberative approach to Ephesians, which deserves more attention than we are able to give it here, for reasons of scope and focus; but see our brief comments (below, 4E).

4. In this chapter we will generally follow and elaborate the path Ched originally plotted out during the Reagan era, which looked at Ephesians' relevance to Cold-War-era Manichaean political dualism (1981). We also lean on the two detailed works that most clearly lift up Ephesians' peace perspective: the older two-volume Anchor Bible Commentary by Markus Barth (1974) and the recent *Believers Church Bible Commentary* by Thomas Yoder Neufeld (2002).

5. Such schools often grew up in antiquity around both Greco-Roman philosophers and Jewish or Christian sages, dating back at least as far as the "company of prophets" alluded to in the Elijah/Elisha cycles (see 2 Kgs 4:1, 38). They were the best means of carrying on the legacy of a deceased teacher or movement leader for minority communities that did not have access to the dominant "media" such as monuments or "official" literary accounts sponsored by great houses or royal courts. It is in this context that we should understand the biblical phenomenon of "pseudepigraphy" (writing an epistle in the name of a beloved, authoritative teacher; see the helpful discussion in Yoder Neufeld, 2002: 359ff.). While we do not think our position on the authorship of Ephesians is decisive to our reading of the text, we think the prospect that it was written by a disciple some thirty to forty years later actually strengthens the epistle's argument. It means that Pauline ideas continued to be compelling two generations later. For detailed and balanced discussions of the authorship question, see Barth (1974: 36ff.), who comes down (softly) on the side of Paul's authorship of Ephesians, and Yoder Neufeld (2002: 24ff., 341ff.), who comes down (equally softly) on the side of a Pauline editor/compiler. He writes: "Ephesians thus probably reflects an animated dialogue within the Pauline 'school' over the implications of the apostolic deposit . . . for churches at the close of the first century" (ibid.: 28).

6. We find it helpful to think analogically here: this is not so unlike our efforts in this book to lift up the genius of Dr. King's life and work forty years after his death, even as we recontextualize it to a new moment. In fact, we consciously aspire to be followers of Jesus "in the tradition of King," similarly perhaps to how the author of Ephesians sought to be a disciple "in the way of Paul."

7. See, for example, Prov 8, where the Hebrew word for "wisdom" is *chokmah*, which has a feminine ending, as does the Greek *sophia*. Jesus images *sophia* as the

mother of many children in Matt 11:19. The image of divine Sophia as a woman is beloved in the Eastern Orthodox Church.

8. This passage echoes Ephesian themes; *sophia* appears no less than fourteen times in 1 Cor 1-2! Ephesians calls this a new "administration" (Gk. *oikonomian*, the word from which "economics" is derived). It means "management of a household," which in antiquity was mostly handled by women, thus resonating with the female imagery of Sophia.

9. What began as a Public Broadcasting Service documentary series on nonviolence in history by this title has become a whole online resource center for how people around the world are using "nonviolent conflict to to achieve democracy and human rights"; see http://www.aforcemorepowerful.org/.

10. The "right hand" image goes back to Ps 110's image of messianic coronation, and appears often in the New Testament (see, e.g., Rom 8:34; Matt 22:44; Mark 14:62).

11. See, for example, the early work of James Cone (1969) and Cornel West (1982). Barbara Holmes's attempt to overturn the ethnocentricity of scientific rationalism from an African American perspective (2002) has an "Ephesians" feel to it. For perspectives on Black biblical interpretation, see Felder (1991) and Callahan (2006); for a white critique of white supremacy in theology, see Perkinson (2004).

12. John of Patmos has a similar vision of a world in which God dwells directly amidst the people: "And I saw no temple (Gk. *naon*) in the city, for the temple is the Lord God the Almighty and the Lamb" (Rev 21:22).

13. These and related works have given rise to an avalanche of responses and further elaborations over the last few years (see, e.g., J. Sanders, 2006). This critical conversation has happily stimulated wide-ranging theological reassessments in many church circles. For resources and bibliographies, see http: //www. preachingpeace.org/NVAStore.html.

14. Docetism (from the Greek *dokeō*, "to seem or appear") was embarrassed by the notion of divine incarnation because of the philosophical premise that the world and the body are evil. Docetists attempted to rescue Jesus from this conundrum by disembodying him; he became a sort of visiting spirit that was never fully resident in the Nazarene flesh that hungered, turned over Temple tables, and hung on a cross. "If Christ suffered he was not God," the docetists were fond of saying; "and if he was God he did not suffer." It is the Christian faith's oldest heresy, and also its most persistent one. It was rightly repudiated by the early church councils, but has nevertheless flourished throughout Christendom. We might say that orthodoxy won the battle and lost the war. The cosmic Savior Christ who dwells in our hearts but has no opinion about racism or the economy or the H-bomb has been thoroughly severed from Jesus the radical Jewish prophet whose political practice got him killed. The docetic tendency is present whenever believers take refuge from engaging the real world by spiritualizing faith and faithfulness—which is to say, most of our North American churches are functionally docetic. The historical consequences of discarding Jesus' body

have been myriad and terrible: the suppression of the body has resulted inevitably in the oppression of bodies and the disappearance of body politics (above, 2B).

15. Theologically this is known as the problem of "theodicy": the struggle to reconcile evil and suffering with an omniscient, omnipotent, and benevolent God. Liberation theologian Jon Sobrino, however, rightly argues that as it regards Jesus' cross, the problem should be redefined as one of "anthropodicy": how can humanity coexist with its own evil (1978: 179ff.)?

16. There are many other ways to "catalogue" atonement images in the New Testament. One worth noting is Gerd Theissen (1992: 159ff.), who identifies two major metaphorical types in Paul, each with three different manifestations: 1. change in social conditions (liberation, justification, and reconciliation); and 2. organic transformation (changing form, death and life, and symbols of union).

17. See Rom 2:8. The Greek *orgē* appears most frequently in Romans (eleven times) and Revelation (six times). Paul's most militant expression of divine judgment is found in 2 Thess 1:9, which uses the vexing phrase "eternal destruction" (Gk. *olethron aiōnion*). But this seems to be responding to a situation in which Christians are being "afflicted" (1:6), and so could be understood as a reference to the *system* of the Roman Empire (as in Rom 1-3; above, 1A). Again we commend Marshall's discussion (2001: 175ff.).

18. See the discussion of Lev 25-26 above, chapter 3 n. 56.

19. Roman writer Juvenal complains at one point that with so many people in prison, "that is how our iron is mostly used; and you may well fear that ere long none will be left for ploughshares, none for hoes and mattocks!" (Wansink, 1996: 47). The Roman underground dungeons were so identified with the horrors of perpetual darkness that they became synonymous with "Hades."

20. See Rev 1:9; 2:10-13; 13:15; 17:5f.; 20:4 for allusions to persecution and death for refusal to worship "the beast." On Revelation, see Friesen (2001) and Howard-Brook and Gwyther (1999), who point out that the only places the Greek term *aikmalōsian* ("prisoner of war") appears in the New Testament are Rev 13:10 and Eph 4:8.

21. This famous phrase comes from Jose Marti, the late-nineteenth-century Cuban independence leader and anti-imperialist, who knew the inside of prisons intimately (1975). Paul's imprisonments were legendary for the church that survived him, as reported for example by Luke in Acts 21:23 and 28:30. Emphasizing this jail legacy, and the moral authority it freighted, was an important literary aspect of later pseudepigraphic epistles (see, e.g., 2 Tim 1:8-12 and Col 4:3, 18). Jail was nothing to be "ashamed" of; indeed, it represented a *bona fide* of Paul's apostolic stature. And for Ephesians, it offered courage to a new generation under persecution.

22. We have learned this from our colleague and mentor Rev. Nelson Johnson (see vol. II, 7B), a Black activist for forty years in Greensboro, North Carolina. Though he has been physically attacked by the Klan and vilified by the white establishment, he continues working for racial and labor justice because he understands that those with race and class privilege are the most wounded of

all, and that African Americans who continue to organize in the tradition of Dr. King carry a moral authority that yet seeks to "save the soul of America."

23. The Greek noun *energeia* (here and 1:19; 4:16) and verb *energeō* (1:11, 20; 2:2; 3:20) appear more often in Ephesians than in any other book of the New Testament.

24. The same transition is made in Rom 12:1 (using the identical phrase *parakalō oun hymas*) and in 2 Cor 6:1, where there is a similar segue from the imperative to the indicative mood (see above, chapter 1 n. 22). The metaphor of "walking" is adopted from the peripatetic philosophers, and means "to conduct an ethical way of life" (the closest Greek equivalent to the Hebrew tradition of *halakah*; see, e.g., Rom 6:4; 8:1, 4; 1 Cor 7:17; 2 Cor 4:2; 1 Thess 2:12; 2 Thess 3:6). It is analogous to the gospel rhetoric of "the Way."

25. The Greek phrase here (*kopiatō ergazomenos tais idiais chersin*) is identical to that in 1 Cor 4:12, where Paul describes his discipleship commitment to manual labor. As noted (above, 1A), this practice was central to his renunciation of patronage, so as to avoid the pitfalls of class entitlement. See Rom 2:21, where the implication is that even the scribal class that upholds the official ethic is complicit in stealing.

26. See vol. II, 6A. The inaugural Plowshares action took place September 9, 1980, when Daniel and Philip Berrigan and six others entered the General Electric Nuclear Missile Re-entry Division in King of Prussia, Pennsylvania, where nose cones for Mk 12A warheads were manufactured. In the spirit of Isaiah's prophecy of beating swords into plowshares, they hammered on two nose cones, poured blood on documents, and offered prayers for peace. They were arrested and initially charged with over ten different felony and misdemeanor counts. They were eventually convicted by a jury of burglary, conspiracy, and criminal mischief and sentenced to prison terms of five to ten years. This action is examined through the lens of Ephesians in Myers (1987a); see also Laffin (2003). For more on the biblical rational for civil disobedience, see Myers (1987b).

27. We recommend Yoder Neufeld's treatment as thoughtful and critical without being dismissive (2002: 253ff.). We are sensitive to the resistance this text engenders; at the same time, we have been publicly scolded at presentations for daring to work from an epistle that includes such "oppressive" passages. But "banning" Ephesians because of the household code is, in our opinion, a huge hermeneutic blunder. Reading the whole epistle through the lens of the code would be like setting aside the Sermon on the Mount because of Matthew's difficult last judgment parables about "weeping and gnashing of teeth"—which few of our critics would advocate. We think it wiser to let the theological and political center of Ephesians direct how we handle parts that *seem* to contradict it, such as the household code.

Of course, we must remain clearly critical of the ways that this and similar New Testament texts have been used to oppress, past and present. But our political reading strategy does not concede the text to those who have interpreted it dysfunctionally in other cases, so why should we do so here? Rather, we should start with the assumption that the dominant "received" meaning probably has

little to do with how a given passage functioned in the earliest Christian movement. In that sense, we give benefit of the doubt to the ancient author, and apply
our "hermeneutics of suspicion" *first* to the history of interpretation. This includes
applying it to contemporary critical scholarship, which exhibits a (modernist)
tendency to feel morally or politically "superior" to texts such as this, despite the
fact that the social location of most academics is far more privileged than that of
any New Testament writer!

28. "Fear" (or "awe"; Gk. *phobos*) is contrasted with "pride" or "presumption"
in Rom 11:20. While "fear of the Lord" is found in 2 Cor 5:11 (see also Acts 9:31)
and "fear of God" in Rom 3:18 and 2 Cor 7:1, the phrase "fear of Christ" appears
only here in the New Testament. Paul uses the example of Christ's "downward
social mobility" in 2 Cor 8:9 to shame the Corinthians' sense of class entitlement.

29. Slaves/servants (Gk. *doulai*) are included in the code because those in
bond-service to a given family were in antiquity considered part of the household.

30. The Greek *prosōpolēpsia* connotes the core Jewish belief that "God is no
respecter of persons" (Rom 2:11; Acts 10:34), and in Jas 2:1-9 it is used twice,
specifically to excoriate a congregation for giving deference to the "rich who
oppress you" (Jas 2:6).

31. The original seems to be "General George Washington, Winter 1777-78,"
a copy of an engraving by John C. McRae after Henry Brueckner, first published
in 1866. Another version, which hangs in Ringwood Manor in New Jersey, is a
painting entitled "The Prayer at Valley Forge." It unashamedly depicts Washington in terms of Christ's prayer in the Garden of Gethsemene, complete with a
gothic arch of the trees behind, and heavenly light illuminating the scene from
above. "The Prayer at Valley Forge," painted by Arnold Friberg to commemorate
the 1976 American bicentennial, is now marketed as a "modern classic." We also
found a recent poster that portrays Washington mystically praying next to a U.S.
soldier in Desert Storm camouflage, against a backdrop of the American flag.
Such images, replete with patriotic and pious commentary, are ubiquitous on the
Web.

32. For more on Christian Peacemaker Teams, see the testimony of Jim
Loney (vol. II, 5B).

33. The phrase is reiterated in Eph 6:13a. The Greek term *methodeias* connotes deceitful, cunning stratagems, and appears only in Ephesians in the New
Testament. Here it is attributed to Satan, but in 4:14 it is correlated to methods of
human opponents that are called *tēs planēs*, which can mean "erroneous," "delu-
sionary" or "deceitful." Apropos, the most direct New Testament warning "not
to be led astray" (Gk. *planaō*) has to do with the heated propaganda that accom-
panies the outbreak of war in Mark 13:5ff. (see Myers, 2006b).

34. See 1:21; 3:10; 1 Cor 15:24; and Wink (1984, 1986). This list seems to
outline a "hierarchy" of political authority, from the local (Principalities) to the
regional ("Powers"), to the "*kosmokratoras* of this present darkness" (only here in
the New Testament, and probably a thinly veiled reference to the imperial politi-

cal machine). Alexander the Great adopted the epithet *kosmokrator* for himself, and it was taken by Roman emperors, though mostly in the late imperial period (see Horsley, 2000). Above (or within) all of these political institutions resides the spirituality of domination.

35. See the testimony of Myrna Bethke, who lost her brother in the World Trade Towers attack, yet refused to be drawn into war fever, choosing instead to travel to Afghanistan to stand with civilian victims of U.S. bombing there (vol. II, 5A).

36. The Greek *agrypnountes* means literally to "sleep out in the open"; doubtless derived from shepherding, it means "to keep vigil," and is used in the closing parable of Mark's apocalyptic discourse (Mark 13:33). The language in Eph 6:18 is very close to Luke 21:36: "Stay awake in each moment, praying [Gk. *agrypneite de en panti kairō deomenoi*] that you may have strength to escape all these things that will take place, so that you may stand . . ." (Gk. *stathēnai*). In both cases the verb is associated with the consciousness of imminent danger.

37. Both adverb and verb mean "openly," and in a public or political context where breaking silence can result in opposition or arrest, "boldly or courageously" (e.g., Acts 2:29; 4:13, 29; 9:27-29; 13:46; 14:3; 18:26; 19:8; 26:26; 28:31; Phil 1:20; Col 1:20; 1 Thess 2:2).

38. From *The Collected Works of Mahatma Gandhi*, XXV-351 and XXVI-292. These volumes are in the public domain and can be found online at http://www. gandhiserve.org/cwmg/cwmg.html or http://www.publicationsdivision.nic.in/ Eng-Pub/Sub-Wise/EG20.HTM. The spinning wheel was displayed at the center of the Indian National Congress flag at the time of independence, though it was later replaced with the Ashoka Chakra (the "wheel of the law" of the third-century B.C. Mauryan emperor Ashoka) to add historical "depth" and separate the national flag from the INC party flag.

REFERENCES

Anderson, Gary
  2002 "From Israel's Burden to Israel's Debt: Toward a Theology of Sin in Biblical and Early Second Temple Sources." In *Reworking the Bible: Apocryphal and Related Texts at Qumran,* edited by Esther G. Chazon, Devorah Dimant, and Ruth A. Clements. Studies on the Texts of the Desert of Judah 58. Leiden: Brill.

Bartchy, Scott
  2003 "Who Should Be Called Father? Paul of Tarsus between the Jesus Tradition and *Patria Potestas." Biblical Theology Bulletin* (Winter) 33:135-47.

Barth, Marcus
  1974 *Ephesians: Introduction, Translation, and Commentary on Chapters 1-3 and 4-6.* Anchor Bible. Garden City, NY: Doubleday.
  1959 *The Broken Wall: A Study of the Epistle to the Ephesians.* Valley Forge, PA: Judson.

Bartlett, Anthony
  2001 *Cross Purposes: The Violent Grammar of Christian Atonement.* Harrisburg, PA: Trinity Press International.

Basser, Herbert W.
  1985 "Derretts 'Binding' Reopened." *Journal of Biblical Literature* 104:297-300.

Bauer, J.
  2006 "Equality or Bust! The 1947 Journey of Reconciliation and the Effort to Desegregate the Jim Crow Transit." Unpublished paper presented at the annual meeting of the Association for the Study of African American Life and History, Atlanta, Georgia, September 26, 2006.

Beker, J. Christiaan
  1982 *Paul's Apocalyptic Gospel: The Coming Triumph of God.* Minneapolis: Fortress.

Bender, Harold S.
  1944 *The Anabaptist Vision.* Scottdale, PA: Herald.

Bennett, Lerone, Jr.
  1994 "Martin or Malcolm? The Hero in Black History—Martin Luther King Jr. and Malcolm X." *Ebony* (February): 68ff.

Berrigan, Daniel, S.J.
  1998 *And the Risen Bread: Selected Poems, 1957-1997.* Edited by John Dear with Ross Labrie. New York: Fordham University Press.

Bishop, Jim
  1994   *The Days of Martin Luther King, Jr.: A Biography*. New York: Barnes & Noble.
Bondurant, Joan
  1958   *The Conquest of Violence: The Gandhian Philosophy of Conflict*. Berkeley: University of California Press.
Bonhoeffer, Dietrich
  1963   *The Cost of Discipleship*. Revised edition. New York: Macmillan.
Branch, Taylor
  2006   *At Canaan's Edge: America in the King Years (1965-68)*. New York: Simon & Schuster.
  1998   *Pillar of Fire: America in the King Years (1963-65)*. New York: Simon & Schuster.
Brock, Rita Nakashima, and Rebecca Ann Parker
  2002   *Proverbs of Ashes: Violence, Redemptive Suffering, and the Search for What Saves Us*. Boston: Beacon.
Brown, Robert McAfee
  1987   *Religion and Violence*. Second edition. (1973). Philadelphia: Westminster.
Bruteau, Beatrice, ed.
  2001   *Jesus Through Jewish Eyes: Rabbis and Scholars Engage an Ancient Brother in a New Conversation*. Maryknoll, NY: Orbis Books.
Burnside, Jonathan
  2007   "Retribution and Restoration in Biblical Texts." In *Handbook of Restorative Justice*, edited by G. Johnstone and D. Van Ness. Portland, OR: Willan Publishing.
Callahan, Dwight Allen
  2006   *The Talking Book: African Americans and the Bible*. New Haven: Yale University Press.
  2000   "Paul, *Ekklēsia*, and Emancipation in Corinth: A Coda on Liberation Theology." In *Paul and Politics*, edited by Richard Horsley. Philadelphia: Trinity Press International.
Carson, Clayton, ed.
  2001   *The Autobiography of Martin Luther King, Jr.* New York: IPM/Warner Books. Available online at: http://www.stanford.edu/group/King/publications/autobiography/.
Carter, Edward
  2003   "Toll and Tribute: A Political Reading of Matthew 17:24-27." *Journal for the Study of the New Testament* 25:413ff.
Carter, Warren
  2001   *Matthew and Empire: Initial Explorations*. Harrisburg, PA: Trinity Press International.
  2000   *Matthew and the Margins: A Sociopolitical and Religious Reading*. Maryknoll, NY: Orbis Books.
Catchpole, E.
  1983   "Reproof and Reconciliation in the Q Community: A Study of the

tradition-history of Matt 18,15-17.21-22/Luke 17,3-4." *Studien zum Neuen Testament und seiner Umwelt* 8:79-90.

Ceresko, Anthony
   1992   *Introduction to the Old Testament: A Liberation Perspective.* Maryknoll, NY: Orbis Books.

Chase, Robert T.
   1998   "Class Resurrection: The Poor People's Campaign of 1968 and Resurrection City." *Essays in History,* vol. 40. University of Virginia. http://etext.virginia.edu/journals/EH/EH40/chase40.html.

Chernus, Ira
   2004   *American Nonviolence: The History of an Idea.* Maryknoll, NY: Orbis Books.

Chow, John
   1997   "Patronage in Roman Corinth." In *Paul and Empire: Religion and Power in Roman Imperial Society,* edited by Richard Horsley. Philadelphia: Trinity Press International.

Collins, R. F.
   2003   "Parables for Priests: The Lost Sheep." *Emmanuel* 109:11-21.

Collins, Robin
   2000   "Girard and Atonement: An Incarnational Theory of Mimetic Participation." In *Violence Renounced: René Girard, Biblical Studies and Peacemaking,* edited by Willard M. Swartley. Scottdale, PA: Herald.

Cone, James
   1992   *Martin & Malcolm & America: A Dream or a Nightmare.* Maryknoll, NY: Orbis Books.
   1969   *Black Theology and Black Power.* New York: Seabury.

Cooney, Robert, and Helen Michalowski, eds.
   1987   *The Power of the People: Active Nonviolence in the United States.* Culver City, CA: Peace Press.

Crosby, Michael
   1988   *House of Disciples: Church, Economics and Justice in Matthew.* Maryknoll, NY: Orbis Books.

Crossan, John Dominic
   2007   *God and Empire: Jesus Against Rome, Then and Now.* San Francisco: HarperSanFrancisco.

Daye, Russell
   2004   *Political Forgiveness: Lesson from South Africa.* Maryknoll, NY: Orbis Books.

Dear, John, S.J.
   2000   *Jesus the Rebel: Bearer of God's Peace and Justice.* Kansas City: Sheed & Ward.

Derrett, J. D. M.
   1983   "Binding and Loosing (Matt 16:19; 18:18; John 20:23)." *Journal of Biblical Literature* 102:112-17.

Dillard, Annie
  1989   *The Writing Life.* San Francisco: HarperCollins.
Dix, G.
  1953   *Jew and Greek: A Study in the Primitive Church.* Philadelphia: West-
          minster.
Douglass, James W.
  2007   *JFK and the Unspeakable: Why He Died and Why It Matters.* Maryknoll,
          NY: Orbis Books.
  2006a *The Nonviolent Cross: A Theology of Revolution and Peace.* Second edi-
          tion. Eugene, OR: Wipf & Stock.
  2006b *Resistance and Contemplation: The Way of Liberation.* Second edition.
          Eugene, OR: Wipf & Stock.
  2000   "The Martin Luther King Conspiracy Exposed in Memphis." *Probe* 7,
          no. 4 (Spring).
Elliott, Neil
  2008   *The Arrogance of Nations: Reading Romans in the Shadow of Empire.*
          Minneapolis: Fortress.
  1994   *Liberating Paul: The Justice of God and the Politics of the Apostle.* Mary-
          knoll, NY: Orbis Books.
Felder, Cain Hope, ed.
  1991   *Stony the Road We Trod: African American Biblical Interpretation.* Min-
          neapolis: Fortress.
Friesen, Steven
  2004   "Poverty in Pauline Studies: Beyond the So-called New Consensus."
          Journal for the Study of the New Testament, 26:323-61.
  2001   *Imperial Cults and the Apocalypse of John: Reading Revelation in the
          Ruins.* New York: Oxford University Press.
Freyne, Sean
  1998   "The Geography, Politics and Economics of Galilee and the Quest for
          the Historical Jesus." In *Studying the Historical Jesus: Evaluations of the
          State of Current Research,* edited by Bruce Chilton and Craig A. Evans.
          Leiden: Brill.
Furnish, Victor Paul
  1968   *Theology and Ethics in Paul.* Nashville: Abingdon.
Gandhi, Mohandas Karamchand
  2001   *Non-Violent Resistance (Satyagraha).* Mineola, NY: Courier Dover
          Publications.
  1983   *Autobiography: The Story of My Experiments with Truth.* Washington,
          D.C.: Public Affairs Press.
George, S. K., and G. Ramachandran, eds.
  1992   *The Economics of Peace: The Cause and the Man* [J. C. Kumarappa]. New
          Delhi: Peace Publishers.
Gibbs, J. A., and J. J. Kloha
  2003   "'Following' Matthew 18: Interpreting Matt 18:15-20 in Its Context."
          Concordia Journal 29:6-25.

Gilligan, James
   1997   *Violence: Reflections on a National Epidemic.* New York: Vintage
           Books.
Girard, René
   2001   *I See Satan Fall Like Lightning.* Translated by J. Williams. Maryknoll,
           NY: Orbis Books.
Goertz, Hans-Jurgen
   1996   *The Anabaptists.* London: Routledge.
Gorringe, Timothy
   1996   *God's Just Vengeance: Crime, Violence, and the Rhetoric of Salvation.* New
           York: Cambridge University Press.
Gottwald, Norman
   1985   *The Hebrew Bible: A Socio-Literary Introduction.* Philadelphia: For-
           tress.
Grieb, Katherine
   2002a   *The Story of Romans: A Narrative Defense of God's Righteousness.* Louis-
           ville: Westminster John Knox.
   2002b   "Deutero-Pauline Letters." In *The New Testament: Introducing the Way
           of Discipleship,* edited by W. Howard-Brook and S. Ringe. Maryknoll,
           NY: Orbis Books.
Hanson, K. C.
   1997   "The Galilean Fishing Economy and the Jesus Tradition." *Biblical
           Theology Bulletin* 27:99-111.
Hanson, K. C., and Douglas Oakman
   1998   *Palestine in the Time of Jesus: Social Structures and Social Conflicts.* Min-
           neapolis: Fortress.
Harding, Vincent
   2008   *Martin Luther King: The Inconvenient Hero.* Second edition. Mary-
           knoll, NY: Orbis Books.
   1990   *Hope and History: Why We Must Share the Story of the Movement.* Mary-
           knoll, NY: Orbis Books.
Herzog, William
   1994   *Parables as Subversive Speech: Jesus as Pedagogue of the Oppressed.* Louis-
           ville: Westminster John Knox.
Hiers, Richard A.
   1985   "'Binding' and 'Loosing': The Matthean Authorizations." *Journal of
           Biblical Literature* 102:233-50.
Hock, Ronald
   1980   *Social Context of Paul's Ministry: Tentmaking and Apostleship.* Philadel-
           phia: Fortress.
Holmes, Barbara
   2002   *Race and the Cosmos: An Invitation to View the World Differently.* Har-
           risburg, PA: Trinity Press International.
Horsley, Richard
   1989   *Sociology and the Jesus Movement.* New York: Crossroad.

1987   *Jesus and the Spiral of Violence: Popular Jewish Resistance in Roman Palestine.* San Francisco: Harper & Row.

Horsley, Richard, ed.

2001   *Hearing the Whole Story: The Politics of Plot in Mark's Gospel.* Louisville: Westminster John Knox Press.

2000   *Paul and Politics.* Harrisburg, PA: Trinity Press International.

1997   *Paul and Empire: Religion and Power in Roman Imperial Society.* Harrisburg, PA: Trinity Press International.

Horsley, Richard, and Neil Silberman

1997   *The Message and the Kingdom: How Jesus and Paul Ignited a Revolution and Transformed the Ancient World.* New York: Grosset/Putnam.

Howard-Brook, Wes, and Anthony Gwyther

1999   *Unveiling Empire: Reading Revelation Then and Now.* Maryknoll, NY: Orbis Books.

Jeschke, Marlin

1988   *Discipling in the Church: Recovering a Ministry of the Gospel.* Scottdale, PA: Herald.

Jesudasan, Ignatius

1984   *A Gandhian Theology of Liberation.* Maryknoll, NY: Orbis Books.

Kellermann, Bill Wylie

1991   *Seasons of Faith and Conscience: Kairos, Confession, Liturgy.* Maryknoll, NY: Orbis Books.

King, Coretta Scott, ed.

1996   *The Words of Martin Luther King, Jr.* New York: Newmarket Press.

Kinsler, Ross, and Gloria Kinsler

1999   *The Biblical Jubilee and the Struggle for Life.* Maryknoll, NY: Orbis Books.

Laffin, Arthur, ed.

2003   *Swords into Plowshares: A Chronology of Plowshares Disarmament Actions, 1980-2003.* Revised edition. Marion, SD: Rose Hill Books.

Leverton, Reed

2006   "'Today You Will Be with Me in Paradise': The Case for Consideration of Restorative Justice as a Component of Christian Doctrine." Unpublished paper posted at: http://www.restorativejustice.org/resources/docs/leverton.

Levinas, Emmanuel

1994   "Cities of Refuge." In *Beyond the Verse: Talmudic Writings and Lectures.* Translated by G. Mole. Bloomington: Indiana University Press.

Levine, Amy-Jill, ed.

2006   *The Misunderstood Jew: The Church and the Scandal of the Jewish Jesus.* San Francisco: HarperOne.

2001   *A Feminist Companion to Matthew.* Sheffield: Sheffield Academic Press.

Lorde, Audre

1984   *Sister Outsider: Essay and Speeches.* Berkeley, CA: Crossing Press.

Lorenzen, Thorwald
2003 *Resurrection, Discipleship, Justice: Affirming the Resurrection of Jesus Today.* Macon, GA: Smyth & Helwys.
Lowery, Richard
2000 *Sabbath and Jubilee.* St. Louis: Chalice.
Lynd, Alice, and Staughton Lynd, eds.
1995 *Nonviolence in America: A Documentary History.* Maryknoll, NY: Orbis Books.
Malina, Bruce, and Richard Rohrbaugh
1992 *Social-Science Commentary on the Synoptic Gospels.* Minneapolis: Fortress.
Marsh, Charles
2005 *The Beloved Community: How Faith Shapes Social Justice, from the Civil Rights Movement to Today.* New York: Basic Books.
Marshall, Christopher
2001 *Beyond Retribution: A New Testament Vision for Justice, Crime, and Punishment.* Grand Rapids: Eerdmans.
Marti, Jose
1975 *Inside the Monster: Writings on the United States and American Imperialism.* Edited by P. Foner. New York: Monthly Review Press.
Marty, Martin, and Den Peerman, eds.
1969 *New Theology No. 6: On Revolution and Non-Revolution, Violence and Non-Violence, Peace and Power.* Toronto: Macmillan.
Matthew, P. K.
1985 "Authority and Discipline: Matt. 16:17-19 and 18:15-18 and the Exercise of Authority and Discipline in the Matthean Community." *Communio Viatorum* 28:119-25.
McDermott, John
1998 *What Are They Saying about the Formation of Israel?* Mahwah, NJ: Paulist.
McNutt, John
1999 *Reconstructing the Society of Ancient Israel.* Louisville: Westminster John Knox.
Meeks, Wayne
1983 *The First Urban Christians: The Social World of the Apostle Paul.* New Haven: Yale University Press.
Meggitt, J. J.
1998 *Paul, Poverty and Survival.* Edinburgh: T&T Clark.
Meier, J. P.
2004 "The Historical Jesus and Grain on the Sabbath." *Catholic Biblical Quarterly* 66:561-81.
Merton, Thomas
1968 *Faith and Violence: Christian Teaching and Christian Practice.* South Bend, IN: University of Notre Dame Press.

Miller, Steven
  2004 "From Politics to Reconciliation: *Katallagete*, Biblicism, and Southern
        Liberalism." *Journal of Southern Religion* (November). Online at http:
        //jsr.fsu.edu/Volume7/Millerarticle.htm.
Molina, Ana Amalia Guzman
  2003 *The Power of Love: My Experience in a U.S. Immigration Jail.* Bilingual
        Version. Washington, DC: Ecumenical Program on Central America
        and the Caribbean.
Myers, Ched
  2006a "A House for All Peoples? Welcoming the Outsider." *Sojourners*
        35/4:20-25.
  2006b "Mark 13 in a Different Imperial Context." In *Mark, Gospel of Action:
        Personal and Community Responses,* edited by John Vincent, 164-75.
        London: SPCK.
  2001a *The Biblical Vision of Sabbath Economics.* Washington, DC: Church of
        the Savior.
  2001b "Beyond the 'Addict's Excuse': Public Addiction and Ecclesial Recov-
        ery." In *The Other Side of Sin,* edited by Susan Nelson and Andrew
        Sung Park. New York: SUNY Press.
  1994 *Who Will Roll Away the Stone? Discipleship Queries for First World Chris-
        tians.* Maryknoll, NY: Orbis Books.
  1993 "The Wilderness Temptations and the American Journey." In *Richard
        Rohr: Illuminations of His Life and Work,* edited by A. Ebert and P.
        Brockman, 143-57. New York: Crossroad.
  1988 *Binding the Strong Man: A Political Reading of Mark's Story of Jesus.*
        Maryknoll, NY: Orbis Books (second edition, 2008).
  1987a "Storming the Gates of Hell: Reflections on Christian Evangelism in
        Nuclear Security Areas." In *Border Regions of Faith: An Anthology of
        Religion and Social Change,* edited by K. Aman. Maryknoll, NY: Orbis
        Books.
  1987b "By What Authority? The Bible and Civil Disobedience." In *The Rise
        of Christian Conscience,* edited by J. Wallis. San Francisco: Harper &
        Row.
  1981 "Armed with the Gospel of Peace: The Vision of Ephesians." *Theology
        News and Notes* (Fuller Theological Seminary) 28:17ff.
Myers, Ched, M. Dennis, J. Nangle, C. Moe-Lobeda, and S. Taylor
  1996 *"Say to This Mountain": Mark's Story of Discipleship.* Maryknoll, NY:
        Orbis Books.
Oakman, Douglas E.
  1986 *Jesus and the Economic Questions of His Day.* Lewiston, NY: Edwin
        Mellen.
Overman, Andrew
  1990 *Matthew's Gospel and Formative Judaism: The Social World of the
        Matthean Community.* Minneapolis: Augsburg Fortress.

Pepper, William F.
    2003   *An Act of State: The Execution of Martin Luther King.* New York: Verso.
Perkinson, James
    2004   *White Theology: Outing Supremacy in Modernity.* New York: Palgrave
            Macmillan.
Pilch, John J.
    2000   *Healing in the New Testament: Insights from Medical and Mediterranean
            Anthropology.* Minneapolis: Fortress.
Pixley, George
    1981   *God's Kingdom: A Guide for Biblical Study.* Maryknoll, NY: Orbis
            Books.
Powell, M. A.
    2003   "Binding and Loosing: A Paradigm for Ethical Discernment from the
            Gospel of Matthew." *Currents in Theology and Mission* 30:438-45.
Prejean, Helen, C.S.J.
    1995   "Dead Man Walking." Speech delivered at an interreligious service to
            protest the death penalty in Albany, New York, January 24, 1995.
Prior, Michael
    1995   *Jesus the Liberator: Nazareth Liberation Theology.* Sheffield: Sheffield
            Academic Press.
Queller, Kurt
    2008   "'Stretch Out Your Hand!' Intertextual Echoes and Metaleptic Sig-
            nification in Mark's Sabbath Healing Controversy Narrative." Ph.D.
            diss., University of Idaho.
Quinn, Daniel
    1992   *Ishmael.* New York: Bantam Books.
Raboteau, Albert J.
    1996   *A Fire in the Bones: Reflections on African-American Religious History.*
            Boston: Beacon.
Raines, John
    1984   "Righteous Resistance and Martin Luther King, Jr." *Christian Cen-
            tury,* January 18, 1984, 52.
Ramshaw, E. J.
    1998   "Power and Forgiveness in Matthew 18." *Word & World* 18:397-404.
Reagon, Bernice Johnson
    2001   *If You Don't Go, Don't Hinder Me: The African American Sacred Song
            Tradition.* Omaha: University of Nebraska Press.
Rhoads, David M.
    1976   *Israel in Revolution, 6-74 C.E.: A Political History Based on the Writings
            of Josephus.* Philadelphia: Fortress.
Rieger, Joerg
    1998   *Remember the Poor: The Challenge to Theology in the Twenty-First Cen-
            tury.* Harrisburg, PA: Trinity Press International.
Ringe, Sharon
    1985   *Jesus, Liberation and the Biblical Jubilee.* Philadelphia: Fortress.

Roberts, Alexander, J. Donaldson, P. Schaff, and H. Wace, eds.
  1994   *The Ante-Nicene Fathers*. Peabody, MA: Hendrickson Publishers.
Rosenblatt, Marie-Eloise
  1995   *Paul the Accused: His Portrait in the Acts of the Apostles*. Collegeville,
         MN: Liturgical Press.
Rossing, Barbara
  2004   *The Rapture Exposed: The Message of Hope in the Book of Revelation*. New
         York: Basic Books.
Rowland, Christopher, and Mark Corner
  1989   *Liberating Exegesis: The Challenge of Liberation Theology to Biblical Stud-
         ies*. Louisville: Westminster John Knox.
Sanders, John, ed.
  2006   *Atonement and Violence: A Theological Conversation*. Nashville: Abing-
         don.
Scott, Bernard Brandon
  1989   *Hear Then the Parable*. Philadelphia: Fortress.
Scott, James
  1987   *Weapons of the Weak: Everyday Forms of Peasant Resistance*. New Haven:
         Yale University Press.
Segundo, Juan Luis
  1976   *Liberation of Theology*. Translated by John Drury. Maryknoll, NY:
         Orbis Books.
Sharp, Gene
  1990   *Civilian-Based Defense: A Post-Military Weapons System*. Princeton, NJ:
         Princeton University Press.
  1973   *The Politics of Nonviolent Action*. 3 vols. Part One: *Power and Struggle*.
         Part Two: *The Methods of Nonviolent Action*. Part Three: *The Dynamics
         of Nonviolent Action*. Boston: Porter Sargent.
  1970   *Exploring Nonviolent Alternatives*. Boston: Porter Sargent.
Smith, D.
  1973   "The Two Made One: Eph 2:14-18." *Ohio Journal of Religious Studies*
         (January): 35ff.
Smith, Kenneth, and Ira G. Zepp, Jr.
  1974a "Martin Luther King's Vision of the Beloved Community." *Christian
         Century* (April 3): 361ff.
  1974b *Search for the Beloved Community: The Thinking of Martin Luther King.
         Jr.* Valley Forge, PA: Judson.
Snyder, T. Richard
  2001   *The Protestant Ethic and the Spirit of Punishment*. Grand Rapids: Eerd-
         mans.
Sobrino, Jon, S.J.
  1978   *Christology at the Crossroads: A Latin America Approach*. Translated by
         John Drury. Maryknoll, NY: Orbis Books.

Spencer, F. Scott
    2005   "Follow Me: The Imperious Call of Jesus in the Synoptic Gospels." *Interpretation* 59/2:142ff.

Swartley, Willard M.
    2006   *Covenant of Peace: The Missing Peace in New Testament Theology and Ethics.* Grand Rapids: Eerdmans.

Swartley, Willard M., ed.
    2000   *Violence Renounced: René Girard, Biblical Studies and Peacemaking.* Scottdale, PA: Herald.
    1992   *The Love of Enemy and Nonretaliation in the New Testament.* Louisville: Westminster John Knox.

Tamez, Elsa
    1993   *The Amnesty of Grace: Justification by Faith from a Latin American Perspective.* Nashville: Abingdon.

Telushkin, Joseph
    1997   *Biblical Literacy: The Most Important People, Events, and Ideas of the Hebrew Bible.* New York: William Morrow.

Theissen, Gerd
    2003   "Social Conflicts in the Corinthian Community." *Journal for the Study of the New Testament* 25:371-91.
    1992   *Social Reality and the Early Christians: Theology, Ethics, and the World of the New Testament.* Minneapolis: Fortress.
    1991   *The Gospels in Context: Social and Political History in the Synoptic Tradition.* Translated by L. Maloney. Minneapolis: Fortress.
    1982   *The Social Setting of Pauline Christianity: Essays on Corinth.* Minneapolis: Fortress.

Thurman, Howard
    1996   *Jesus and the Disinherited.* Second edition. Boston: Beacon.

Trible, Phyllis
    1984   *Texts of Terror: Literary-Feminist Readings of Biblical Narratives.* Philadelphia: Fortress.

Tutu, Desmond
    1999   *No Future without Forgiveness.* New York: Image/Doubleday.

Van Aarde, Andries
    2001   *Fatherless in Galilee: Jesus as Child of God.* Harrisburg, PA: Trinity Press International.

Wainwright, Elaine
    1998   *Shall We Look for Another? A Feminist Rereading of the Matthean Jesus.* Maryknoll, NY: Orbis Books.

Wansink, Craig S.
    1996   *Chained in Christ: The Experience and Rhetoric of Paul's Imprisonments.* JSNT Supplements. Sheffield: Sheffield Academic Press.

Washington, James M., ed.
    1986   *A Testament of Hope: The Essential Writings and Speeches of Martin Luther King, Jr.* San Francisco: HarperSan Francisco.

Weaver, J. Denny
   2001   *The Nonviolent Atonement.* Grand Rapids: Eerdmans.
   1987   *Becoming Anabaptist: The Origin and Significance of 16th Century Anabaptism.* Scottdale, PA: Herald.
Weisman, Ze'ev
   1998   *Political Satire in the Bible.* Atlanta: Scholars Press.
Wengst, Klaus
   1987   *Pax Romana and the Peace of Jesus Christ.* Philadelphia: Fortress.
West, Cornel
   1982   *Prophesy Deliverance! An Afro-American Revolutionary Christianity.* Philadelphia: Westminster John Knox.
Wilder, Amos
   1982   *Jesus' Parables and the War of Myths.* Philadelphia: Fortress.
Williams, James G.
   1991   *The Bible, Violence and the Sacred: Liberation from the Myth of Sanctioned Violence.* San Francisco: Harper Books.
Wink, Walter
   1992a *Engaging the Powers: Discernment and Resistance in a World of Domination.* Philadelphia: Fortress.
   1992b "Neither Passivity nor Violence: Jesus' Third Way (Matt 5:38-42 par.)." In *The Love of Enemy and Nonretaliation in the New Testament,* edited by Willard Swartley, 102-25. Louisville: Westminster John Knox.
   1986   *Unmasking the Powers: The Invisible Forces That Determine Human Existence.* Philadelphia: Fortress.
   1984   *Naming the Powers: The Language of Power in the New Testament.* Philadelphia: Fortress.
Witherington, Ben
   1995   *Conflict & Community in Corinth: A Socio-Rhetorical Commentary on 1 and 2 Corinthians.* Grand Rapids: Eerdmans.
Yoder, John Howard
   1972   *The Politics of Jesus: Vicit Agnus Noster.* Grand Rapids: Eerdmans.
Yoder Neufeld, Thomas
   2003   "'In the Middle': Biblical Reflections on Restorative Justice." Unpublished paper delivered to the Mennonite Central Committee Restorative Justice Network, Winnipeg, February 14-15. Online at http://mcc.org/canada/restorativejustice/resources/articles/neufeld.html.
   2002   *Ephesians: Believers Church Bible Commentary.* Scottdale, PA: Herald.
Young, Frances, and David Ford
   1987   *Meaning and Truth in Second Corinthians.* Grand Rapids: Eerdmans.
Zehr, Howard, and Barb Toews, eds.
   2004   *Critical Issues in Restorative Justice.* Monsey, NY: Criminal Justice Press.

SUBJECT INDEX

SCRIPTURE INDEX

Mark (*continued*)

2:10	38, 43, 45	3:20-34	31	8:31	43
2:12	35	3:21	44, 45, 131n21	8:32	132n31
2:13	36, 43			9:14-29	131n16
2:13-17	31, 42	3:21-35	44	9:25	132n30
2:13-3:6	36-43	3:22	45	9:42-49	138n26
2:14	26, 36	3:22-30	45	10:13	132n30
2:15	37	3:22ff.	44	10:17-31	132n28
2:16	37, 38	3:23	46	10:28f.	30
2:17	37, 131n22	3:24	46	10:35ff.	132n31
2:18	37	3:25f.	46	10:45	96
2:18-22	31, 37, 42	3:26	47	10:46-52	131n16
2:19	38	3:27	46, 131n22	10:47	25
2:21f.	38	3:28	46, 134n38	10:47ff.	43
2:23	37	3:29f.	46	11:1-10	47
2:23-28	37, 38, 42	3:31	45	11:1-23	22
2:23-38	31	3:31-34	45	11:1-13:2	42
2:24	38	3:32	45	11:9	133n31
2:25b	38	3:33	45	11:10	134n38
2:25f.	38	3:35	45	11:11-25	47
2:27	38	4:1	36	11:15-17	46
2:28	38, 43	4:1ff.	62	11:15ff.	84
3:1	39	4:8	62	11:17	134n38
3:1f.	38	4:10-12	72	11:27-12:17	47
3:1-6	40, 42, 48	4:11	45	11:27ff.	46
3:1-16	31	4:39	132n30	12:13-17	137n17
3:3	39	4:41	43	12:31	55
3:4	38, 39, 40	5:1	26	12:35-40	47
3:5	38, 39, 40, 132n27	5:1-20	131n16	12:41-13:2	47
		5:21-43	131n16	12:42	135n9
3:5a	40	5:25ff.	33	13:2	22, 46, 84
3:5b	40	5:42	131n21	13:3-8	47
3:5c	40	6:1-6	133n33	13:5-13	47
3:6	39, 132n27	6:3	130n9	13:5ff.	147n33
3:7	43	6:7ff	133n33	13:8	134n38
3:7-12	31	6:13-30	133n33	13:9-13	47
3:7-35	43-48	6:14-16	23	13:14-23	47
3:7ff.	43	6:14-30	24	13:24-33	47
3:8	43	6:17-29	23	13:33	148n36
3:9f.	43	6:23	134n38	13:34-37	46
3:11	43	6:51	131n21	13:34f.	134n38
3:12	43, 132n30	7:24-30	131n16	14:1ff.	47
3:13	44	7:31-37	131n16	14:6	132n28
3:13-19	31	8:18	72	14:7	132n28
3:14-19a	44	8:22-26	26, 131n16	14:43ff.	133n33
3:14f.	43	8:27	33	14:55ff.	133n31
3:19a	133n33	8:27-30	43	14:58	84
3:19ff.	44	8:27-9:1	42	14:61	43
3:20	44	8:28f.	43	14:62	43, 144n10
3:20f.	45	8:29	43	14:67	25
		8:30-33	132n30	15:2f.	43

Also by Ched Myers

Binding the Strong Man
A Political Reading of Mark's Story of Jesus

ANNIVERSARY EDITION

ISBN 976-57075-797-6

"This is, quite simply, the most important commentary on a book of
scripture since Barth's *Romans*."

—*Walter Wink*

"Bound to become a classic in the field of gospel studies . . . Ched Myers
has produced a commentary that is potentially as revolutionary as the
very gospel account it portrays"

—*Sojourners*

"Myers has produced a commanding and coherent political commentary
on the Gospel of Mark, distinguished in its grasp of biblical and social
scientific scholarship and amazingly lucid in its style and argument. . . . A
cogent and venturesome biblical embodiment of liberation theology."

—*Norman K. Gottwald*

"Twenty years later, *Binding the Strong Man* still has the ability to push
its readers into a fresh new perspective on what it means to be in
discipleship with the Human one who seeks to realize the Reign of God
in our social, historical, spiritual, and political landscape."

—*Brian Blount*

Since its publication in 1988, *Binding the Strong Man* has been widely
recognized as a landmark in contemporary biblical criticism. Applying a
multi-disciplinary approached called "socio-literary method," Myers
integrates literary criticism, socio-historical exegesis, and political hermeneutics
in his investigation of Mark as a "manifesto of radical discipleship."

Please support your local bookstore, or call 1-800-258-5838.
For a free catalog, please write us at
Orbis Books, Box 302
Maryknoll, NY 10545-0302
or visit our website at www.orbisbooks.com.

Thank you for reading *Ambassadors of Reconciliation*.
We hope you enjoyed it.

Also by Ched Myers

"Say to This Mountain"
Mark's Story of Discipleship
Ched Myers, Marie Dennis, Joseph Nangle, OFM,
Cynthia Moe-Lobeda, Stuart Taylor

ISBN 1-57075-100-5

"A remarkable book . . . The authors provide timely, compelling, demanding exegesis."
—*Walter Brueggemann*

"A rare and wonderful book. Rooted in the best of scholarship. . . it enlivens our hearts and engages our minds for the work of social transformation."
—*Bill Wylie-Kellermann*

This "team-authored," popular-level version of Ched Myers's monumental study of Mark, *Binding the Strong Man*, adapts its socio-literary method of reading to a work ideal for study and reflection by groups or individuals with limited background in biblical scholarship.

Who Will Roll Away the Stone?
Discipleship Queries for First World Christians

ISBN 0-88344-947-1

"This compelling call to discipleship is radical, rigorous, honest, and inviting."
—*Jim Wallis*

Ched Myers exposes the social and spiritual "stones" that impede us in our development and growth as Christians. "In every age," writes Myers, "disciples despair that the story has ended, only to discover that the stone 'has been rolled away,' reopening the possibility—and imperative—of following the Way of Jesus."

Please support your local bookstore, or call 1-800-258-5838.
For a free catalog, please write us at
Orbis Books, Box 302
Maryknoll, NY 10545-0302
or visit our website at www.orbisbooks.com.

Thank you for reading *Ambassadors of Reconciliation*.
We hope you enjoyed it.